A FRAMEWORK FOR
FAITH

A FRAMEWORK FOR FAITH

LUNDENSIAN THEOLOGICAL METHODOLOGY
IN THE THOUGHT OF RAGNAR BRING

BY

THOR HALL

114632

LEIDEN
E. J. BRILL
1970

*To my
little family*

CONTENTS

PART THREE

BRING'S LIMITS

PREFACE

The Bring family name came into Swedish ancestral registers by way of Norway. This Norwegian writer came into the theological community by way of Sweden. Yet the contact between Lund and myself was not established until I had settled in the United States.

In the preface to the first edition of this work—my academic dissertation entitled *A Study of Lundensian Theological Methodology as Represented in the Thought of Ragnar Bring*—I expressed the sentiment that to study Lundensian theology properly, one needs to be outside the Scandinavian "stone wall", beyond the watershed of this school of thought. This judgment still stands. However, since then I have found myself drawn into close personal friendships with the men in Lund—the emeriti as well as the active faculty—and this relationship has increased my understanding of Lundensian thought and deepened my grasp of its underlying presuppositions. The present work is the result of this development. Compared with the dissertation of 1962, it is an entirely different book, though much of the material may be recognized. The main difference—besides improvements in style and organization—is in the critical assessment of Bring's thought and the constructive presentation of viable alternatives. Bring, in typical kindness, invited me to undertake such endeavors following the presentation of my dissertation. The third part of this book is an attempt to respond to that invitation.

I am indebted to many people, in Lund, at Duke University, and—closest—in my family. During three different visits to Lund, one day in 1963, one month in 1966, and one year in 1968-69, I have been graciously received and magnanimously helped in matters both practical and theoretical, by the faculty as a whole and by many individuals. The three emiriti most closely related to my subject, Bishop Gustaf Aulén, Bishop Anders Nygren, and Professor Ragnar Bring, continue to amaze me by their vitality and youthful outlook. I shall long treasure their spirited conversation.

At Duke University, my indebtedness is both personal and institutional. Professor Robert E. Cushman, Dean of the Divinity School, who suggested the topic for this research and also directed my dissertation, has continued to encourage and provide opportunity for an ongoing interest in theological methodology. The William R.

Perkins Library and the Divinity School Library have given unrestrict-
ed support in every way. The Graduate Department of Religion and,
more recently, the Research Council of the University have provided
financial support at various times. For all and to all I am most grateful.

This book is dedicated to my little family: my wife Gerd, who
with all other meaningful things also contributed directly by giving
the Bibliography its final form, and our son Jan Tore, who with
much else often helped—and occasionally upset—my sense for the
English language. They know my gratitude.

Lund
Valborgsmässoafton
1969   T.H.

ABBREVIATIONS

DhL	=	Bring, *Dualismen hos Luther*
FTG	=	Bring, *Förhållandet mellan tro och gärningar inom luthersk teologi*
KrT	=	Bring, *Kristendomstolkningar i gammal och ny tid*
LUÅ	=	Lunds universitets årsskrift
NmPh	=	Bring, *Wie ist nicht-metaphysische Philosophie möglich?*
STK	=	Svensk teologisk kvartalskrift
STU	=	Bring, *Till frågan om den systematiska teologiens uppgift*
ToR	=	Bring, *Teologi och religion*
UUÅ	=	Uppsala universitets årsskrift
ZST	=	Zeitschrift für Systematische Theologie

INTRODUCTION

Theological methodology is an elusive concept. It covers the philosophical presuppositions behind a given system of theological reflection. It includes the relationships between philosophy and theology, theology and religion, religion and other aspects of human experience. It centers on understanding the nature of faith, but it comprises also the more practical questions concerning the procedures involved in doing theology. Hence the general form of the title of this work, *A Framework for Faith*.

The study of theological methodology is of fundamental importance to the theological endeavor. It is surprising, therefore, that many of the twentieth century theological movements that sought to reclaim theology from the grip of its nineteenth century captivities to reason, philosophy, criticism, or the scientific worldview have allowed the concern for theological content—the recovery of certain essential Christian emphases—to overshadow the problems of theological method, thus neglecting the task of formulating a contemporary intellectual rationale for theology. What methodological interest there was in these movements came to focus on certain preliminary theological questions, such as the nature of revelation, the authority of Scripture, the dynamics of the God-man encounter, and the Word of God, all of which were considered from the perspective of theology itself. Some representatives of the twentieth century theological recovery have been working in undeniable dependence on dialectic principles of thought. Others have been informed by existentialist emphases. Still others have based their systems on various forms of philosophical-theological correlation. But only in very few instances were any theoretical questions raised concerning the philosophical commitments underlying the various approaches to theology, and more seldom yet were they raised in such a way as to facilitate a dialogue between theologians and the contemporary intellectual community. The new theologies of the twentieth century were quite conscious of the peculiar characteristics of Christian faith and thought, but they were less able to establish how this particular expression of human spirit and intellect relates to other aspects of our experience. The radical criticism leveled at theology by representatives of the so-called modern mindset has not until very recently made penetration into the theo-

logical circles, and only a few representatives of the present generation
of theologians have responded by taking an honest interest in the
contemporary intellectual situation. By and large, the theological
community of the twentieth century has concerned itself with intra-
theological concerns, particularly the recovery of essential Christian
faith content, leaving aside the problem of how to find a place for
Christian faith and thought in the thoughtworld of our contemporaries
in general.

In one school of thought contributing to the theological recovery,
the combination of these two concerns has been consciously attempted,
namely in the faculty of theology at the University of Lund, Sweden,
during the period from the second to the sixth decade of this century.
It is, in fact, the peculiar way in which this double interest was pursued
by the leading men of this faculty that has given Lundensian theology
its distinctive character and forms its major contribution to the theology of our era. In this school, a radical type of philosophical criticism
was developed, providing the theoretical basis for a modern philosophy of religion. On these foundations, there emerged a series of
clear delineations of the nature and function of theology, resulting
in the formulation of a specific method of theological research and a
claim, on behalf of systematic theology, to scientific respectability.
Against the background of these methodological endeavors, and
utilizing the scientific method that had been hammered out, the
Lundensian scholars proceeded to analyze the characteristic emphases
of an explicitly Protestant theological tradition, seeking to recover the
understanding of essential Christian faith content by an intensive
study of the particular historical tradition within which this theology
professedly stands. In short, Lundensian theology aimed at a double
distinction: It desired at one and the same time to be both intellectually
respectable and theologically responsible. It aspired to be both truly
scientific and fully evangelical.

It is the purpose of the present work to investigate one aspect of
Lundensian theology, its theological methodology. We are interested
in its strength and its weaknesses, its promises and its failures. We
shall focus our attention on a leading proponent of this methodology
from the time of its inception to the early sixties, Professor Ragnar
Bring. The reasons for this choice of subject are clear and simple.
Within twentieth century Swedish theology, Bring in many ways
stands as a central figure, ranking—although he is a man of unassuming
stature—a head above the crowd in any theological company, whether

among the philosophers of religion, the Luther scholars, the interpreters of Scripture, or the methodologians. [1] For decades he has served as a catalyst and a unifier of many important trends in modern Swedish theology. He has assimilated into his thinking significant contributions of Nathan Söderblom and Einar Billing, the early exponents of the theological recovery in Sweden. He has learned much from the encounter with the strongest men in Swedish philosophical circles in our century, Axel Hägerström and Adolf Phalén, and he has succeeded in some measure in bridging the gap between philosophical criticism and systematic theology. He recognized early the fundamental values in the thought of Gustaf Aulén and Anders Nygren, the two major lights in Scandinavian theology in our age, and as Aulén's successor in the chair of systematic theology at Lund and Nygren's colleague there for a decade and a half, he took upon himself the task of clarifying their thought and expanding their views both on methodological matters and in the interpretation of central Christian themes. Entering freely into the theological debate, Bring has been engaged in significant discussions with theologians of other schools of thought, particularly those of a dialectic, irationalistic, or psychologistic orientation.

Carefully, he has avoided superficial controversies or issues that are ultimately reducible to terminological preferences. He has attempted, instead, to uncover and identify the underlying assumptions in his opponents' views. He has never been a strict, partisan theologian. Though his orientation is clearly Lutheran, he has not become a narrow-minded sectarian. His own theological stance has not jeopardized his respect for other ways of thinking. The basis for his judgments is directly related to his perpetual concern for intellectual honesty and authentic evangelical faith.

When Ragnar Bring retired in 1962 from the chair he had held for twenty-eight years at the University of Lund, he left behind a record of excellence both in quality and length of tenure which even in Scandinavia is hard to match. Unlike many of the top scholars in Sweden, he was not taken out of his academic involvements by the

---

[1] Anders Nygren pays a similar tribute to Bring. Cf. "Ragnar Brings teologiska insats," *Nordisk teologi, Ideer och män*, Lund: Gleerup (1955), pp. 293-296. He describes Bring's contributions to Luther-research as "of fundamental importance", his exegetical work as giving new understanding of "the central problem of theology, the relationship between the law and the gospel," and his philosophical analyses as "strong" and „independent".

church's call to the episcopacy. What his influence has been in the Swedish church, through the generation or two of ministers trained under his guidance, and in Swedish theology, through his own diligent authorship and through the direction he has given as adviser and friend to many young scholars working under him, is not easily assessed or articulated. His central position in Swedish theology is well indicated by his long tenure as editor of *Svensk teologisk kvartalskrift* from 1937 to the present time. As editor, he has sought consistently to make this respected journal an open forum for theological debate, striving particularly to provide young scholars an opportunity to find their place in the theological community.

Ragnar Anders Ebbe Bring was born on July 10, 1895, in Skara, Sweden. His father, Gustaf I. M. Bring, held a doctorate of philosophy from the university at Uppsala. He had done advanced work under the personalistic idealists of the Boström-Geijer tradition [1] and had successfully defended his academic dissertation before the philosophical faculty. Ragnar Bring, probably on his father's suggestion, went to Uppsala to work for a *fil. kand.* degree, a professional degree given in any one of several fields, philosophy, philology, history, psychology, etc. Bring's field was philosophy, and his teachers at Uppsala were two critical philosophers who had radically altered the direction of the philosophical faculty, Axel Hägerström in practical philosophy and his fellow positivist Adolf Phalén in theoretical philosophy. These men were giving the Uppsala-theologians Einar Billing and Nils J. Göransson a difficult time, charging theology with all the errors of subjectivistic arbitrariness and metaphysical speculation. [2] Billing and Göransson did not have the philosophical stamina to take up the challenge. If they had the necessary sophistication for such debate, it did not manifest itself in a direct response to their colleagues in the philosophical faculty. Their own philosophical orien-

---

[1] Christoffer Jacob Boström was the school-forming philosopher at Uppsala from 1838 to 1863. At the time of his death, three of the four professorates in philosophy in Sweden were held by his avowed disciples, and "half a century after his death his ideas (were still in) full actuality in Swedish philosophy." *Svensk biografiskt lexikon*, Vol. 6, p. 523.

[2] Cf. Phalén, "Kritik av subjektivismen i olika former med särskild hänsyn till transcendentalfilosofien," and Hägerström, "Kritiska punkter i värdepsykologien," both in *Festskrift tillägnad E. O. Burman*, Uppsala: Akademisk bokhandel, 1910. Also Hägerström, "Om moraliska föreställningars sanning," in his *Socialfilosofiska uppsatser*, Stockholm: Bonnier, 1939. Hägerström's views on metaphysics are clearly delineated in his "Selbstdarstellung," *Die Philosophie der Gegenwart in Selbstdarstellungen*, Vol. 7, Leipzig, 1929, pp. 136 ff.

tation was more influenced by the idealistic trends that had formerly dominated Swedish philosophy from the time of Boström.

Bring completed his *fil. kand.* degree in 1917 and planned to go on to study theology. But he did not feel at home in the theological atmosphere at Uppsala; his eyes were turned toward Lund. In contrast to the faculty of theology at Uppsala, the theologians in Lund had begun to face up to the challenge of philosophical criticism. Gustaf Aulén had already during his Uppsala period published a study of the place and purpose of systematic theology,[1] and by 1917 it was obvious that Aulén and his colleague Magnus Pfannenstill in Lund were trying to justify theology against the charges of subjectivism and metaphysics by reference to the Ritschlian understanding of faith as a principle of personal commitment and religious trustfulness. Bring decided that if he was to do theology it would have to be in Lund. He went there in 1919.

While Bring was studying for his *teol. kand.* degree (the professional degree for ministers of the Swedish church) under Aulén, Anders Nygren also came to Lund. Nygren had served pastorates for a few years, following his graduation from the university in 1912, and he returned now to complete his *licentiat* (a degree roughly corresponding to a master's) in philosophy and pursue his doctorate in theology. Bring received his *kandidatur* in theology in 1923. By that time Nygren had been serving as *docent* in philosophy of religion for two years, being groomed for the chair soon to be vacated by Pfannenstill. The two were very close. Bring was especially impressed with Nygren's approach to the problems raised by the Uppsala-philosophers. When Nygren became professor of systematic theology and ethics in 1924, Bring was hard at work on his *licentiat* in theology, which he received in 1926. Continuing his work toward the doctorate while holding a position as amanuensis at the university library, Bring presented his dissertation entitled *Dualismen hos Luther* in 1929 and was immediately appointed *docent* under Aulén.[2] The school-forming triumvirate at Lund was established.

---

[1] *Uppenbarelse och historia i den nutida teologien. En studie til dogmatikens läge och uppgift*, Uppsala: Almquist & Wiksell, 1912. Aulén was a student under Söderblom in Uppsala and became his *docent* (research assistant and lecturer) in 1907. In 1913, he moved to Lund, where he followed Pehr Eklund as professor of systematic theology, a position which he held for twenty years.

[2] This was a direct result of his succesful dissertation, a book which in Aulén's estimation immediately made Bring a leading Swedish Luther scholar, worthy of the legacy from Söderblom, Billing, and Göransson, and of comparison with

Bring left Lund for a short period to accept an appointment as professor of systematic theology at the Swedish-speaking university academy at Åbo, Finland, where he served until 1934. It was during his tenure at Åbo that the problems of theological methodology challenged him to a preliminary response. In a book entitled *Till frågan om den systematiska teologiens uppgift* (literally, on the question of the task of systematic theology),[1] published in 1933, he sought to take account of the modern developments in the encounter between theology and the modern mindset, showing himself dependent on Aulén and Nygren but able also to advance their views in creative ways. With this work, and another book published a year later under the title *Förhållandet mellan tro och gärningar inom luthersk teologi*,[2] Bring proved himself ready to shoulder the burden of the dual task taken up by the Lundensian faculty: the development of a theology which was to be scientific in method and evangelical Christian in content. He returned to Lund in 1934 to succeed Aulén (who had been elected bishop of Strängnes) in the chair of systematic theology, thus settling down to a long career of distinguished academic work as teacher, writer, editor, guest lecturer, visiting professor, trusted colleague and friendly adviser. He retired in 1962, but only pro forma. In recent years, he has held short term positions at the universities of Chicago, Berlin, Copenhagen and Oslo, and his productivity as author shows no signs of slackening. He continues to make his home in Lund, where his two teachers and colleagues and friends, Gustaf Aulén and Anders Nygren, also have settled in their retirement.[3] All of them still active, they make up the most uncommon group of *teologie studerande* found anywhere. We may yet expect the men who gave *Lundateologien* its place among the major schools of theology in the twentieth century to produce new crops of ripe fruit in their mature years.[4]

Runestam, Ljunggren, Bohlin, and von Engeström—not to mention Nygren and Aulén himself. *STK*, 6, 1930, p. 357.

[1] LUÅ, N. f., Avd. I, Bd. 29, 1, 1933.

[2] Acta Academia Aboensis, Humaniora IX, Helsingfors: Åbo Akademi, 1934.

[3] Aulén returned from Strängnäs as *biskop emeritus* in 1952; Nygren retired from the see of Lund in 1958 and moved back to the house he had built while teaching at the university.

[4] Aulén has published several important volumes in his retirement, among them *Reformation och katolicitet*, Stockholm: Diakonistyrelsen (1959), and *Dramat och symbolerna*, Stockholm: Diakonistyrelsen, 2nd ed. 1965. He still works daily at his desk. Nygren is hard at work on a major book on the philosophy of religion, hoping to finish it within the year. He has also given time to a forthcoming volume in the

Of Ragnar Bring's writings, only the most important shall be listed here.[1] In addition to the three works already mentioned, they include *Teologi och religion* (a further development of his methodological standpoints),[2] *Kristendomstolkningar i gammal och ny tid* (a collection of essays on methodological issues),[3] *Wie ist nicht-metaphysische Philosophie möglich* (a principal development of his philosophy of religion),[4] *Bibelns auktoritet och bibelns bruk* (signifying a shift to more biblically oriented studies),[5] *Pauli brev till galaterna. Tolkning* (a theological commentary on Galatians),[6] and *Att lyda bibeln. Luthers förhållande till bibelns bud* (combining his interests in Luther and in biblical theology).[7] To the English-speaking world, Bring is known mainly for his *Commentary on Galatians*,[8] for his little book *How God Speaks to Us: The Dynamics of the Living Word*,[9] for his contributions to a volume of essays by Swedish theologians, entitled *This is the Church*,[10] and for an essay in the *festschrift* in honor of Anders Nygren, *World Lutheranism of Today*.[11] In Germany, Bring is somewhat better known as a Luther-scholar in the succession of Holl and Hirsch and as a biblical theologian of a more conservative form-critical orientation. His published works in the German language include a translation of his study of the relation of faith and works in Lutheran theology, *Das Verhältnis von Glaube und Werken in der*

Library of Living Theology series, edited by Charles W. Kegley, entitled *The Theology of Anders Nygren* (to be published *Philosophy and* by Southern Illinois University Press). Bring continues his studies in the area of biblical theology, focusing particularly on the concept of the law. He has prepared a volume of articles and essays under the title *Christus und das Gesetz*, Leiden: Brill, 1969. He is also contemplating a collection of studies in the philosophy of religion.

[1] A near complete bibliography of Bring's writings through 1955 is included in the *festskrift* published in honor of his sixtieth birthday, *Nordisk teologi, Ideer och Män*, 1955, pp. 297-311. Additional items of more recent origin are included in our Bibliography, cf. pp. 255 ff., below.

[2] Lund: Gleerup (1937).

[3] Stockholm: Diakonistyrelsen, 1950.

[4] Lund: Kungliga humanistiska vetenskapssamfundet i Lund, Årsberättelse 1939-40.

[5] Lund: Gleerup (1958).

[6] Stockholm: Diakonistyrelsen, 1958.

[7] Stockholm: Diakonistyrelsen, 1961.

[8] Translation of *Pauli brev till galaterna*, and published by Muhlenberg Press (now Fortress), Philadelphia, in 1961.

[9] Philadelphia: Fortress Press, 1962.

[10] "The Subjective and the Objective in the Concept of the Church," *This is the Church* (translation of *En bok om kyrkan*), Philadelphia: Muhlenberg Press (1952).

[11] Stockholm: Diakonistyrelsen, 1950.

lutherischen Theologie; [1] a translation of his book on Luther's concept
of the Bible, *Luthers Anschauung von der Bibel;* [2] several contributions
to the *Luthertum* series; [3] and a number of articles in theological
journals and anthologies.[4] Translations of his *Commentary on Galatians*
and of *How God Speaks to Us* have recently appeared in German also.[5]

In recognition of his standing among contemporary theologians,
Bring has received many honors. A *festschrift* in his honor, entitled
Nordisk teologi. Ideer och män,[6] was published in 1955 on the occasion
of his sixtieth birthday. Honorary degrees have been awarded him
by the universities in Erlangen, 1952; Aarhus, 1953; Åbo, 1955; and
Rock Island, Ill., 1960.

The present study of Ragnar Bring's thought is limited in purpose
and does not claim to be a definitive analysis of all his contibutions
to twentieth century theology. We are interested in the theoretical
framework of his theology, particularly his way of holding together
a modern emphasis on scientific objectivity in theological method and a
positive commitment regarding the content of Christian faith. Our main
concern will be to uncover and understand the basic elements of
Bring's methodology, from the critical-philosophical foundations
of his epistemology to the practical-theological procedures of motif-
research. But we shall also want to ask questions, reveal weaknesses,
perhaps even suggest answers.

The first part of the book, Chapters I-III, is devoted to the background of Bring's work. Attempts are made to place the Lundensian
school of theology in relation to other major movements of thought

---

[1] München: Kaiser Verlag, 1955.

[2] *Luthertum*, Hft. 3, 1951.

[3] "Lutherische Theologie angesichts der ökumenischen Arbeit," *Luthertum*,
Hft. 1, 2, 1951; "Die paulinische Begründung der lutherischen Theologie,"
Luthertum, Hft. 17, 1955.

[4] "Ein Versuch dogmengeschichtlicher Neuorientierung," *Theologisches Literaturblatt*, 53, 1932, pp. 257 ff; "Glaube und Werke, " *ZST*, 12, 1934-35, pp. 498 ff;
"Der Glaube an die Zukunft und die Hoffnung auf das ewige Leben," *Lutherische
Rundschau*, 4, 1954, pp. 225 ff; "Luthers Lehre von Gesetz und Evangelium als
der Beitrag der lutherischen Theologie für die Ökumene," *Luther-Jahrbuch*, 26,
1957; "Christologie und Gottes Monarchie," *Die Leibhaftigkeit des Wortes*, Hamburg: Furche-Verlag (1958); "Die Erfüllung des Gesetzes durch Christus,"
Kerygma und Dogma, 5, 1959; "Der Mittler und das Gesetz," *Kerygma und Dogma*,
12, 1966; "Die Erfüllung des Gesetzes. Vergleich zwischen Paulus und Luther,"
*Vierhundertfünfzig Jahre lutherische Reformation. 1517-1967. Festschrift für Franz
Lau*, Berlin: Evangelische Verlags Anst., 1967.

[5] *Der Brief des Paulus an die Galater*, Berlin: Lutherisches Verlaghaus, 1967;
Das göttliche Wort. Grundfragen unseres Glaubens, Gütersloh: Gerd Mohn, 1964.

[6] Cf. p. 7, note 1.

in the twentieth century and to draw some guidelines through those historical traditions of Swedish theology from which Bring emerged. One entire chapter is given to a study of Anders Nygren's early contributions to the development of a critical philosophy of religion and the formulation of a theoretical basis for *motivforskning*. The second part of the book, Chapters IV-VIII, contains a series of detailed analyses of Bring's own methodology, his fundamental philosophical commitments, his development of Nygren's non-metaphysical approach to the philosophy of religion, and his definition of the nature and task of scientific systematic theology. Special attention is given to Bring's keen critique of the subjectivistic and metaphysical tendencies in contemporary theology. The third part of the book, a concluding chapter and an appendix, offers a critique of Bring's methodological work, giving particular attention to the shortcomings that have become apparent along the way, and proposing a way to fulfill Bring's intentions and bring his theological methodology into correspondence with the critical presuppositions. Thus the present author hopes to make Lundensian methodology better known, to advance it one step further, and in doing so to give credit to the men whose thinking became his starting point for meaningful theological existence in our time.

PART ONE

BRING'S BACKGROUND

CHAPTER ONE

SWEDISH CONTRIBUTIONS
TO THE MODERN THEOLOGICAL RECOVERY

Commenting on the English edition of a Swedish theologian's work in the field of biblical theology, a well known British theologian remarked: "In the past, great teachers like Aulén and Nygren have convinced us that from Sweden there is much that we may thankfully receive." [1] This is undoubtedly correct; but in the typical manner of a British understatement, the comment misses more than it contains. Modern Swedish theology—and particularly the theology emanating from the University of Lund since the second decade of this century— has contributed much to Christian faith and thought in our time. However, some of the most important contributions of the Lundensian theologians are as yet hidden in the less recognized aspects of their thought, namely the thoroughgoing methodological examinations on which their theological work is based. The theological community has acclaimed the Swedes for their creative leadership in the renewal of Luther-research,[2] for their initiatives in the current revival of interest in the doctrine of the church,[3] for their incisive and penetrating studies of the historical development of certain Christian doctrines,[4] and for significant individual contributions to systematic

---

[1] Alan Richardson, in his preface to Gustaf Wingren's *The Living Word*, Philadelphia: Muhlenberg Press (1960), p. 9.

[2] Cf. Edgar Carlson, *The Reinterpretation of Luther*, Philadelphia: Westminster Press (1948). The main credit of Swedish theology, according to Daniel Day Williams, is its Luther studies. *What Present-Day Theologians Are Thinking*, New York: Harper (1959), p. 47.

[3] Cf. J. R. Nelson, *The Realm of Redemption: Studies in the Doctrine of the Nature of the Church in Contemporary Protestant Theology*, London: Epworth Press (1951). Note the positive estimation of Gustaf Aulén's contributions to the study of the sacraments; Walter Marshall Horton, *Christian Theology: An Ecumenical Approach*, New York: Harper (1958). General recognition is also given the cooperative work by Swedish theologians, *En bok om kyrkan*, Stockholm: Diakonistyrelsen, 1942 (in German translation, 1951; in English, *This is the Church*, 1952).

[4] Best known outside of Scandinavia are Gustaf Aulén's *Den kristna försoningstanken*, Stockholm: Diakonistyrelsen, 1930 (in English, *Christus Victor*, London: S.P.C.K., 1931); Anders Nygren's *Den kristna kärlekstanken genom tiderna*, Stockholm: Diakonistyrelsen, Vol. I, 1930, Vol. II, 1936 (in English, *Agape and Eros*, Philadelphia: Westminster Press, 1953); and Gustaf Wingren's *Skapelsen och*

and biblical theology.[1] But outside of Scandinavia, theologians have largely left untouched the painstaking methodological groundwork of the Lundensians—except for some more or less incidental references where other aspects of their thought are the main topic.[2] Most non-Scandinavian theologians would perhaps be able to identify the source of the method of motif-research, but only a very few people abroad have been able to penetrate the Lundensians' philosophical discourses and to appreciate the solidity of the methodological foundations on which *motivforskningen* is built.[3]

---

lagen, Lund: Gleerup, 1958 (in English, *Creation and Law*, Philadelphia: Muhlenberg Press, 1961).

[1] Gustaf Aulén's *The Faith of the Christian Church*, Philadelphia: Muhlenberg Press (1960), had gone through four editions in Sweden before its first English translation in 1948. The second English translation takes account of Aulén's extensive revisions, incorporated in the fifth Swedish edition. A sixth, further revised edition was published in Sweden in 1965. In the biblical field, the most important translations into English are Anders Nygren's *Commentary on Romans*, Philadelphia: Muhlenberg Press (1949); Ragnar Bring's *Commentary on Galatians*, Philadelphia: Muhlenberg Press (1961); and Gustaf Wingren's *The Living Word*, 1960.

[2] The most serious studies of the Lundensian methodology published in English are Nels S. Ferré's *Swedish Contributions to Modern Theology*, New York: Harper (1939), and Bernhard Erling's *Nature and History: A Study in Theological Methodology with Special Attention to the Method of Motif-Research*, Lund: Studia Theologica Lundensia, No. 19, 1960. Shorter treatments of Swedish methodology are found in Edwin E. Aubrey, *Present Theological Tendencies*, New York & London: Harper, 1936; Denzil G. M. Patrick, "Some Trends in Contemporary Theology," *The Student World*, 31, 1938, pp. 363-377; Ragnar Bring, "Die neuere schwedische Theologie," *Ekklesia*, II, 5, *Die Kirche in Schweden*, Gotha: Klotz, 1935, pp. 70-90; Ragnar Bring, "Einige Blätter aus der schwedischen Lutherforschung," *ZST*, 8, 1931, pp. 615-670; Carl Gustaf Carlfelt, "Recent Swedish Theologians and Their Theology," *Journal of Theology of the American Lutheran Conference*, VII, 1942, pp. 481-510; Leiv Aalen, "Principal Systematic Problems of Present-Day Scandinavian Theology," *Lutheran World*, III, 1956, pp. 45 ff; Gustaf Wingren, "Swedish Theology Since 1900," *Scottish Journal of Theology*, 1956; Anders Nygren, "The Religious Realm of Meaning," *The Christian Century*, July 16, 1958, pp. 824 ff; and Bernhard Erling, "Swedish Theology from Nygren to Wingren," *Religion in Life*, Spring 1961, pp. 196-208. The appearance before long of Charles W. Kegley, ed., *The Philosophy and Theology of Anders Nygren*, in the "Library of Living Theology" series, will in considerable measure serve to open the Lundensian methodology to the international theological community.

[3] In America, a few academic dissertations have treated Lundensian methodology, or some aspect of it, with some understanding of its intentions; cf. William A. Johnson, *The Religious A Priori. A Critical Evaluation of the Philosophy of Religion of Anders Nygren, with Particular Reference to his Dependence upon Schleiermacher*, Columbia-Union, 1960; George Rudolph Gordh, *Criticism of Reason in Contemporary Theological Methodology*, University of Chicago, 1941; and Elder M. Lindahl, *On Relating Philosophical Inquiry to Religious Convictions, with Special Reference to the Early Writings of Bishop Anders Nygren*, Northwestern, 1966.

The reason for this lack of understanding for Lundensian methodology is twofold. In the first place, the language barrier drastically limits the accessibility of the primary sources. Virtually none of the works contributing to the development of this theological method has been translated into other languages. A list of Nygren's major works from the period between 1919 and 1923, for example, includes the titles of four books without which no man can claim to understand the Lundensians' work; namely *Det religionsfilosofiska grundproblemet*; *Religiöst apriori, dess filosofiska förutsättningar och teologiska konsekvenser*; *Dogmatikens vetenskapliga grundläggning*; and *Filosofisk och kristen etik*. None is available except in the Swedish language. Nygren's magnum opus, *Agape and Eros*, which was probably the work that the British theologian had in mind when complimenting him as a 'great teacher', includes only a short sketch of motif-research as theological method. Aulén's *The Faith of the Christian Church*, the work most often identified as the definitive presentation of Lundensian theology, contains an introductory chapter on methodological questions, but it is limited in its impact, partly because of Aulén's well guarded style, partly because non-Scandinavian readers have no way of understanding its theoretical foundations. A little book by Gustaf Wingren, *Theology in Conflict*, published in 1958,[1] includes a chapter that is sharply critical of Nygren's methodology, and this has helped to bring one of the sharpest controversies in modern Swedish theology before a larger audience. However, Nygren has complained—quite justifiably—that since his own methodological works are not available in English he has been placed in an awkward position by the appearance of Wingren's work.[2] This problem has been reduced somewhat by the subsequent publication of the English edition of Nygren's popularly styled *Det bestående i kristendomen* (English title, *The Essence of Christianity*),[3] but the international theological community is still without the material most needed for the understanding of the Lundensians' work.[4]

---

[1] Philadelphia: Muhlenberg Press (1958).

[2] The sharp methodological exchange between the two occurred during 1955/56. Cf. Nygren, "Till teologiens metodfråga," *STK*, 32, 1956, p. 22; also pp. 122 ff; 284 ff.

[3] Translated by Philip Watson, London: The Epworth Press (1960).

[4] The most important of these are, by Anders Nygren, *Det religionsfilosofiska grundproblemet*, reprinted from *Bibelforskaren*, 1919-1921, Lund: Gleerup, 1921; *Religiöst apriori, dess filosofiska förutsättningar och teologiska konsekvenser*, Lund: Gleerup, 1921; *Dogmatikens vetenskapliga grundläggning*, *LUÅ*, N.f., Avd. I, Bd.

There is another side to the matter. The reason for the lack of understanding of the theoretical underpinnings of Lundensian theology may also be found in the general disinterest, in Europe as well as in America, toward the hard core methodological problems that are preliminary to the theologian's work. Very few of the theologians involved in the neo-orthodox recovery of theology during the 1920's and 1930's, following the collapse of post-Ritschlian humanism and social gospel liberalism, had the inclination or the leisure to uncover and reconsider the deep running philosophical issues to which the theologians of the late nineteenth and the early twentieth century had been forced to take a stand. Karl Barth, who became the patriarch of the new theology, fathering the ideas as well as the language of most other theologians of the time, made a conscious commitment to avoid not only the philosophical point of view but even the philosophical problems of ordinary men of thought. In his own *prologomena* to theology, Barth restricted himself to the theological perspective, centering his own methodological consider-ations on the revelational concept of "the Word of God" and claim-ing it as the principle of both knowledge and truth.[1] Emil Brunner, who soon found Barth's revelation epistemology too narrow, attempt-ed to widen the concept of revelation by relating it to reason as a possible point of contact for the divine truth confronting man. But in developing the dialectic of „the divine-human encounter", Brunner persisted in his original point of view, starting with "revelation as the subject of a Christian theory of knowledge" or "as a doctrine of believing knowledge... the foundation and the norm of all knowledge

---

17, 8 (1922); *Filosofisk och kristen etik*, LUÅ, N.f., Avd. I, Bd. 18, 8 (1923); *Filo-sofi och motivforskning*, Stockholm: Diakonistyrelsen (1940); and by Ragnar Bring, *Till frågan om den systematiska teologiens uppgift* (hereafter STU), 1933; *Teologi och religion* (ToR), 1937; *Wie ist nicht-metaphysische Philosophie möglich?* (NmPh), 1939-40. Other important methodological works on the Swedish scene are, by Torsten Bohlin, *Tro och uppenbarelse*, Stockholm: Diakonistyrelsen, 1926; *Kierkegaards dogmatiska åskådning*, Stockholm: Diakonistyrelsen, 1925; by Arvid Runestam, *Wilhelm Herrmanns teologi. En kritiks studie*, Uppsala: Förtattaren, 1921; by Hjalmar Lindroth, *Schleiermachers religionsbegrepp. Förutsättningar och konsekvenser*, UUÅ, 1926, Teologi, Bd. 1; and by John Cullberg, *Religion och vetenskap. Till frågan om den systematiska teologiens vetenskapliga grundläggning*, Stockholm: Diakonistyrelsen, 1930. In addition, it is imperative for anyone who seeks to understand Swedish theology in the twenthieth century to take note of important materials published in the excellent theological quarterly, *Svensk teologisk kvartalskrift* (*STK*), started in 1925 under the leadership of Gustaf Aulén, Arvid Runestam, *et. al.*

[1] Cf. *Church Dogmatics*, Vol. I, Part I, 2, 6 and 7.

of faith," [1] thus proving himself bound within the circles that hold Barth captive. The situation was not much different in the thought of Paul Tillich. Laying the groundwork for his "method of correlation", he began his methodology with what he calls an "epistemological" consideration, but it was soon evident that Tillich's "epistemology" has little to do with what this term normally means. He did not develop a theory of knowledge. His epistemology represents, instead, a theological process by which the human situation, "reason", is interpreted in such a way as to require divine truth, "revelation", in order to avoid conflicts and gain meaning.[2] Tillich's starting point is, in essence, the same as Barth's and Brunner's. Their "epistemology" is not epistemological in the sense that it contains a common-sensical theory of the nature of human knowledge, religious knowledge included. It is a part of their system of theology, and it either ignores the realities of the intellectual situation or theologizes about them.

One illustrious exception to this general disinterest in the theoretical background of theology is provided by the so-called history of religion school. Here the analysis of the nature of religious experience, so important for the understanding of the nature of theology, was undertaken in several different ways: William James approached the subject from an empirical-psychological point of view; Nathan Söderblom and Joachim Wach pursued the matter in historical-sociological categories; and Rudolf Otto, the dean of the movement, worked mostly on the philosophical-theological definition of the essence of religion. In a comment aimed directly at systematic theology, Otto advised that "no one ought to concern himself with the 'Numen ineffabile' who has not already devoted assiduous and serious study to the 'Ratio aeterna'." [3] Theologians, however, did not seem to get the point. The work of the psychologists and sociologists and philosophers of religion was generally dismissed as falling under the rubric of "anthropocentrism", and the contributions of Otto came to have importance more for theological terminology than for theological methodology. Characteristically, the theological community generally acclaims Otto as the author of *Das Heilige*, all but forgetting that he also wrote *Die Kantisch-Fries'sche Religionsphilosophie*.

---

[1] *Revelation and Reason*, Philadelphia: Westminster Press (1946), pp. 3, 12.
[2] Cf. *Systematic Theology*, Vol. I, Chicago: University of Chicago Press, 1951, p. 94.
[3] In the preface to the first English edition, *The Idea of the Holy*, New York: Oxford University Press, 1958, p. XXI.

One should not, in retrospect, judge the leaders of the twentieth century theological recovery too harshly, however. They were faced with a theological situation in which the bankruptcy of the nineteenth century was announced simultaneously by members of the theological community and the society to which they had addressed themselves. The theological announcement took the form of two books, both of which revealed—although in different ways—the process of steadily diminishing returns into which nineteenth century theological methodology had brought the scholars of the faith: Adolf von Harnack's *What is Christianity*, published in 1900, and Albert Schweitzer's *The Quest of the Historical Jesus*, published in 1905. Schweitzer's book offered a thorough reevaluation of the historical-critical approach to Christology, pointing in no uncertain terms to the hopelessness of the attempt to obtain knowledge of Christian truth by scientific textual research. Harnack's work marked the mature stage of the nineteenth century understanding of Christianity. It was thought by many to inaugurate a new era for theology; but it came, instead, to symbolize the end of an era. Harnack's historical analyses of the essential content of Christian faith had resulted in an interpretation that was closer to the ideas of the Enlightenment and the nineteenth century humanism than to the theology of Paul or Luther.

And then the political announcement came, setting a brutal period to all the social optimism of liberal progressivistic theology: World War I, the Versailles Treaty, the Great Recession, the rise of Nazi Germany, World War II. Theology was forced to cope with crisis—crisis in its own camp, crisis in its environment.

The tools for coping with the crisis of theology were twofold, rising out of and transcending the limits of nineteenth century historical research. One was the application of historical methods to the study of historical theology, particularly Reformation theology, and most especially Luther's thought; the other was the utilization of historical-textual criticism as a means for the study of biblical theology, particularly New Testament theology, and most especially Paul's thought. Luther-research had slowly established itself, through the efforts of men like Otto Ritschl, Fr. Loofs, O. Scheel and others, as a respectable scientific discipline; and with the work of Karl Holl, E. Hirsch, P. Althaus, F. Kattenbusch and many more, it bloomed into a veritable Luther-renaissance that could not but influence the mood of theology in general. The most spectacular tool of theological renewal, however, was the radical reversal in the general estimation of Paul's influence on Christian thought that was inaugurated so decisively with Karl Barth's theological commentary, *The Epistle to the Romans*, first published in 1918 and reissued in a completely revised edition in 1921. With this work, and with the subsequent writings of Barth, Fr. Gogarten, Emil Brunner and others, European theology moved quickly into an era of recovery and reconstruction. It was characterized by a determined rejection of the nineteenth century idealization of man and nature, and an unyielding opposition to the humanization of Christianity; its own aim was to lead the church back to a traditional but renewed Christian understanding of God, man, sin, salvation, and the Kingdom of God. When "crisis theology" finally gained self-consciousness, therefore, its attention came to focus almost exclusively on the recovery of essential Christian doctrinal emphases. The problems concerning the contemporary philosophical context and the modern conceptualization of doctrine—the methodological backdrop of nineteenth century theology—were largely laid aside. The neo-orthodox community of scholars reasoned that the nineteenth century methodological framework was precisely what was to blame for the theological crisis. As a consequence, in opposing the results of this methodology, the leaders of the renewal movement made short process with the presuppositions of this theology as a whole.

When we come to consider how the Lundensian theology of the same period fits into the picture of theological crisis and recovery, it is immediately clear that this theology is different. The Lundensians responded to the crisis not by way of singular concentration on the content of faith. They did emphasize the need of a deeper understanding of the essence of Christianity, but they were also concerned to discuss the dynamics of such an understanding in the context of the contemporary intellectual situation. The Lundensian theologians were concerned with the renewal of evangelical Christian theology, to be sure; but they understood also that such a renewal can never be accomplished by way of a methodology which proposes to disregard the contemporary problems of mind and culture. What in their view was needed in order to bring theology through its crisis and on to a full awareness of its nature and content was partly a new understanding of the traditional emphases of evangelical Christian faith, partly a thorough-going reexamination of the epistemological and philosophical presuppositions for theology itself. As the present leader of Lundensian theology, Gustaf Wingren, says:

"An examination of the programme (the return of theology to the Word of God) can only take place as a part of a thorough-going analysis of the methodology of theology. This task has been attempted in Sweden with an interest and thoroughness scarcely paralleled elsewhere and has been given a wide setting within the philosophy of religion—reference to the work of A. Nygren and R. Bring alone suffices." [1]

Pursuing their double interest in the content and the method of authentic Christian theology, the Lundensians sought their way back to the sources from which, in their view, modern theology must learn its lessons: the Reformation theology of Luther, and the critical philosophy of Kant and Schleiermacher. The two poles from which the modern Lundensian theology has taken its orientation are thereby identified: Luther-research and critical philosophy. The former gives guidance in regard to theological content; the latter is the starting point in methodological matters.

The story of Swedish Luther-research does not fall within the limits of this book. Its importance, however, must be clearly recognized. It is interesting to note that the Swedish theological community claims to have initiated the Luther-renaissance in Europe some time before Karl Holl came on the scene.[2] Nathan Söderblom and Einar Billing, from the beginning of their academic careers at Uppsala in the early years of this century, gave unequivocal indications of what was to be a major tradition in Swedish theological scholarship in the twentieth century. Many young scholars were inspired by their example and leadership.[3] Whether or not the Swedish claim holds, one may safely say that they have been "foremost in the reinterpretation of the reformer's doctrine" [4] and that they have approached the study of Luther with an energy and a depth of perspective which is unmatched anywhere else. They take justifiable pride in their work, and they have reaped a rich harvest from it; their work on Luther has contributed significantly to the shaping of their own theology.

While the Swedish contributions to the study of Luther's the-

---

[1] *The Living Word*, 1960, p. 23.

[2] Gustaf Aulén, "Det teologiska nutidsläget," *STK*, 5, 1929, pp. 123 f; Ragnar Bring, *Dualismen hos Luther* (DhL), Stockholm: Diakonistyrelsen, 1929, p. 17, footnote 38. Cf. also Aulén's review of this work, *STK*, 30, 1954, p. 237.

[3] Cf. Hjalmar Lindroth, *Lutherrenässansen i nyare svensk teologi*, Stockholm: Diakonistyrelsen, 1941, p. 7; and E. Rodhe, "En blick på de trenne sista decenniernas svenska teologi," *STK*, 3, 1927, pp. 325 f.

[4] Daniel Day Williams, *What Present-Day Theologians Are Thinking*, 1959, p. 47.

ology definitely identify the Scandinavian theological recovery with the neo-orthodox renewal movements on the European continent, one should note that the Lundensians' interest in philosophical criticism, and particularly their attachment to the epistemology of Kant and the philosophy of religion of Schleiermacher, definitely distinguishes them from their Barthian counterparts. A comparison between Karl Barth and the leading Lundensian methodologians, Anders Nygren and Ragnar Bring, is quite instructive at this point.

In an interesting passage in his *Protestant Thought from Rousseau to Ritschl*,[1] Barth delineates three alternative ways of evaluating the relevance of Kant's philosophy for theology. The first possibility is to accept the Kantian premises and, on their basis, to proceed to execute the Kantian program in various ways (more "compactly" or more "freely"). This is the way of the rationalists of the late eighteenth and early nineteenth centuries and the leaders of the Kant-revival in the second half of the nineteenth century, Ritschl and Herrmann. The second possibility is to accept Kant's basic methodological presuppositions and to widen his *a priori* to include not only the categories of theoretical and practical reason, but also a religious *a priori*. This attempt to correct Kant, according to Barth, is Schleiermacher's and De Wette's way, and it was influential in the so-called positive or conservative theology of the nineteenth century as well as in the liberal theology of the late nineteenth and early twentieth century. Both of these alternatives give evidence that "theology desires in principle to keep the Kantian terms for peace." In his own judgment, however, a theology which pursues any one of these lines is bound to become "the direct continuation of the theology of the Enlightenment." To avoid this, a third approach must be taken, Barth's own. That is to question not only Kant's conception of religion, but to refuse the Kantian scheme altogether. As a theologian, Barth desires to speak of religion not in terms of a human function, "religion within the limits of reason," but as having to do with "the other side, the significant point to which this function is related and whence it springs, the dealings...of a God who is not identical with the quintessence of human reason...."[2] This is Hegel's and Marheineke's and Dorner's line, says Barth, and it is the only way by which theology can gain independence in relation to philosophy. It consists in

---

[1] New York: Harper, 1959, pp. 190 ff.
[2] *Ibid.*, p. 191.

"theology resigning itself to stand on its own feet in relation to philosophy, in theology recognizing the point of departure for its method in revelation, just as decidedly as philosophy sees its point of departure in reason, and in theology conducting, therefore, a dialogue with philosophy, and not—wrapping itself up in the mantle of philosophy—a quasi-philosophical dialogue." [1]

The Lundensians part company with Barth here—and at a rather elementary point, one might add. Critical philosophy, in their view, is not the cause of the theological crisis; on the contrary, it points the way to the solution. We shall have occasion to analyze how Nygren and Bring attach their methodology to certain elements in Kant's and Schleiermacher's thought, attempting to develop a modern philosophy of religion that would represent a consistent application of the critical presuppositions of the masters. The Lundensians approach Kant, then, more in line with the second of Barth's alternatives than either the first or the third. They are particularly sensitive—more so, they claim, than either Kant or Schleiermacher themselves—to any metaphysical tendencies, whether these appear in the form of a Hegelian desire to speak of absolute reality as if one had knowledge of it or in the form of a positivistic, inner-worldly identity-philosophy. Barth's desire to speak of "the other side" is, in Nygren's and Bring's view, philosophically invalid. So also is the philosophical-theological "dialogue" which Barth advocates. It simply sets the two disciplines over against one another as opponents, each making claims to absoluteness of insight and finality of truth. No significant dialogue is possible between contending systems of metaphysics. Dialogue between philosophy and theology can only be established if both parties recognize their own particular area of competence, agree to respect the special interests and perspectives which they both bring to the encounter, and thus observe both the autonomy and the interaction of the two disciplines. The relationship between theology and philosophy is best defined, according to the Lundensians, in terms of two different but complementary functions. Karl Barth, on his side, does not see the possibility of such a relationship between the two. In his view, theology ought to take up "the Hegelian demands" rather than give in to the Kantian terms for peace. [2]

It is evident, then, that the Lundensian approach to the recovery of

---

[1] *Ibid.*
[2] *Ibid.*, pp. 299 f.

theology belongs to a tradition of thought that is entirely different from its continental, Barthian correlary. Morton White, in *The Age of Analysis*, describes the two main traditions of twentieth century philosophy as "the hedgehogs" and "the foxes": those, on the one hand, "who are content to know the many little things in life" and those, on the other hand, who "strive to know one big thing" above all other things.[1] While Barth is apparently prepared not only to join the foxes, but to take up discussion with others among them, the Lundensians appear to be quite satisfied with participating in the humble tradition of the hedgehogs.[2] There is definitely an empiricistic trend in their thought; the influence of philosophical positivism is evident in their methodology; their philosophy is a brand of critical analysis; and their theology is defined as an objective, descriptive science. The object of theology is faith—the Christian faith as historically given, available for investigation and interpretation by responsible men who work according to scientific principles of research. The aim of theology is simply the understanding of faith, not the definition of absolute truth .As Ragnar Bring says,

> "these are two separate and distinct tasks: to show what is the right and genuine Christian faith, and to prove by some scientific verification that this faith is right. To show what is genuinely Christian is certainly the task of systematic theology; but to try to show that this represents an understanding of life which is 'right' or represents 'truth' is a different task, and must not be mixed with the first one." [3]

Notice, in contrast, the following pronouncement by Barth concerning the task of theology:

> "It should not be concerned with manifestations of life in general, with some kind of expressions, declarations, avowels, assertions and symbols attempting to express the inexpressible in some form or another, nor with a kind of verbal music-making, nor with a description of conditions or circumstances, nor even with a view of essentials, however deep, but with truth, with a kind of knowledge which does not have its foundation in some kind of given thing, as such, but in the link of this given thing with the final origin of everything given. If theology does not speak the truth in this sense, then

---

[1] *The Age of Analysis*, New York: New American Library (1957), p. 18.

[2] Wingren, in "Några karakteristiska drag i modern teologi," *STK*, 27, 1951, pp. 241 ff, makes a comparison between dialectic theology and Lundensian thought and finds the Lundensians to be influenced by the history of religion school, critical philosophy, and Schleiermacher, while dialectic theology is more dependent on form criticism, existential philosophy, and Heidegger.

[3] *STU*, 1933, p. 180.

in what sense can it assert that it is speaking of God?...A theology whose basis was merely historical, merely psychological, merely phenomenological, could in fact stand in...(a) questionable shadow. And did not nineteenth century theology to a large extent stand indeed in this shadow when and after it passed by Hegel's doctrine? " [1]

Against this background, we find it difficult to understand Nels Ferré's recurring evaluation of Lundensian theology as being "definitely Barthian", made up of "the results of the modern '*Lutherforschung*' heavily spiced with Barthian thought." [2] Barthian thought has, in fact, never had much of a market in Scandinavia.[3] Most of the major theologians in Sweden have been sharply critical of dialectic theology. Torsten Bohlin at Uppsala, for example, made it clear already in 1925 that the Swedish theological recovery should be distinguished clearly from dialectic trends of thought.[4] Aulén has been eager to

---

[1] *Op. cit.*, p. 299.

[2] *Swedish Contributions...*, 1939, pp. 24, 28. This book was republished by Harper & Row, New York, in 1967 (Torch Book edition). Ferré's impressions of Lundensian thought apparently have not changed.

[3] In private conversation, Anders Nygren once made the comment that "We have not turned Barthian in Sweden, because we never really needed Karl Barth here." For the same sentiment, cf. Ragnar Bring, *ZST*, 8, 1931, pp. 669 , note 1; and Gustaf Wingren, *Svensk teologi efter 1900*, Stockholm: Sveriges kristliga studentrörelse, 1958, pp. 13 f. Very few studies of Karl Barth's thought have originated in Sweden; only three are of consequence, namely John O. Cullberg, *Das Problem der Etik in der dialektischen Theologie, I. Karl Barth*, UUÅ, 1938, 4; Gustaf Wingren's *Gott und Mensch bei Karl Barth*, *Luthertum*, Hft. 2, 1951; and Benkt-Erik Benktson, *Den naturliga teologiens problem hos Karl Barth*, Lund: Gleerup, 1948. This last work is hailed by Regin Prenter as "the beginning of a squaring of accounts" between Swedish theology and Barth, "with whom they evidently have had difficulties coming to terms before." *STK*, 25, 1949, p. 258. Benktson has recently broadened his critique of Barth by comparing him with Bonhoeffer and Tillich; cf. *Christus und die Religion. Der Religionsbegriff bei Barth, Bonhoeffer und Tillich*, Stuttgart: Calver Verlag (1967).

[4] In two very incisive articles on the subject, *STK*, 1, 1925, pp. 156-176, 219-232, and in his book *Tro och uppenbarelse*, 1926, Bohlin expresses the following criticisms of dialectic theology: Its absolute qualitative distinction between God and man is a metaphysical distinction and not a religious one; it is not primarily a contrast between two concepts of God, but an instance of a general and abstract philosophical polarity of time and eternity. Thus, neither man's sin nor his salvation is understood in a fully ethical-religious way. Furthermore, although it denies a point of contact in man to which eternity may connect itself, dialectic theology defines eternity as the opposite of everything *"diesseits"*—which means in dialectic dependence of the world. Thus, dialectic theology operates within the problematics of immanentism. Should it attempt to free itself from this by denying the dialectic relationship between the *diesseits* and eternity, the result will be that revelation is entirely heterogeneous to man, completely tangential to history. This makes Christology problematic, incarnation becomes modalism, and faith is interpreted in exclusively ideal-forensic terms.

make the same point.[1] In a manner that is characteristic of his own interests, Ragnar Bring made the comment in 1937 that the weakness of dialectic theology is that "it does not so far seem to have found methodological clarity." [2] This is exemplified, in Bring's view, by the Barthian interpretation of Schleiermacher. In opposing Schleiermacher's psychologistic tendencies, the Barthians overlook other important methodological contributions of his, thus proving themselves bound within an understanding of theology which is totally out of step with the modern situation. Likewise, in their reaction to Harnack's understanding of Christianity, the dialectic theologians make a "crisis type response" and do not meet the challenge of this theology by way of an objective evaluation of Harnack's methods and use of materials. To oppose Harnack's views is one thing, says Bring; to reject his methods of investigation without closer analysis is altogether different.[3]

There is, as we have seen, little to indicate any family relationship between the Swedish theological recovery and continental neo-orthodox movements of thought. Certain features, such as the influence of Reformation theology and the emphasis on the theocentric character of the Christian faith, are common to both, but this does not cover up the fact that certain radical differences in their philosophical orientation make their theological methodology, their understanding of the nature of faith, and their view of the function of theology completely incompatible. In the Swedish theological community—of which the Lundensian school forms the strongest flank in the twentieth century—dialectic theology is valued generally for having

---

[1] Aulén emphasizes particularly the polemic character of dialectic theology, arguing that a purely negative relationship to the theology one seeks to counter-act easily means that one becomes "negatively dependent" on one's opponents. "Det teologiska nutidsläget," *STK*, 5, 1929, pp. 130 f. Cf. also "Inför Einar Billings sextioårsdag...," *STK*, 7, 1931, pp. 236 f.

[2] *ToR*, 1937, p. 148. Bring does point out that dialectic theology, in its critique of the so-called theology of experience, is not returning to a pre-critical metaphysics. *STU*, 1933, pp. 35 f. However, in structuring its opposition to humanistic idealism on the absolute qualitative distinction of God and man, dialectic theology proves itself bound within the idealistic philosophical framework. *STK*, 10, 1934, p. 385. To set the dialectic contrast between God and creature in the place of Harnack's contrast between the ethical and the physical does not necessarily mean that the idealistic framework has been erased. *ToR*, 1937, pp. 202, 214.

[3] *Ibid.*, p. 183. Bring does not blame Harnack for trying to understand the historical material on the basis of certain opinions concerning its essential meaning; Harnack goes wrong where he forgets that his opinions are only hypothetical. He is at fault, in other words, for not being scientifically responsible. *Ibid.*, pp. 184 f.

spearheaded the renewal of Protestant thought on the continent of Europe, but it is blamed for having left half the task aside: the methodological groundwork. In their own work, the Lundensians have combined the efforts to recover the essential Christian emphases of faith and doctrine with equally significant endeavors in the interest of developing an understanding of theology as a modern discipline of thought. The main problem of contemporary theology, clearly identified and consciously acknowledged by the Lundensian theologians, is how and in what sense Christian systematic theology can be made both positively Christian and strictly scientific.[1] It has been their aim to develop a methodology that will assure both. Whether they have succeeded or have failed we shall not at this point venture to adjudicate. Their attempts at constructing such a methodology form the central plot in the story of the Lundensian school of theology. It shall be the story we pursue in the following chapters as we seek to explicate the methodological contributions of one of its leading proponents, Ragnar Bring. Our evaluation of the plot must wait until we are sure that we understand the Lundensian way.

---

[1] This is the problem raised by Nygren in *Dogmatikens vetenskapliga grundläggning*, 1922, and by Bring in *STU*, 1933. The term "scientific" is intended in the broad sense common to the European academic community, not in the restricted sense of the natural sciences.

CHAPTER TWO

METHODOLOGICAL TRENDS IN MODERN SWEDISH THEOLOGY

As background for our understanding of Ragnar Bring's thought, an attempt must be made to draw out certain features in the landscape of twentieth century Swedish theology as a whole. Our purpose here is simply to describe the "problematics" [1] involved and to make the reader conversant with the main elements of the discussion between the major theologians on the Swedish scene. No exhaustive treatment can be undertaken here. What is intended is primarily to identify the particular philosophical and theological succession within which Lundensian theology—and especially Ragnar Bring —belongs, and secondarily to relate this tradition to other alternatives on the scene.

The two main centers of theology in Sweden, the universities at Uppsala and Lund, are both characterized by peculiar brands of patriotism, and the friendly antagonism between them is often considerable, particularly during periods when the two theological faculties are dominated by somewhat different traditions of thought.[2] There is clear evidence of this relationship, at least to outsiders, in the competitive spirit with which the two schools are vying to take the theological initiative from time to time, each faculty putting its prominence and creativity in the balance against the incontestable contributions of the other. As a fair generalization, one may de-

---

[1] The Swedish language has some useful terms to refer to the dynamics of theological and philosophical discussions, namely *frågeställning*, meaning literally "question position", the way one poses problems, or *problematik*. Since there are no immediate synonyms in English, I shall make a corresponding noun by adding an s to the adjective "problematic", using it to refer to the whole context of a discussion, *i.e.* the internal structure of it as well as the constellation of questions to which it relates.

[2] One should note that although the two schools traditionally served as seminaries for the training of ministers, the church itself does not have jurisdiction over theological education. The theological faculties have not, therefore, been conformed to any ecclesiastical or confessional standards; they have been free to develop—though not without criticism from large groups of conservative churchmen—in step with the theological community at large. Asserting the consequences of this freedom to the fullest, the two faculties have now proposed a plan for reconstructing *theologicum* into a *religionsvetenskaplig* (science of religion) faculty (proposal dated March, 1968).

scribe the last half of the nineteenth century as a period of Lundensian domination in Swedish theology. Then, at the beginning of the twentieth century, the theological initiative passed to Uppsala for a period of approximately twenty years, after which the Lundensian faculty regained the leadership once more, now under the influence of Aulén and Nygren, Bring and Wingren. This is not to say, of course, that Uppsala had nothing to contribute to the theology of the late nineteenth century or that the Uppsala theologians since the 1920's have been unimportant men. It only serves to indicate where the growing edge of theology is most clearly apparent and where the theological work is marked by the greatest relevance to the continuing development of Christian theology at large. It is significant to note that the intermittant exchange of theological primacy between the two schools has not happened in mutual isolation or by way of internal developments exclusively. On the contrary, in each case when the theological initiative was seen to pass from the one school to the other the new leaders were strongly influenced by the other faculty. The development of Swedish theology shows a considerable degree of continuity and consistency, therefore, even though the issues have been many and the discussions lively at each stage.

SWEDISH THEOLOGICAL TRADITIONS

When Aulén in a 1954 article on the Lundensian theological tradition considered the possibility of finding some element of thought that could be said to characterize the school's faculty during the last one hundred years, he was led to confess that there is very little evidence of any identifiable continuity in content. [1] He is undoubtedly correct. Methodologically, the Lundensian scales have swung from the express Kantian commitments of the leader of the so-called "reform faculty", [2] Martin Eric Ahlman, to the Hegelianism of the leaders of the so-called "great faculty" in the middle of the nineteenth century,[3] among them E. G. Bring, and back again to the modified

---

[1] "Lundensisk teologisk tradition," *STK*, 30, 1954, pp. 230 ff.

[2] A group of liberal minded theologians, dominating the faculty at the University of Lund from the late 1820's to the early 1850's, and expressing definite interests in the creation of a scientific theology in the Enlightenment tradition.

[3] These were the theologians who published the conservative, highly ecclesiastically oriented *Swensk kyrkotidning*, between 1855 and 1863, and who attempted to develop a grand synthesis between Hegelian philosophy and orthodox Lutheranism. Cf. Gustaf Aulén, *Martin Eric Ahlman och Ebbe Gustaf Bring. En teologisk strid i Lund på 1840-talet*, LUÅ, N. f., Avd. I, Bd. 14, 5, 1918; Erik Wallgren,

Kantianism of the modern Lundensians. Nevertheless, there is a certain formal tradition involved. Common to all these men—and to Swedish academic theology at large—is a deep-rooted interest in philosophical and methodological questions.[1] Common also is a rather loose attachment to the great German philosophers and theologians. This may have something to do with the situation of theology within the modern Swedish community. Theology was here set within a milieu of increasing intellectual emancipation and free thought. The authority of the theologian to establish the ground-rules for his own discipline of thought was widely questioned. Intellectual selfrespect demanded that the theologian relate his work to the prevailing philosophies in university and culture, and this meant primarily entering into dialogue with the philosophers close at hand. The great philosophical and theological movements on the continent did exert its influence on the Swedish scene, of course, but they were not transplanted into the Scandinavian soil intact. Scandinavians have always had a tendency to modify and ,,scandinavianize" imported viewpoints;[2] this gives the intellectual community both a certain contact with the world at large and a certain independence in relation to the major schools of thought. We find Swedish theologians exhibiting these Scandinavian traits no less than Swedish philosophers do.

A few examples will be illustrative.

At the time of the "great faculty", there was a general squaring of accounts among Swedish philosophers, some of whom were followers of Hegelianism proper, as interpreted by J. J. Borelius, while others became disciples of a more personalistic modification of idealism represented by the influential Uppsala-philosopher Chr. J. Boström and his immediate successor, Axel Nyblaeus.[3] The theolo-

---

Individen och samfundet. Bidrag till kännedom om samfundstänkandet i Swensk kyrko-tidning 1855-63, Lund: Studia Theologica Lundensia, 16, 1959; and Ragnar Bring, "Swensk kyrkotidnings teologi. Reflexioner med anledning av Erik Wallgrens avhandling *Individen och samfundet,*" STK, 35, 1959, pp. 153-174.

[1] "The methodological questions have never ceased to engage the interest since (the time of the "great faculty")." Gustaf Aulén, STK, 30, 1954, p. 232.

[2] Cf. H. Höffding, *A History of Modern Philosophy,* II, Dover Publ., 1955, pp. 283 ff; E. Ryding, *Den svenska filosofins historia,* Stockholm: Natur och Kultur (1959).

[3] Boström expressed in the beginning of his career a close attachment to a speculative transcendentalist philosophy, but he came soon to develop a sharp critique of this standpoint, particularly of its tendency to reject individuality or personal experience and its preference for pantheistic metaphysics. His own view can be described as personalistic-idealistic theism; it shows considerable influence

gians at Uppsala and Lund did not participate directly in the sometimes heated discussions, but it is obvious that their interest in the outcome was considerable. The sympathies of the "great faculty" were to begin with clearly on the side of the Hegelian camp; it seemed to give the greatest promises for the grand theocentric synthesis which they were committed to produce.[1] However, several factors influenced them to move in the direction of the Boströmian modifications. The Hegelianism of the "great faculty" was closely correlated with a commitment to Lutheran orthodoxy and a traditional Swedish high church ecclesiology. The theological program of these nineteenth century Lundensians was constructed accordingly. They did not intend to pursue a synthesis of a speculative, transcendent, and purely theoretical nature; theirs was a practical, cultural, and ecclesiological interest.[2] Their theology rested on three pillars: God, the church, and the nation. Having thus turned their attention away from the transcendent and to the historical, Boström's philosophy at once came closer to hand. At first, the theological community had been rather suspicious of Boström's thought.[3] But as time went on, it was evident that the experiential reorientation of philosophy which Boström presented opened the door for a fuller theological-philosophical conjunction than the traditional Hegelian speculation had. Typically, when E. G. Bring's son, Gustaf Bring, in 1876 published his dissertation on *Immanuel Kants förhållande till den filosofiska teologien*, a work which is written from a clearly identifi-

---

from Leibnitz' nomadology as well as Schleiermacher's brand of personalism. *Svenskt biografiskt lexikon*, Vol. 5, pp. 520 ff.

[1] In an article on E. G. Bring, *ibid.*, Vol. 6, pp. 250 ff, E. Rodhe points out that Bring, in an effort to overcome Schleiermacher's phenomenological tendencies, sought to develop a synthesis of the subjective and the objective in terms of God, who is defined as "the identity of thought and being." In religion, God reveals himself to man, and in this revelation man finds himself as man. He does not think his own thoughts any more; his life is "nothing but the free necessity of the progressing spiritual laws of God." E. G. Bring openly professes his dependence on Hegelian theologians like Marheineke and Daub. He is said to have been highly impressed by Martensen's *Dogmatik*—the work that Kierkegaard so strongly opposed.

[2] Ragnar Bring, "*Svensk kyrkotidnings* teologi...," *STK*, 35, 1959, p. 162. "The men of *Svensk kyrkotidning* accepted certain Hegelian thoughts, but the acceptance included reconstruction and incorporation into an independent Swedish theology. This was already evident when these thoughts were brought into contact with a doctrine of the church dominated by the idea of Christian culture." *Ibid.*, p. 157.

[3] Cf. E. Rodhe, "En blick på de trenne sista decenniernas svenska teologi," *STK*, 3, 1927, pp. 220 ff.

able Boströmian standpoint, even E. G. Bring seems to have been satisfied with it.

The philosophical idealism of nineteenth century Swedish theology cannot be described by way of continental parallels, then; German classifications such as "left wing" or "right wing" Hegelianism are not applicable on the Swedish scene. Should we ask whether theological classifications such as "Ritschlianism" are appropriate to describe any major tradition in Swedish theology, the answer is, again, only partially. One can find very few examples of open and avowed discipleship in relation to nineteenth century German theology. At best, the influence of the continental schools of thought is limited. At Uppsala, for example, the theological faculty was so enveloped in Boströmian idealism during the 1880's and 90's that when Ritschlian thought finally began to manifest itself among a few men, it was primarily the definition of faith as an expression of personal trust rather than assertion of doctrinal truth that interested them. The Uppsala-theologians took no part in the Ritschlian refutation of metaphysics.[1] Similarly, in Lund, where the successor to the "great faculty", Pehr Eklund, was attempting to incorporate the new continental trends into his thought, the elements he found most useful were Ritschl's concept of faith and Schleiermacher's interest in the definition of essential Christianity.[2] But via Ritschl's influence, Eklund was also brought to the study of Luther. This not only convinced him that Ritschl's concept of faith was true to the evangelical Christian understanding of religion; it revealed to him that other aspects of Ritschlian theology represented something less than "the purest of the gospel." [3] In short, Ritschl had no strait-laced disciple in Eklund.[4]

As the twentieth century began, so did a new era for Swedish theology. The new generation of theologians now taking over were definitely more open to the developments on the continent. At Uppsala, the dominating orientation was still inspired by Boström, but as the pressures of the scientific worldview and the historical-

---

[1] Gustaf Aulén, "Nathan Söderblom och nutida svensk teologi," *STK*, 2, 1926, p. 6; E. Rodhe, *op. cit.*, p. 221.

[2] *Ibid.*, pp. 222 f; cf. Bring, "Einige Blätter aus der schwedischen Lutherforschung," *ZST*, 8, 1931, pp. 618 f.

[3] Lindroth, *Lutherrenässansen...*, 1941, pp. 29 f.

[4] Edvard Rodhe calls him "supremely free of all theological partly lines; he never became, in the terminology of the nineties, a 'Ritschlian'." *STK*, 3, 1927, p. 223.

critical methods of biblical scholarship increasingly came to bear on theology, younger men like Söderblom and Billing began to search for fresh perspectives. They did not, however, become pure-bred Ritschlians.[1] Söderblom counted himself basically a disciple of Ritschl,[2] but he had no patience with the Ritschlian separation of subjective value judgments and objective truth. Söderblom never relinquished the view that faith leads to a deeper knowledge of reality than that which rational analysis produces.[3] Billing, who openly confessed his dependence on the methodology of Wilhelm Herrmann, obviously did not feel obliged to restrict himself to Ritchlian categories when developing his philosophy of history.[4] The same freedom in relation to Ritschl was also characteristic of Magnus Pfannenstill, Eklund's contemporary in Lund. Under the impact of an anti-metaphysical intellectual climate, Pfannenstill found himself rescued by the ethical-religious understanding of faith which he learned from the Ritschlian school of thought. Particularly important to him was Herrmann's view of the role of Christian experience as theological starting point. However, as the Ritschlian frame of reference seemed to develop an increasingly more inner-worldly character and Harnack became the authority to follow, Pfannenstill left the Ritschlian path.[5]

The absence of direct discipleship in relation to nineteenth century German theology should not blind us to the fact that there are strong Ritschlian undercurrents in the mainstream of Swedish theology in this century. They may, as the Swedes are prone to say, be the results of independent thought. Their formulation may be entirely indigenous to the Swedish Lutheran mindset, but they show that this theology stands within the framework of a typical Ritschlian problematics, nevertheless. In the *festskrift* honoring Bring, *Nordisk teologi. Ideer och män*, von Engeström discusses the legacy of Ritschl in modern

---

[1] Cf. Bring, *op. cit.*, pp. 619, 621; Runestam, *Svensk kyrka och teologi i dag*, Stockholm: Diakonistyrelsen, 1953, p. 9; and S. von Engeström, "Arvet from Albrecht Ritschl i den svenska teologien," *Nordisk teologi...*, 1955, p. 187. All three agree that the Ritschlianism of Söderblom and Billing was never consistent.

[2] Rodhe, *op. cit.*, p. 213, describing the struggle over Ritschlianism at Uppsala, points out that Söderblom's role was that of a defender of Ritschlian methodology.

[3] von Engeström, *op. cit.*, p. 191.

[4] Bring argues that Billing's dramatic view of history is a continuation of the Hegelian tendencies in the "great faculty", only that Billing exchanges monism for a dualistic perspective. Cf. "*Svensk kyrkotidnings* teologi...," *STK*, 35, 1959, pp. 166 f.

[5] Cf. Lindroth, *op. cit.*, pp. 31 ff; Rodhe, *op. cit.*, pp. 225 f.

Swedish theology and identifies three particular elements which must be ascribed to this source: first, the thesis that religious propositions are statements of value judgment, utterances concerned with religious meaning or the experience of salvation, and not functioning as metaphysical statements concerning the nature of reality in general; second, the explicit rejection of the juridical interpretation of God and the emphasis on love as the essence of the Christian God-concept; and third, the experience of Christian life in the context of vocation rather than in individual pietistic devotion.[1] Von Engeström is right. These emphases constitute something of a unifying principle in modern Swedish theology. One can find all these elements of the Ritschlian legacy echoed with special strength in Lundensian thought. And there are others.

Aulén, in the 1954 article referred to earlier, identifies three areas of consensus which he considers characteristic of Swedish theology as a whole during this century: a) the interest in and attachment to Luther, b) the interpretation of the church as "the community of grace", and c) the emphasis on "the purest of the gospel" or on essential Christianity.[2] Aulén's judgment is easily corroborated. Certainly, no other single item can be said to typify Swedish theology in this century—being its trade-mark, so to speak—as does Luther-research. "One may say without hesitation that the history of systematic theology in our country, from the beginning of this century until now, is in essence identical with the history of Swedish Luther-research in the same period," says Hjalmar Lindroth.[3] He is paraphrasing an earlier statement by Ragnar Bring: "Die Geschichte der systematischen Theologie in Schweden ist eine Geschichte der Lutherforschung." [4] So uniform is the Swedish orientation around Luther that Karl Barth was led to say that with Swedish theologians, "all God's ways...must end with Luther!" [5]

---

[1] One should note, however, that there is no unanimity in Swedish theology concerning the significance of personal religious experience. The influence of W. Herrmann can be found in Söderblom, Billing and Runestam, while Aulén and the other Lundensians have been more strictly Ritschlian in this respect. Their emphasis on the social aspects of Christian faith has been held within the context of the doctrine of the church, and consequently it has not developed into a social gospel. But the Lundensians have taken a stand against the subjectivistic tendencies of "the theology of experience." Cf. below, pp. 38; 42 f.

[2] "Lundensisk teologisk tradition," STK, 30, 1954, pp. 230 f.

[3] Lindroth, op. cit., p. 7.

[4] Bring, "Einige Blätter...," ZST, 8, 1931, p. 613.

[5] Benkt-Erik Bengston, STK, 36, 1960, p. 218.

Again, the central place of ecclesiology is certainly recognizable in the curriculum of Swedish theological concerns. It is so at Uppsala, where the so-called "young church" movement sprang to life in the early part of the century under the leadership of J. A. Eklund, Einar Billing, and Manfred Björkquist, [1] and where the current renewal of Swedish "high church" ecclesiology is centered. It is so also at Lund, where the nineteenth century revivalistic-pietistic influence of Henrik Schartau [2] and the high-churchly ecclesiology of the "great faculty" [3] were succeeded in the 1920's and 30's by the double barreled evangelical-ecclesiastical emphases of Gustaf Aulén and Yngve Brilioth.[4]

Finally, it is undoubtedly true that Swedish theology has been united in the pursuit of essential Christianity. This concern came to focus perhaps most clearly in the Lundensian response to the challenges of the Ritschl-Harnack tradition of thought, but it has been the aim of Swedish theologians of many persuasions and in various periods, whether the essence of faith was expressed in terms of biblical fundamentalism, Hegelian synthesis, confessional Lutheranism, or scientific historical motif-research.

RAGNAR BRING'S THEOLOGICAL PEDIGREE

From the general picture of the background of modern Swedish theology, we move now to a closer view of the particular historical succession from which Ragnar Bring emerges. In a sense, one may

---

[1] Rodhe refers to this movement as a "romantic" one, *STK*, 3, 1927, p. 316. For a thorough study of Billing's concept of the church, cf. Gösta Wrede, *Kyrkosynen i Einar Billings teologi*, Uppsala: Studia Doctrinae Christianae Upsaliensis, 5, 1966.

[2] Schartau, a West-Swedish Lutheran minister in the early nineteenth century, was heavily indoctrinated with Lutheran orthodoxy and Württemberg pietism. Bring, *op. cit.*, indicates that Schartau had a certain influence among students and faculty at the University of Lund.

[3] Bring suggests that the reason the strong churchly traditions in Sweden were not broken under the impact of nineteenth century pietism and its corollaries, religious individualism and congregationalist sectarianism, lies in the influence of the "great faculty" and of its publications, particularly *Swensk kyrkotidning. STK*, 35, 1959, pp. 169 f.

[4] The following titles represent the more important contributions of these men in the development of Lundensian ecclesiology; by Yngve Brilioth, *Nyanglikansk renässans*, Vol. I-III (1921-1923); *Svensk kyrkokunskap* (1933); *Kyrkokristendom* (1935); *Kampen om kyrkan* (1937); by Gustaf Aulén, *Till belysning av den lutherska kyrkoidén, dess historia och dess värde* (1912); *Evangeliskt kyrklighet* (1916); *Evangeliskt och romerskt* (1922); *Liturgiska förnyelsesträvanden och evangelisk kristendom* (1928); *Gammalkyrkligt och reformatoriskt* (1930); *Reformation och katolicitet* (1959).

say that he is an heir to all the main family traits of the Swedish theological traditions. But such a description of a single theologian is not very helpful. Bring, as well as any other individual theologian, constitutes a particular theological personality. One may point to the general configuration of a theologian's background and environment, but unless one knows the personal choices and commitments which have been made along the way, by the man himself and by those who can be considered his theological ancestors, one does not understand the man. We shall therefore look in a little more detail at those Swedish theologians who have contributed most to the formation of the context in which Ragnar Bring came to theological consciousness and in relation to which he found his own decisive stance.

Pehr Eklund. The most impressive—and most popular—theologian in Sweden in the 1890's and the early 1900's was undoubtedly Pehr Eklund in Lund. With the charming familiarity that characterizes students' relationship to popular teachers, Eklund was called—in his absence—just Pehr, and his colleagues generally regarded him the incarnation of the Lundensian scholar: the articulate, humorous, wide-ranging intellectual who is distinctive and recognizable in all that he does and says.[1] His ways and views can still be found influencing Lundensian thought. The reference here is not simply to his emphasis on Luther-research and his strong interest in identifying "the purest of the gospel". In Eklund's theological words, among which *Den apostoliska tron i Martin Luthers katekesutläggning*, published 1897-99, ranks as the major accomplishment, it is the unique way in which he defines the "purely evangelical"—the essence of Christianity—that has engaged the greatest interest. This essence, according to Eklund, lies in the Christian concept of faith, and the Christian concept of faith is clearest expressed in Luther's explications of the attitude of "trust in God".[2] There are those among the Swedish Luther scholars who analyze Luther's concept of faith in a different way, particularly in regard to the relation of trust and assertion of doctrine,[3] but Pehr

---

[1] Cf. Aulén, *STK*, 30, 1954, p. 229.

[2] *Den apostoliska tron i Martin Luthers katekesutläggning*, Hft. 1-5, Lund: Gleerup, 1897-99, pp. 78. f.

[3] So, for instance, Magnus Pfannenstill, *Luthers tro såsom förtröstan och kunskap*, Lund, LUÅ, N.f., Avd. I, Bd. 14, 4, 1918, where Luther is found to emphasize both trust and assertion of doctrine; Nils J. Göransson, *Luthers reformation. Historisk-psykologisk trosskildring*, Stockholm: Norstedt, 1920, pp. 238 ff, where faith is seen as personal acceptance and application of the Word of God; Sigfrid von Engeström, *Luthers trosbegrepp. Med särskild hänsyn till församhällandets betydelse*, Uppsala: UUÅ, Teologi 3, 1933, where the objective references in Luther's

Eklund's interpretation, closely parallel to Holl's later emphases, has held its position and is still influential in the tradition to which Ragnar Bring belongs.

Another contribution of Pehr Eklund's theology, a practice which to some extent is still kept alive in Lundensian thought, is the peculiar way in which he distinguishes the true evangelical faith, "the purest of the gospel", from various distorted interpretations of Christianity. Eklund usually spoke of three such distortions: a) the scholastic-orthodox-legalistic, b) the intellectualistic-rationalistic-theoretical, and c) the emotionalistic-pietistic-mystical.[1] Eklund used this scheme with such assurance and regularity of pattern that his students, with typical and charming disrespect, called his groupings "Pehr's cliches". This tendency to schematize and pigeon-hole types of doctrine, historical periods, or hypothetical alternatives, often dangerous in its oversimplification, is still in evidence in the historical-theological analyses of Aulén, Nygren, and Bring.

Nathan Söderblom. After the 24th of September, 1901, Pehr Eklund was no longer the greatest theological genius in Sweden. On that date, Nathan Söderblom gave his first lecture as professor at Uppsala, and it became the event from which Swedish theology reckons time in the modern period.[2] Gustaf Aulén, who was a student at Uppsala then, speaks of the event in 1926, in an article on "Nathan Söderblom och nutida svensk teologi." [3] The most striking innovation, in the eyes of the students, was the new emphasis on research, i.e. the scientific, historical investigation of the realities of religious thought and experience. Söderblom's words, "Not less science but more science, and with it new humility and new strength," became the seed of a new era for the theological community in Sweden. It manifested itself not only in a new respect for serious research among the theologians; it took expression also in a new attitude of respect for and acceptance of theology on the part of the academic community

conception of faith are coming to the fore and faith is identified as the humble assertion of God's will and work described in the doctrines; and Gustaf Ljunggren, *Synd och skuld i Luthers teologi*, Stockholm: Diakonistyrelsen, 1928, where the objective references of faith are emphasized together with its paradoxical nature.

[1] Cf. Rodhe, *STK*, 3, 1927, pp. 222-224; Aulén, *STK*, 30, 1954, pp. 233 f.

[2] Two excellent biographies of Söderblom are, by Tor Andrae, *Nathan Söderblom*, Uppsala: Lindblad, 1931; and by Bengt Sundkler, *Nathan Söderblom. His Life and Work*, Lund: Gleerup, 1968.

[3] *STK*, 2, 1926, pp. 3-19.

and the intellectuals.[1] This in itself was a major advance for Swedish theology, but the principal effect was more far-reaching yet. The most significant result of Söderblom's initiative was that theology under his influence received new methodological orientation and began to direct itself toward new materials and new tasks. Theology was defined as the science of religion. The object of study was historical religion—not only Christianity, but religion in general.[2] We shall find these themes again in Aulén, Nygren, and Bring.

Söderblom's importance for Swedish theology lies not only in his starting point, of course. With his respect for scientific research, Söderblom also revealed what Aulén calls a "praise-worthy accuracy with regard to the genuine"— the genuinely religious, the character-istically Christian, and the purely evangelical.[3] Thus, already in Söderblom do we find the combination of concerns which came to typify the Lundensians: scientific methodology and genuine Christian content. His approach is well illustrated in his very influential study of the nature of religion, *Uppenbarelsereligion*.[4] Söderblom analyzes the religions of the world, attempting to classify them according to type. First he draws a basic distinction between what he calls "natural" and "prophetic" religions. Characteristic of the former is that they develop in step with the cultural evolution in general, while the latter take their rise in some form of revelation and are not tied in with the stages of cultural growth.[5] Pursuing this perspective further, Söderblom goes on to distinguish, within "prophetic" or "revelation-al" religion, between a higher and a lower kind, or between a "general" and a "special" revelation.[6] This latter category of religion, the Christian, is characterized by a "peculiar awareness of the activity of the divine." It is theocentric and, in a revelational sense, even mystic.[7]

---

[1] Important, in this respect, was Söderblom's book on *Studiet av religionen*, Stockholm: Ljus, 1907.

[2] *Ibid.*, pp. 3, 99.

[3] Aulén, *op. cit.*, p. 8.

[4] First published in *Skrifter i teologiska och kyrkliga ämnen tilägnade C. A. Toren*, Uppsala: Schultz, 1903; 2nd ed., Stockholm: Diakonistyrelsen, 1930.

[5] For a brilliant analysis of Söderblom's philosophy of religion, cf. Erland Ehn-mark, *Religionsproblemet hos Nathan Söderblom*, Lund: Gleerup, 1949.

[6] "The facts of history impress upon faith in revelation the typological dis-tinction between a general and a special revelation." *Naturlig religion och religions-historia*, Stockholm: Bonnier, 1914, p. 110.

[7] Söderblom's analysis of the nature of mysticism is, perhaps, one of the most important of his contributions to the understanding of religious experience; his distinction between "infinity-mysticism" and "personality-mysticism" has since

With this emphasis on a peculiar experience of the divine, Söderblom moves from the analysis of the history of religion to the psychology of religion, his second major field of interest. Here the Lundensians leave Söderblom and go their own ways. At Uppsala, followers of Söderblom like Runestam, Bohlin, and von Engeström have been more open to these references to subjective religious experience; the Lundensians have explicitly disassociated themselves from such an interest. It represents, in their estimate, a tendency in the direction of the psychologism of Schleiermacher and Herrmann, and Lund distrusts such tendencies intensely. This differentiation in the response to Söderblom' interest in subjective religious experience marks the beginning of a fundamental distinction between two separate traditions in Swedish theology in this century, namely—for want of better descriptions—the Aulén-line and the Runestam-line. We shall have occasion to observe some facets of the debate between these two traditions at a later point. For Lundensian thought, the fear of subjectivity has had the effect that many of the important insights in Söderblom's analyses of religion, for example the distinction between "infinity-mysticism" and "personality-mysticism", are all but lost. All that remains is a strictly methodological (or theoretical) principle having to do with the distinction between the *eros* and the *agape* motifs, or between "egocentricity" and "theocentricity".[1] However, in the emphasis on revelation as characteristic of the prophetic-Christian understanding of religion, the Lundensians are in line with Söderblom.

A third major contribution of Söderblom comes into focus at this point: the emphasis on "dualism" as a distinctive feature of prophetic-Christian faith.[2] This was a bold step by Söderblom, particularly in view of the optimistic, life-asserting monism which was propounded by Ritschlian theology,[3] and so he had to qualify it well. In a series of consistent arguments, Söderblom shows that the dualism which is typical of prophetic religion is not the familiar metaphysical bifurca-

---

been generally adopted among philosophers of religion. Cf. *Uppenbarelsereligion*, 1930, pp. 87 f.

[1] Bring, in typical Lundensian fashion, calls the distinction of "personality-mysticism" and "infinity-mysticism" "eine äusserst fruchtbare Arbeitshypothese"; and he uses it as such, but only in a theoretical context, not with reference to religious experience. "Einige Blätter...," *ZST*, 8, 1931, pp. 624, 626, 627 ff. Cf. Aulén's refusal to use the term "mysticism" in connection with Christian faith, *The Faith of the Christian Church*, 1960, p. 46, footnote 2.

[2] Cf. Söderblom, *op. cit.*, pp. 61 f.

[3] F. ex. in H. H. Wendt, *Christentum und Dualismus*, Jena: G. Neuenhahn, 1909.

tion of nature and spirit; it is, instead, "practical, ethical, and religious" in character.[1] These are themes that are taken up, with much greater assurance—and greater clarity—by Aulén, Söderblom's star student at Uppsala, and by Bring, Aulén's successor in Lund.[2]

Einar Billing. At Söderblom's side in Uppsala, after 1908, was a young colleague, Einar Billing, whose father, Gottfrid Billing, had been educated at the university of Lund under the influence of the "great faculty". Einar Billing, who in his own studies had experienced the clash between "the great religious synthesis"—the emphases of his father and the Hegelian tradition—and the new exegetical principles which he found in the historical-critical school of Wellhausen,[3] was especially concerned to develop a modern philosophy of history which would leave room for both detailed historical research and an over-all synthetic interpretation. He found the starting point for his interpretive stance in Söderblom's analyses of the nature of prophetic-revelational religion,[4] and he took his approach to historical studies from another colleague at Uppsala, the great historian Harald Hjärne.[5] Armed in this way, Billing proceeded to construct his own interpretation of history with such concentration and forcefulness that it has inspired Swedish theology ever since. We shall consider here only a few important points left by Billing as a legacy to Lundensian theology.[6]

First, there is the strong emphasis on the dynamic-dramatic nature of history. Billing identifies the dramatic interpretation of history as characteristic of the prophetic-Christian understanding, in contrast to the cyclical-Greek interpretation of life and the evolutionistic-humanistic view of the world. The dynamic force of history, in Billing's view, is God's will; the drama of history is God's drama.

---

[1] *Op. cit.*, p. 62.

[2] Cf. Bring's positive estimation of Söderblom's thought at this point, *op. cit.*, p. 624.

[3] He tells of this experience in his *Herdabref till prästerskapet i Västerås stift,* Stockholm: Sveriges kristliga studentrörelse, 1920.

[4] Bring points out that Billing expanded Söderblom's views into a general theory of religious knowledge; *DhL*, 1929, p. 9.

[5] Cf. Rodhe, *STK*, 3, 1927, pp. 221, 313. Hjärne had broad interests in scholarship, politics, national and international conditions, and was widely influential in late nineteenth and early twentieth century Scandinavia. He was concerned also with the relation of church and state, and this gave Billing his point of contact.

[6] We find no need to mention further his fundamental importance in spurring Swedish scholarship toward Luther-research. For these aspects, cf. Bring, "Einige Blätter...," *ZST*, 8, 1931, p. 621; Wingren, *Svensk teologi....*, 1958, p. 10; and Lindroth, *Lutherrenässansen....*, 1941, pp. 7 f.

The conception of God as actively working in human history became, in fact, the ruling idea in Billing's theology. It was determinative for the understanding of the nature of Christian faith which he developed in his book *De etiska tankarna i urkristendomen i deras samband med dess religiösa tro*,[1] and it was decisive for the interpretation of Christology which he presented in an influential monograph on *Försoningen*,[2] a work which has been of formative importance for Lundensian explications of the atonement, primarily Aulén's, but also for Nygren's and Bring's.

From Billing's dramatic interpretation of history, the step is not long to a closer definition of the dynamic force of history in terms of Söderblom's dualism. God is active in history, but so are his "enemies". God's action in the world meets with oppostion; it takes on the nature of a "struggle", and history becomes a cosmic drama. It is shaped, as it were, in the dynamic interplay between "the powers of destruction" and "God's will to salvation". All things in life fall under the influence of one or the other of the dueling powers. On the one side stand the devil, self, sin, death; on the other, God, faith, grace, eternal life. In its essence, the drama takes shape as a continuing confrontation between egocentricity and theocentricity.[3]

According to Billing, even the Christian message—directed as it is to both sides of the dramatic conflict—is structured in terms of a series of "strenge Alternativen",[4] namely law and gospel, wrath and love, judgment and redemption. As a matter of fact, the correlation between the dualistic structure of the Christian message and the dualistic interpretation of life and history is so close that Billing's disciples—and the Lundensians foremost among them—often combine the negative aspects of the message with the "powers of destruction" in the world, speaking of the law, wrath, and judgment of God much the same way they refer to sin, death, and the devil.[5] This may, at times, seem confusing to the non-initiated. Moreover, on the positive side of the correlation, Billing connects the Christian

---

[1] Uppsala: Schultz, 1907.

[2] Uppsala: Almqvist & Wiksell, distr., 1908.

[3] Anders Nygren is a close follower of Billing in this respect; his *Agape and Eros* takes essentially the same approach as Billing's *De etiska tankarna....* We shall see that Ragnar Bring makes use of the same methodological perspective. Cf. below, pp. 190 ff.

[4] Bring, *op. cit.*, p. 632.

[5] See f. ex. Nygren's *Commentary on Romans*, 1949, and Aulén's *Christus Victor*, 1931, which are particularly clear instances of this practice.

message and actual history so closely that the symbols of God's "will to salvation", the incarnation, the gospel, and the church are seen as "real acts of God", "God manifesting himself objectively" in Christ,[1] in the Word, and in the Church.[2] It is this positive side of the Christian message which is identified as the "essence of the gospel". To many of Billing's disciples, this approach has seemed helpful. It concentrates the understanding of Christianity around the basic motifs of love (*agape*) and redemption. The Lundensians have proven themselves particularly faithful disciples of Billing in this respect. However, one problem has continually risen to haunt them: the relationship between law and gospel within the Christian faith.[3]

A second important facet of Billing's influence in Swedish theology appears in his conscious attempt at establishing a scientific methodology for theological research. No depth analysis of this method can be undertaken at this point,[4] but certain leading ideas must be mentioned. There is, first, Billing's stress on historical research in combination with a systematic principle of interpretation.[5] Theological research is defined in terms of "type-description". It is undertaken by way of a double analysis: a) a *längdsnitt* (literally length-cut) of the historical development through the centuries, and b) a *tvärrsnitt* (literally cross-cut) of the actual situation at each important junction in history.[6] According to Billing, the central core of a certain idea can become clear to a scholar only as he observes it under many shifting

---

[1] Christ is, in other words, "ein zusammenhängendes Gotteshandeln." Bring, *op. cit.*, p. 631.

[2] The Word of God represents "God's own doing in and with us what in the days of Christ he did through him". Billing, *Luthers storhet*, Stockholm: Sveriges kristliga studentrörelse, 1917, pp. 27 f. The church, in Billing's view, is a sign of the forgiveness of sins to the people of the land. Cf. his *Herdabref*, 1920; *Folkkyrkan och förkunnelsen*, Stockholm: Sveriges kristliga studentrörelse, 1912; and *Den svenska folkkyrkan*, Stockholm: Sveriges kristliga studentrörelse, 1930. See also Gösta Wrede, *Kyrkosynen i Einar Billing's teologi*, 1966.

[3] One of the most consistent criticisms of Lundensian thought—perhaps especially directed toward Nygren's *Agape and Eros*—is that this theology oversimplifies the *agape* motif to the extent that it becomes incapable of containing the full spectrum of motifs that actually characterize the Christian faith. Bring's continuing consideration of the law in relation to the gospel is evidence of the Lundensian concern to counter this criticism. Cf. *Christus und das Gesetz*, 1969.

[4] For three different estimates of Billing's methodology, cf. Wingren, "Einar Billings teologiska metod," *Nordisk teologi...*, 1955, pp. 279-292; Lindroth, "Logos—Ordet," *Ordet och tron*, 1931, pp. 93-107; and Bring's chapter, "Billings tvenne metodiska tendenser," in *STU*, 1933, pp. 109-158.

[5] This method is formulated already in his study of *Luthers lära om staten*, Uppsala: Almqvist & Wiksell, 1900, p. V.

[6] Billing explicates this procedure in *De etiska tankarna...*, 1907.

circumstances and in several contingent forms. What remains constant in spite of all the relativities of historical change constitutes the essence of an idea. This systematic-historical method has had wide following within Swedish theology in this century, and Lund is especially indebted to it.

There is another facet of Billing's methodology that has been a point of contention, however. Billing presses on, beyond the purely historical method that he outlined in *Luthers lära om staten* and utilized in *De etiska tankarna i urkristendomen*, to claim that the task of systematic theology is not fulfilled until the theologian also sets the results of his historical investigations into a larger framework interlocking historical reality and absolute truth.[1] The theologian must ask the question of truth; he must concern himself with the interplay of historical facts and the facts of faith, "the connection between God's acts and man's ordinary life".[2] He must never be satisfied with history per se or with researching a certain system of ideas or analyzing a variety of psychological experiences. Instead, as the prophets do, he must "interpret God's election-history, its system, its inner unity,"[3] and relate it to ordinary reality.

It is obvious that the scientific intentions of Billing's methodology have been broken through and disrupted at this point. It is clear also that no such theology can remain in good standing under the scrutiny of critical scientists and philosophers set against all subjectivism and metaphysics. Billing knew this, and in the later years of his academic career he attempted to defend his methodology against the criticism of Hägerström and Phalén by distinguishing between two separate ways to valid knowledge. "Self-reflection" was for him the theoretical principle that characterizes objective scientific knowledge; "self-realization" was his term for the knowledge attained by personal involvement in the object of knowledge.[4] After Billing, this way of approaching the question of the relationship between science and religion, or between theoretical knowledge and religious knowledge, has been taken up and developed further by Billing's successors at

---

[1] Cf. *Universitet och kyrka*, Stockholm: Sveriges kristliga studentrörelse, 1923, p. 12.

[2] *Herdabref*, 1920, p. 50.

[3] *Försoningen*, 1908, p. 115.

[4] There is no explicit delineation of this distinction from Billing's own pen, but his lectures are said to have stressed the point repeatedly. Cf. von Engeström, "Arvet från Ritschl...," *Nordisk teologi...*, 1955, pp. 191 f.

Uppsala, Runestam,[1] Bohlin,[2] and Lindroth.[3] The Lundensians, however, departed from Billing at this point, setting out instead to rectify what appeared to them to be inconsistencies in Billing's methodology.[4] We have here another manifestation of the fundamental split between the Aulén-line and the Runestam-line in Swedish theological methodology. Both lines claim Söderblom and Billing as their teachers, but their attachment to the masters is of radically different kinds.[5]

Gustaf Aulén. When Gustaf Aulén moved from Uppsala to Lund in 1913, he left behind a theology which had become increasingly unsatisfactory to him. Aulén had begun his career as a disciple of Söderblom and Billing. Together with Billing he had sought to find an answer to the problems of theological methodology, but while Billing found himself helped by Wilhelm Herrmann's position and thereby entered into the orbit of "experience-theology", Aulén was more prone to strike out in a different direction.[6] His move to Lund came, in a sense, to signify an open break with the past, and his subsequent acquaintance with Anders Nygren came to set his

---

[1] Cf. "Gudstro och självkännedom," *Ordet och tron*, 1931, pp. 124-142.

[2] Cf. "Vetenskap—troslära—förkunnelse," *Gåva och krav. Skrifter tillägnade Manfred Björkquist*, Stockholm: Sveriges kristliga studentrörelse, 1934.

[3] *Op. cit.*

[4] Cf. Aulén, "Inför Einar Billing's sextioårsdag...," *STK*, 7, 1931, p. 239. Gustaf Wingren, who has consistently gone his own ways in methodological matters, has recently suggested a return to Billing's theological perspectives. He considers the predominance of critical philosophical and methodological standpoints since 1920 a digression in comparison to the primary task of theology, the explication of the meaning of the Word of God; *Einar Billing. En studie i svensk teologi före 1920*, Lund: Gleerup, 1968.

[5] The following sources mark the Lundensian standpoint in relation to the proponents as well as critics of Billing's (and Billing inspired) conceptions of theology: Aulén, "Troskunskap och vetenskap," *STK*, 1, 1925, pp. 360-371 (which is his answer to Runestam's challenge, pp. 355-360 in the same issue); cf. also *STK*, 2, 1926, pp. 90-104, for the further discussion between Aulén and Runestam; Nygren, "Religionens sanningsfråga och religionsvetenskapen," *STK*, 4, 1928, pp. 192 ff; "Är den religiösa sanningsfrågan ett vetenskapligt problem eller icke?," *STK* 4, 1928, pp. 305 ff; "Till frågan om teologiens objektivitet," *Teologiska studier tillägnade Erik Stave*, Uppsala: Almqvist & Wiksell, 1922; "Hur är filosofi som vetenskap möjlig," *Festskrift tillägnad Axel Hägerström*, Uppsala & Stockholm: Almqvist & Wiksell, 1928; and Bring, "Kristen tro och vetenskaplig forskning. Några reflexioner med anledning av den populära debatten om tro och vetande," *STK*, 25, 1949, pp. 201-243; cf. also his running discussion of Runestam, Bohlin, Lindroth, and Billing, *STU*, 1933 (cf. below, pp. 122 ff; Chapter VI).

[6] "Among Swedish theologians, Gustaf Aulén has probably more than any others expressed himself in direct opposition to the Ritschlian influence on systematic theology." Lindroth, *op. cit.*, p. 91. Cf. Aulén, "Inför Einar Billings sextioårsdag...," *STK*, 7, 1931, pp. 236 f.

course for the future.[1] The next twenty-five years saw the development of a significant new "school" of theology at Lund, and Aulén was at the center of events all along. Certain emphases and perspectives that had been typical of the Uppsala teachers were, as we shall see, still retained, but since the methodological framework of the new theology was entirely different, due particularly to a difference in philosophical orientation, these emphases also came to have a different meaning. A full explication of Aulén's contributions to Swedish theology cannot be attempted here.[2] Only those points shall be included which can be said to characterize the Aulén-line in Swedish theology, and they are explicated only in so far as they became determinative for the shaping of Ragnar Bring's thought.

Aulén's theological starting-point is the interest, inherited from Söderblom, in identifying the unique character of Christian faith. The Christian faith is a historical reality, objectively given, available as an object for the theologian's study.[3] The theological task is to investigate the Christian faith in its historical givenness, to bring to light its characteristic affirmations, and to explicate their theological significance.[4] As the theologian approaches the historical Christian faith, however, he is met by a confusing multiplicity of materials and a great variety of witnesses testifying to a number of different concepts of essential Christianity, and with this multiplicity there emerges a necessity for selection and evaluation.[5] Theology must, therefore, assume the functions of a critical science. It must seek to define a criterion for the evaluation of the various historical forms of Christian faith, and it must identify that decisive factor which makes faith a *Christian* faith or which constitutes the center of this faith.[6] Aulén

---

[1] When Nygren made his debut into theological scholarship with the dissertation *Religiöst apriori...*, 1921, he was a relatively unknown man; he did not belong to a specific school and was not a disciple of any one theologian. During the formal disputation of this work, it was Aulén who perceived most clearly the capacities of the young scholar and who expressed greatest appreciation for his book. Bring, "Anders Nygrens teologiska gärning," *STK*, 16, 1940, p. 315.

[2] We have mentioned already Aulén's contributions to Swedish ecclesiological thought (cf. *supra*, p. 34, note 4). His work in the area of Luther-research need not concern us here. Cf. Lindroth, *Lutherrenässansen...*, 1941, pp. 33 ff; Bring, "Einige Blätter...," *ZST*, 8, 1931, pp. 635 ff. See, f. ex., Aulén, *Die Dogmengeschichte im Lichte der Lutherforschung*, Gütersloh: Bertelsmann, 1932.

[3] Aulén, *The Faith of the Christian Church*, 1960, p. 2.

[4] *Ibid.*, p. vii.

[5] *Ibid.*, p. 65.

[6] *Ibid.*, pp. 7 f.

defines this center Christologically, as "the act of God in Christ",[1] but only hypothetically. He argues that since the Bible is the primary and decisive witness to the faith its authority must be ultimate in any doctrinal context.[2] Christian theology must have a clear biblical orientation.

Against this background, one is not surprised by Aulén's strong interest in the history of dogma.[3] He is, in fact, a masterful practitioner of Billing's *längdsnitt* and *tvärrsnitt* technique. His character sketches of individual Christian doctrines, from their biblical roots, through their formative period and historical development, to the varieties of interpretation vying for primacy in the present,[4] prove him worthy of the compliment he once paid Söderblom: he has a "praise-worthy accuracy with regard to the genuine." But there is a danger of over-simplification in Aulén's analyses. He approaches his subjects typologically, much in the manner of Eklund's schematization and pigeon-hole approach. Centuries are characterized in sweeping descriptions; periods are categorized in terms of dialectical contrasts: The sixteenth century equals the Reformation; the seventeenth, Orthodoxy; the eighteenth, Enlightenment; the nineteenth, Humanism (or Psychologism, or Historicism). The New Testament, the Early Church, and the Protestant Reformation belong together in a positive alliance. Medieval Scholasticism, Post-Reformation Orthodoxy, and Modern Rationalism are united in a devious conspiracy.[5] Reading Aulén, one need not wonder at the persistant recurrence of the criticism that Lundensian research lays a straitjacket on history, that it approaches historical events "with ruler and measuring tape", and that its critical-historical investigations are designed to prove the value of Lund's own theological commitments.

A second facet of Aulén's work comes into focus here, namely his strong sense of theological mission and his conviction of a call to

---

[1] *Ibid.*, p. 35.

[2] *Ibid.*, pp. 64 f.

[3] See, f. ex., his classical history of dogma, *Dogmhistoria*, Stockholm: Nordstedt, 1917.

[4] See, f. ex., *Den kristna tankens tolkning av Jesu person*, Uppsala: Norblad, 1910; *Den kristna gudsbilden genom seklerna och i nutiden*, Stockholm: Diakonistyrelsen, 1927; and *Den kristna försoningstanken (Christus Victor)*, 1930.

[5] "Generally speaking, it is true to say that Aulén's divisions and evaluations of periods have been widely accepted in the Swedish history of ideas.... The long perspective, the total evaluation of Christianity and of the history of Christian thought, has not been up for serious debate (in Sweden) after Aulén and Nygren." Wingren, *Svensk teologi efter 1900*, 1958, pp. 19, 20 f.

theological recovery. As he was surveying the theology of the last few centuries, Aulén found little to be pleased with. In his view, evangelical theology was now as unfaithful to Luther as Medieval theology had been to Augustine.[1] Particularly unsatisfactory, in Aulén's estimation, was the theology of the nineteenth century, crystallized in the Ritschlian-Harnackian interpretations of the shape and content of Christian faith. So, in an important article in the first issue of *Svensk teologisk kvartalskrift*,[2] Aulén gives explicit notice of the break with Ritschlianism which he had been preparing for some time.[3] He analyzes the various emphases of this theology, its "historicism", its "individualism", and its "moralism", pointing out that these are nothing but distortions of what was originally the most important aspects of Ritschl's thought: the historical orientation, the emphasis on personal religion, and the ethical concern. As he saw it, what had been the strength of Ritschlian theology had now turned into its weakness. To counteract the Ritschlian deterioration and attempt to recover lost ground, Aulén stresses three points which in his view are essential to the theological renewal: a) the application of a dynamic-dramatic view of history, b) the emphasis on religious life as life in community, and c) the understanding of faith as theocentric God-relationship.

Aulén's three points are immediately recognizable as his inheritance from Uppsala. As a matter of fact, Aulén makes no effort to claim that the new theology he stands for is a Lundensian invention. On the contrary, he is eager to show that *Lundateologien* belongs in a historical tradition which includes Billing, Söderblom, Luther, Irenaeus, and Paul. The only distinction he claims for the new theology at Lund is that it stands united in opposition to orthodox dogmatism, pietistic exclusiveness, and humanistic rationalism or idealism.[4] In Aulén's view, the particular task of Lundensian theology at the present is to break through the idealization of man and the humanization of the Christian faith.[5] This is the prevailing distortion of modern Christianity, and the future of the faith depends on its being overcome.

---

[1] Aulén, "Den evangeliska teologiens tvänne huvudskeden...," *STK*, 2, 1926, pp. 232-252.

[2] "Sekelskiftets teologi. En återblick," *STK*, 1, 1925, pp. 61-80.

[3] Cf. also *I vilken riktning går nutidens teologiska tänkande?*, Stockholm: Sveriges kristliga studentrörelse, 1921; and *Kristendomens själ. Tillika ett ord om gammal och ny teologi*, Stockholm: Sveriges kristliga studentrörelse, 1922.

[4] "Lundensisk teologisk tradition," *STK*, 30, 1954, pp. 241 ff.

[5] "Det teologiska nutidsläget," *STK*, 5, 1929, pp. 130 ff.

In approaching the weaknesses of modern theology, however, the Lundensians were not to retreat from the modern situation, identifying themselves with the theology of an earlier day and acting as if modern developments in thought and methodology had never taken place.[1] The new theology must be at home in the contemporary age. It must utilize all the resources of a modern discipline of research and reflection. Advances in scientific methodology, developments in idea-historical and event-historical scholarship, progress in logic and linguistics, new approaches in hermeneutics, all these are modern contributions that a responsible theology can appropriate in its search for the understanding of essential Christian faith. The new Lundensian theology is definitely a modern theology, then, not a return to old orthodoxies.

This brings us to a third aspect of Aulén's theology which has influenced the Lundensian approach to theological methodology in significant ways: his definition of the nature of systematic theology. Systematic theology, according to Aulén, is not to be defined as "faithful thinking", or even as "thinking about faith". It is an analytical discipline, concerned entirely with "investigating and elucidating a certain area of research," namely "the Christian understanding of the relationship between God and man, and the idea of God which is characteristic of the Christian faith." [2] Theology cannot be a normative or demonstrative (apologetic) discipline. It does not determine faith or prove its validity; it only analyzes the faith that actually exists.[3] Again, theology is not identical with philosophy of religion. The two have different functions altogether. Philosophy of religion is a critical investigation of the nature of religious life, and it seeks to determine the place of religion within man's total experience; [4] systematic theology is an analytical examination of the various manifestations of Christian faith, and it seeks to identify and explicate the essential meaning of historical Christianity.

Aulén has thereby made a delimitation of the role and function of theology which has stayed with the Lundensian school through thick and thin. We shall not stop to make evaluations here, except

---

[1] Aulén ascribes part of the credit for revealing the inadequacies of Harnack's interpretation of Christianity to the methodological advances of form criticism and to historical-typological research. Cf. "Från den teologiska samtiden," *STK*, 6, 1930, p. 214.

[2] *The Faith of the Christian Church*, 1960, pp. 3 f.

[3] *Ibid.*, p. 4.

[4] *Ibid.*, p. 10.

to say that in their eagerness to establish systematic theology as a scientific discipline, free of all subjectivism, normativity, and all other features that would jeopardize its respectability in the eyes of modern men, the Lundensians seem to have swept an entire dimension of theology quietly under their rug, namely that theology which makes up the material that systematic theology analyzes. Aulén persists in calling it "faith". Occasionally he speaks of "manifestations" of faith, or of "ideas", "expressions", even "documents". It is, of course, nothing but theology— "faith reflection", so to speak. Why the Lundensians persist in ignoring *this theology*, all the while sweeping the surface of their methodological rug to prove that systematic theology is a clean science, is an open question for the moment. We shall want to return to it below.[1]

Aulén sharpens his definition of systematic theology further by insisting that theology must be explicitly distinguished from rational metaphysics.[2] Speculative philosophy moves in entirely different circles from those of Christian faith; besides, metaphysics is suspect from a logical point of view. Faith is a religious activity, not a theoretical one. It does not consist in a rational explanation of the universe; it talks about God and his acts in history, and it bases its utterances on revelation.[3] Aulén has thus stated what is perhaps the most characteristic notion in the Lundensian methodology—and he has, at the same time, made his contribution to the shaping of the most confusing element in Lundensian thought. That faith is "religious" and not "theoretical" is clear enough, at least to those who understand the Lundensian terminology. Also, one can understand why the Lundensians are eager to distinguish metaphysics from faith. But Aulén's delineations of the distinction between metaphysical world explanation and Christian God-talk, between "theoretical" and "revelational" utterances, suffer from a basic weakness which is evident in most Lundensian theology, namely the unwillingness to draw the full consequences of the Lundensian methodology in reference to the understanding of the nature of theological language. We shall have occasion to return to this point later.[4] Strangely, with

---

[1] Cf. below, pp. 117 ff.

[2] Bring points out that Aulén's opposition to metaphysics increased in sharpness between the 2nd and the 3rd edition of *The Faith...*, i.e. between 1924 and 1931. *STK*, 7, 1931, pp. 366 f. One can easily see Nygren's influence begin to make itself felt in this period.

[3] *Op. cit.*, pp. 11 f.

[4] Cf. below, Chapter IX.

all his contributions to modern theology, Aulen's work seems particularly vulnerable to linguistic confusion. That is perhaps the reason so many of his readers miss the radical nature of his methodology and still think of him as a rather conservative dogmatician.

Other aspects of Aulén's attempts at clarifying the nature of systematic theology—and of his difficulties—are evident in the distinctions he draws between theology and psychology of religion and between theology and "historicism". Since faith is religious, theology is different from psychology of religion, he says.[1] Every affirmation of faith is a statement about God and his activity; it does not deal with empirical reality or psychological experience. "Psychology of religion concerns itself exclusively with the religious subject, while systematic theology deals with a relationship in which the revelation of God is the decisive factor." [2] The theologian, therefore, is not concerned with faith as a psychological or sociological phenomenon, but with "faith in a theological sense." [3] Similarly, since theology is determined in reference to the revelation of God it is different from the historicism which locates the acts of God at particular points in time.[4] The Christian faith does not limit the actuality of God within a static framework, but looks at revelation, instead, as a "continuous series of divine acts." [5] This does not mean, however, that theology disregards the individual manifestations of God in history or that it ignores the decisive and ultimate act of God, the culmination of revelation, in Christ. [6] Revelation is *both* something given in history *and* a continuous, active process.[7] It is continuous in history, but it can never be identified with anything historical. Consequently, systematic theology is not simply a historical discipline, although its material is historically given.[8]

A fourth and final aspect of Aulén's contribution to the shaping of Lundensian thought comes into view at this point: the interpretation of revelation as a dynamic process of divine self-impartation. Aulén is a true disciple of Söderblom and Billing here. He says that God, in his relationship to man, not only gives certain gifts; he gives himself, his love, for his nature is love.[9] However, God's active love, *agape*, is constantly being refused by man and opposed by God's enemies. It

---

[1] *Op. cit.*   [2] *Ibid.*, p. 13.
[3] *Ibid.*, p. 20.   [4] *Ibid.*, pp. 49, 46.
[5] *Ibid.*, p. 29.   [6] *Ibid.*, p. 36.
[7] *Ibid.*, p. 39.   [8] *Ibid.*, p. 65.
[9] *Ibid.*, p. 37; cf. "Lundensisk teologisk tradition," *STK*, 30, 1954, p. 236.

has to hold its own at all points against hostility and rejection. Revelation, therefore, takes the form of "a tense drama".[1] Its history is fraught with struggle, but Christ is Victor. Thus Aulén transmits from Uppsala that feature of thought which has given Lundensian theological symbolism its distinct character: its dramatic-dualistic outlook and its dynamic-eschatological orientation.[2] Söderblom and Billing have obviously influenced Aulén in this direction, but there is an important reservation in Aulén's relationship to his Uppsala teachers. He has felt obliged to free himself from the pitfalls of Billing's metaphysical perspective. Billing thought of the dramatic-dualistic outlook as the key to a grand "prophetic" insight into the synthetic meaning of history. Aulén's perspective carries no such claim to absolute validity or objective truth.[3] As a theologian, he does not wish to rise on the wings of speculation or grasp at the truths of "the other side". The dramatic-dualistic outlook functions, in Aulén's use of it, simply as a theological hypothesis—perhaps the chief one—whereby the systematic theologian seeks to understand the deepest motifs of Christian faith.[4]

Gustaf Aulén's methodology is not a completed structure. It certainly cannot be said to represent the Lundensian approach in all its facets.[5] But it is significant in that it identifies the problems of modern theology and suggests directions for the pursuit of solutions. Anders Nygren and Ragnar Bring saw these problems and heard Aulén's suggestions, and with their individual capabilities endowed for precisely such a task these men proceeded to construct a philosophical substructure and a theoretical superstructure which made Aulén's preliminary idea-sketch into a full-fledged methodological framework for faith. Thus Lundensian theology was beginning to find its new self.

---

[1] *The Faith...*, 1960, p. 38.

[2] This is Aulén's own description of Lundensian thought; cf. "Det teologiska nutidsläget," *STK*, 5, 1929, pp. 126 ff.

[3] Bring, *DbL*, 1929, pp. 14 f.

[4] "Eine gefundene Auffassung über den Inhalt eines Motifs, z. B. des dualistischen, ist also als eine Arbeitshypothese anzusehen, die im Laufe der Untersuchung immer mehr verfeinert und schärfer bestimmt wird." Bring, "Einige Blätter...," *ZST*, 8, 1931, p. 665.

[5] Both Bring and Wingren point to the fact that Aulén's thought did not reach any definite or exact methodological orientation until Anders Nygren came on the scene. Wingren, *Svensk teologi efter 1900*, 1958, p. 17; Bring; "Teologisk literatur. Några randanmärkningar till vissa den svenska systematiska teologiens senaste landvinningar," *STK*, 7, 1931, pp. 365 f.

CHAPTER THREE

LUNDENSIAN METHODOLOGY AS FORMULATED BY ANDERS NYGREN

The most original thinker among the Lundensians, and the one who undoubtedly meant the most for the early development of the modern Lundensian methodology, is Anders Nygren. His primary interest, from the beginning of his career and into his retirement, has been in the areas of epistemology and philosophy of religion. Early in his philosophical studies, Nygren discovered what was to become his intellectual orientation throughout. He realized that all the philosophies of metaphysical idealism and speculative rationalism were falling under the ban of the Kantian criticism of reason, and he became convinced that philosophy in the future must take the Kantian challenge seriously. So Nygren became a critical philosopher.[1]

In his confrontation with Kant, Nygren was particularly intrigued by the new vistas opening up in the so-called transcendental analytic,[2] but he was dissatisfied with Kant's own use of the method. In the first place, there were elements in Kant's thought which were clearly inconsistent with his own refutation of metaphysics.[3] Then there

---

[1] It is not necessary to continue the already extended discussion whether or not Nygren's criticism is in fact Kantian. Einar Tegen, in an early exchange with Nygren, *Bibelforskaren*, Vol. 39-40, 1922-1923, charged Nygren with setting aside important aspects of Kant's thought. Nygren accepted the criticism with the simple defense that he did not intend to give an historical explication of the full structure of Kantian philosophy; his approach to Kant was, rather, motivated by a "systematic interest", designed to uncover that which "bore the future in its bosom." *Ibid.*, pp. 285 f. Hjalmar Lindroth, in an article entitled "Anders Nygrens kriticism i förhållande till Kants och Schleiermachers," *Nordisk teologi...*, 1955, pp. 167-186, reissues the charge that Nygren took one element from Kant's critical philosophy and made it the basis of a criticism of another brand. Nygren's recent comment, in private conversation, is characteristic of his reaction to such critique: "Kantian or not, that is not the question. I say, why not discuss *my* views?"

[2] Nygren's main analyses of Kant's transcendental deductions are found in *Religiöst apriori*, 1921, pp. 206-215, and in *Dogmatikens vetenskapliga grundläggning*, 1922, pp. 70-74.

[3] Cf. *Filosofi och motivforskning*, 1940, pp. 34 f, where Nygren discusses Kant's attempt to define a synthetic principle of apperceptive unity or an "oberste Prinzip alles Verstandesgebrauchs." This represents, to Nygren, a break with the original presuppositions of criticism, and it shows that Kant himself was not entirely free from the impact of idealistic metaphysics.

were certain basic weaknesses in Kant's definitions of the categories of experience. As a theologian-philosopher, Nygren was especially concerned with the place of religion within the spectrum of *a priori* categories. He could not accept Kant's way of reducing religion to a subspecies of ethical experience. To subsume religion under the awareness of "the categorical imperative" stood for him as a misunderstanding of the nature of religious experience. In raising this point, Nygren found himself at one with Schleiermacher; in fact, he came to consider Schleiermacher the major proponent of consistent criticism.[1] By his defense of the categorical autonomy of religious experience, Schleiermacher not only laid the foundations for a modern concept of theology; he opened the door also to the accomplishment of a major philosophical task, namely the transcendental deduction of the religious *a priori*.[2]

Seldom has any student of Schleiermacher given a more penetrating exposition of the philosophical intentions of the German master—or a keener critique of his shortcomings—than that presented in Nygren's *Dogmatikens vetenskapliga grundläggning*.[3] By way of a series of analyses of Schleiermacher's major works, *Kurze Darstellung*, *Dialektik*, *Reden*, and *Die Christliche Glaube*, Nygren identified with sure philosophical instinct the leading ideas in the development of Schleiermacher's thought. He found Schleiermacher concerned with the central problem of the modern philosophy of religion, the question of the nature of religious experience, and he proceeded to show how Schleiermacher applied the Kantian transcendental analytic without falling into Kant's errors and jeopardizing the uniqueness of the religious category. According to Nygren, Schleiermacher did reveal tendencies, in his earlier works, toward the same metaphysical inconsistencies which are evident in Kant's thought.[4] But in *Die*

---

[1] Nygren has no hesitation in calling Schleiermacher "the critical philosopher *par preference.*" *Dogmatikens vetenskapliga grundläggning*, 1922, p. 69.

[2] For Nygren's analysis of Schleiermacher's so-called "regressive method", see *ibid.*, pp. 74-81.

[3] It is lamentable that this work has not been translated into other languages. It would be the basis of a renewed respect and appreciation for the work of Schleiermacher, and it would be a most valuable source of information for the general discussion of Lundensian methodology. Cf. Nygren's recent comments on the lasting importance of Schleiermacher (on the occasion of the 200th anniversary of his birth), "Om det levande förflutna. Till Schleiermacherminnet 1968," *STK*, 44, 1968, pp. 197-203.

[4] Nygren shows that the "Ursein, in welchem der Gegensatz zwischen Begriff und Gegenstand aufgehoben ist," which Schleiermacher sets up as the ultimate presupposition for valid knowledge, represents a confusion of the epistemological

Christliche Glaube, Schleiermacher made himself free of such tendencies,[1] and the result was a philosophy of religion—albeit rudimentary— which points the way for the modern philosopher. The most urgent task of philosophy of religion, as Nygren saw it, was to complete the transcendental deduction of the religious *a priori* in a consistently critical manner and thus establish religious experience as an autonomous and unique dimension of life. Nygren assumed this responsibility and endeavored to address himself to the subject in his second book, entitled *Religiöst apriori*.

Nygren's philosophical interests have never been purely theoretical; the most dominating concern throughout his career has been Christian apologetics. During his early years as a theology professor, he was deeply hurt by the sweeping criticism leveled against theology—and especially systematic theology—by the positivistic philosophy at Uppsala and the objectivistic scientism of the modern academic community. He felt himself obliged to join forces with those who sought to rescue the honor of theology by establishing a methodology that would secure both the intellectual respectability and the theological authenticity of the discipline. By the beginning of the century, Swedish philosophy had made a radical turn away from the Hegelian idealism and the personalistic transcendentalism of the Boström tradition to the neo-Kantian criticism of the Hägerström-Phalén variety.[2] Hägerström and Phalén cracked

---

principle of validity and the ontological principle of reality. *Op. cit.*, pp. 88, 91. Schleiermacher has thus "broken with criticism." *Ibid.*, p. 85. Lindroth, in the article referred to (cf. p. 51, note 1), claims that Nygren misunderstands Schleiermacher's concept of criticism. *Op. cit.*, pp. 179 ff. This critique has no bearing on Nygren's work, however; Nygren's concern is not to explain Schleiermacher's type of critcism, but to draw from Schleiermacher the elements which in Nygren's own view are representative of what criticism ought to be.

[1] Nygren indicates that Schleiermacher moved away from the tendencies toward "identity-philosophy" (a term used by Swedish philosophers to describe the tradition of philosophy that finds the center of meaning and reality and knowledge in one ultimate being—the *grand-être*, being itself), evident in his *Dialektik*, into a more consistent criticism, represented by the transcendental deduction of the category of religion which appears in *Die Christliche Glaube. Op. cit.*, pp. 91, 96.

[2] Cf. Ryding, *Den svenska filosofins historia*, 1959, pp. 89 ff, for a quick sketch of the Swedish movement toward neo-Kantian thought led by the philosophers Erik Olof Burman, Vitalis Nordström, Hans Larsson, Axel Hägerström, and Adolf Phalén. The problems of knowledge and faith have long dominated the interest of Swedish philosophers; this is reflected in the perennial engagement of philosophers and theologians in discussions concerning the relation of faith and reason. The latest flare-up over this problem occurred in the late 1940's and early 1950's, when Lundensian methodology was sharply criticized by empiricists and

the philosophical whip mercilessly over all subjectivism and arbitrariness of method. Their philosophy became the rocks and reefs through which no speculative and unscientific construction piloted by theologians could sail without shipwreck. Nygren did not even want to try to get a traditional theology through. Instead, he accepted the dictum that theology must find its place among the sciences, as one among them, scientific in method, descriptive in purpose, objective, non-normative in nature.[1]

Anders Nygren thus began his philosophical and theological career with a double task before him: He wanted to formulate a philosophy of religion which was free from metaphysical and identity-philosophical involvements; and he desired to construct a theological method which would avoid, as far as possible, the charges of subjectivism and arbitrariness. He found the basis for his philosophy of religion in philosophical criticism, selecting those elements in Kant and Schleiermacher which met the specifications; and he located the guideposts for his theological method in the school of comparative religion, represented so brilliantly in Sweden by Nathan Söderblom, and in the Wellhausen tradition of critical historical research, made indigenous to Sweden by the mediation of Einar Billing and Gustaf

---

positivists forming school around the widely popular, culture-radical philosopher Ingemar Hedenius.

[1] Nygren has commented in private conversation that there was no direct dependency involved in his relationship to Hägerström and Phalén. In fact, the impression of some Uppsala theologians that the Lundensians fell for positivism and thus betrayed their colleagues is utterly unwarranted. Hägerström and Phalén reduced religion to illusion or myth; the only reality that could be accommodated by their concept of experience was material, rational, or logical reality, that which is reducible to the categories of time, space, and causality. While Nygren, following certain aspects of Schleiermacher's criticism, proceeded to develop a concept of experience which included the validity of a religious *a priori* category, this procedure was sheer nonsense from the standpoint of Hägerström. Cf. Jarl Hemberg, *Religion och metafysik. Axel Hägerströms och Anders Nygrens religionsteorier och dessas inflytande i svensk religionsdebatt*, Stockholm: Diakonistyrelsen (1966). Hemberg's book has its strength in the analysis of Hägerström's concept of reality and subsequent theory of religion. His discussions of Nygren and Bring, however, suffer from the tendency to apply the results of the study of Hägerström to these men's epistemological considerations, thus projecting Hägerströmian problems into the Lundensians' thoughtworld. A closer attention to the internal structure of Nygren's and Bring's thinking would have convinced Hemberg of the illegitimacy of his undertaking; neither Nygren nor Bring are conscious of discipleship in relation to Hägerström. They did not set out to confirm, revise, or disprove Hägerström's philosophy. They took account of some of the challenges that Hägerström threw at the religious enterprise, but they did not feel that Hägerström necessarily set the terms for peace.

Aulén. It is our purpose here to summarize—and only summarize—
the most important elements in Nygren's contributions to Lundensian
methodology.[1]

NYGREN'S PHILOSOPHICAL GROUNDWORK

As Nygren begins to consider what kind of philosophy is required
as groundwork for scientific theology, he immediately decides that
it must have positive relations to human experience and empirical
science, while it must reject all tendencies to metaphysics. This
double requirement puts the philosopher in a difficult dilemma, however: It seems that when philosophy desires to be scientific, it loses
the right to speak of universals; but when it wants to deal with universals, it seems by necessity metaphysical and unscientific.[2] How
can this evil circle be broken? That is the question Nygren has in
mind as he entitles the first chapter of *Filosofi och motivforskning*, "How
is philosophy as a science possible?" [3]

In trying to answer this basic question, Nygren immediately
decides that two clarifications are necessary: In the first place, explicitly, philosophy cannot be called scientific in the same sense that
the empirical sciences are. It is a "science of universals", not a
"science of particulars"; a "science of principles", not a "science of
experience". Secondly, as a scientific investigation of principles,
philosophy must not be confused with speculation or metaphysics.
Its task is not to identify and define the essence of being or the ultimate
nature of existence. It studies, rather, the logical presuppositions for
human knowledge and experience. Philosophy, to Nygren, is not
an ontological discipline; it is primarily epistemology, or as he
terms it, "analysis of logical presuppositions", "presuppositional
analysis".[4] As such, it is preliminary to all the sciences and all
knowledge. It is, in a sense, the queen of the sciences.

---

[1] In the attempt to sketch Nygren's principal methodological commitments, we
shall draw mainly on the concentrated presentations in *Filosofi och motivforsking,*
1940. However, side glances will be made to *Religiöst apriori*, 1921; *Dogmatikens
vetenskapliga grundläggning*, 1922; and *Den kristna kärlekstanken* (*Apage and Eros*),
1930.

[2] *Filosofi och motivforskning*, 1940, p. 11. This dilemma is very similar to the
difficulties faced by Moore and Russell, and expressed so well in Wittgenstein's
Tractatus logico-philosophicus, 1922.

[3] This chapter was first published in the *festskrift* for Axel Hägerström in
1928. Cf. *supra*, p. 43, note 5.

[4] *Op. cit.*, p. 39.

These delimitations of the nature of philosophy are, of course, inspired by Kant's refutation of idealism and speculative reason, presented in *Critique of Pure Reason*, 1781. Nygren shows his dependence on Kant even more explicitly when he comes to consider the philosophical method. It is evident to Nygren—as it was to Kant—that the so-called "empirical" method is useless in doing philosophy; the reason is simply that the logical presuppositions which the philosopher pursues are not given in empirical reality. The same problem appears in the "rational" or "deductive" method, also. According to Nygren, secondary or tertiary suppositions are not causally related to first presuppositions; and they do not, therefore, provide a basis for the deduction of the *a priori* presuppositions. Such observations do not make legitimate a position of "absolute scepticism", however. Scepticism, as Nygren sees it, is a useless philosophical stance; nothing can be built on such foundations, and anything that is attempted ends in contradiction.[1] Instead, the philosophical analysis of presuppositions must start at the opposite pole: It must build on the fundamental assumption that human experience is significant, that valid judgments can be made, and that there is a way to analyze the relationship between human experience and the universal principles which form the logical presuppositions for its significance.[2]

There is, then, in Nygren's opinion, a logical necessity for assuming a certain connection between empirical reality and transcendent principles; meaningful experience would be impossible without a set of presuppositions that are logically consistent. This connection is not to be understood in terms of ontological concepts or definitions of reality, however; the ontological perspective leads inevitably to identity-speculation and metaphysics. Nygren defines it, rather, in terms of the epistemological concept "validity". In assuming that human experience is significant and that valid judgments can be made, one has at the same time assumed the logical participation of that which is given in experience with certain transcendent presuppositions for the possibility and validity of all experience. By philosophical or presuppositional analysis, it should be possible to identify the

---

[1] Cf. Nygren's settlement with scepticism, "Den religionsfilosofiska apriori-frågan," *Kristendomen och vår tid*, 17, 1922, p. 68.

[2] This represents the fundamental philosophical commitment in Nygren's thinking; he returns to it again and again, considering the starting point of his entire system. Cf. *Filosofi och motivforskning*, 1940, p. 17; *Det religionsfilosofiska grundproblemet*, 1921, pp. 67 f; and *Religiöst apriori*, 1921, pp. 210 f.

various formal categories or *a priori* presuppositions that underlie and govern meaningful experience.[1]

The method for investigating the principal presuppositions of valid experience is, for Nygren, a twofold one:[2] Its first facet is *conceptual analysis*. This has to do with all the preliminary work of clearing away the propositional material that is either conceptually inconsistent or of secondary importance. The material that is subject to conceptual analysis includes the pre-scientific consciousness of man, the axioms and assumptions operative in the empirical sciences, as well as the history of philosophical reflection. The conceptual analyst allows only such experiential or propositional material through to the inner chambers of philosophical analysis that proves itself logically consistent and representative of basic dimensions of human experience. The next step is the transcendental analysis, or as Nygren prefers to call it, the *analysis of formal presuppositions*. Here, the object is not simply to sort out the conceptual material and identify the various categories of experience; the purpose is, rather, to identify the logical presuppositions that underlie the various areas of meaning and inform the propositional material involved. This double-barreled method is, of course, Kant's own. Nygren considers it the most important element in philosophical criticism, the element which points toward the future of philosophy, and he makes it his own without significant deletions or additions.

As a result of the philosophical analysis—the preliminary conceptual analysis and the principal presuppositional analysis, as Nygren describes it—a series of formal or transcendental principles, the *a priori* categories, are uncovered; they are the logical presuppositions of which it can be shown that only as they are assumed to be valid can one speak of meaningful human existence at all.[3] Says Nygren:

---

[1] Bernhard Erling, *Nature and History*, 1960, makes the basic mistake of introducing into Nygren's thought a content-defined concept of validity that functions as a criterion by which to determine "the valid", in distinction from "the invalid", or truth from falsehood. Cf. pp. 30 f. He also interprets Nygren's assumption of validity as having reference only to the theoretical area of experience, where mathematical necessity and general causality are the commonly accepted presuppositions of validity. In Erling's view, Nygren is left with the problem how to establish the validity of the ethical or the religious experience. *Ibid.*, p. 74. Such ideas, however, are not in line with Nygren's. See further my essay, "Nygren's Ethics," in Charles W. Kegley, ed., *The Philosophy and Theology of Anders Nygren*, Southern Illinois University Press (forthcoming).

[2] *Filosofi och motivforskning*, 1940, pp. 24 ff.

[3] "Only that has the right to stand as a philosophical principle or a primary

"...We have to do with (several) large and distinct areas of meaning, each ruled by their specific categories. It is the task of philosophy to perform its presuppositional analysis in each of these areas and thus to open the way to an inclusive theory of the categories." [1]

At this point, obviously, the Kantian concept of *a priori* categories plays a certain role in Nygren's thought. However, on the basis of his own definition of the nature and function of the categories Nygren finds Kant's concept of transcendental *a priori* inadequate, on two counts: First, it tends to exclude or deny independent validity to one major area of experience and meaning which, as Nygren sees it, cannot possibly be eliminated or reduced to another dimension of experience without seriously affecting one's understanding of man's life as a whole, namely the area of religious experience. Also, it includes a metaphysical attempt at tying the various categories together under one "ultimate principle of apperception". Consequently, Nygren rejects Kant's scheme and approaches instead Schleiermacher's philosophy of religion. Particularly important to Nygren's thought are certain passages in the *Reden* where Schleiermacher seeks to establish religious experience as an area of experience *sui generis*, having its own autonomous validity quite apart from the dimensions of "knowing" (the theoretical categories) and "doing" (the ethical category).[2] Taking his direction from Schleiermacher and to a certain degree extending his views, Nygren proceeds to identify four major areas of experience to which independent identity and validity cannot be denied, each being governed by its own unique presuppositional category.[3] They are: a) knowledge (dependent on the formal category of "the true"), b) aesthetic (presupposing the category of "the beautiful"), c) ethic (connected with the category of "the

---

presupposition of which it can be said that only on the basis of its acceptance is experience or validity at all possible." *Ibid.*, p. 31. By this definition, Nygren hopes to have provided an objective basis for the philosophical discussion of the *a priori* categories. On this basis, the different philosophies of principles would not appear to stand in stark and irreconcilable contrast to one another; anyone claiming to have identified an *a priori* principle should be able to show— by way of transcendental analytic—that without this presupposition, experience itself would be logically impossible.

[1] *Ibid.*, p. 40.

[2] Nygren seeks to correlate the philosophical position of the *Reden* with the theological position of *Die christliche Glaube* and to analyze the continuity as well as the inconsistencies in Schleiermacher's thought. Cf. *Dogmatikens vetenskapliga grundläggning*, 1922.

[3] Further presuppositional analysis might, according to Nygren, show that there are others.

good"), and d) religion (answering to the category of "the eternal".[1] All human experience is thus divided into distinct areas or contexts of meaning, and each of these areas has a unique and independent principle of meaningfulness. Every experience, event, or proposition which is given in man's life, empirically or historically, must be understood in terms of "its own proper context of meaning", *i.e.* within

---

[1] Cf. *Agape and Eros*, 1953, pp. 42f. In this connection, E. Tegen's critique of Nygren, *Bibelforskaren*, 39-40, 1922-23, pp. 305ff, is relevant. He distinguishes between what he calls Kant's "narrow" deductions, *i.e.* the efforts to determine the *a priori* principles of validity in each individual area of experience, and a "broad" deduction, designed to show that beyond the multiple categorical presuppositions there is a mutual interdependence by which the many principles are united into one. There are indications that Nygren, in the early stages of his thought, presses for such a broadening. Cf. "Till frågan om den transcendentala methodens användbarhet inom religionsfilofien," *Bibelforskaren*, 40, 1923, pp. 273-293. His emphasis, however, falls on the *methodological* unity of the transcendental deductions undertaken in the various areas of experience, not on any *material* or *absolute* unity of all categories within one supercategory. *Ibid.*, p. 289. Nygren occasionally suggests that the category of "eternity" might serve as an ultimate principle of unity. "Är evighetskategorien en religiös kategori?," *Kristendomen och vår tid*, 17, 1922 pp. 220-241. He recognizes, however, that this is dangerous ground. In *Filosofisk och kristen etik*, 1923, pp. 109 ff, Nygren explains what he means by the attempt to "broaden" the transcendental deduction. He draws a sharp line between a *general* philosophical use of the concept "eternity" and the *particular* use of it in describing the religious category. Many of Nygren's commentators have missed this important distinction; so f. ex. Ferré, *Swedish Contributions...*, 1939, p. 201, who finds Nygren claiming that the religious category is the fundamental principle of experience, the basic presupposition without which all human experience is impossible. If this is the case, it is of course quite right to say that the religious category for Nygren has become "a content-defined concept of validity" with "a metaphysical flavor." One should be quite sure, however, that one understands Nygren's use of the concept "validity" before making such snap judgments. In *op. cit.*, Nygren makes a radical turn away from his earlier double use of the term "eternity". He now speaks of the relationship between the various presuppositional categories ("narrowly" deduced) and the principle of unity between them ("broadly" deduced) in terms of "secondary" and "primary" validity. The individual *a priori* represent "several forms of secondary validity". There is the principle of causality, the presupposition for the validity of theoretical judgments; and there is "eternity", the presupposition for the validity of religious experience. Beyond these individual categories of validity, there is a formal principle, a "primary" or "presuppositional validity", which says simply that *if an individual judgment is valid, certain presuppositions must be valid also.* One should note this formulation, for Nygren is not here saying that if the presupposition is valid, experience is also authenticated. Such an inversion of Nygren's perspective leads to distortions both of his theory of experience and his philosophy of religion. Nygren assumes the validity of experience; that is the dramatic difference between him and Kant. It is also the basic difference between a philosophy riddled with ontological problems and one that undertakes the presuppositional analysis confident of its logical justification.

the specific area and under the particular categorical presupposition to which it is related and in view of which it is meaningful.[1]

Nygren formulates the following maxim in order to clarify the relationship between the empirical-historical realities of man's existence and the categorical presuppositions for their meaningfulness— it is, in a sense, his hermeneutical principle: The categorical *a priori* function as so many formal, fundamental questions; the experiential material contains various content-determined answers. In order to understand a specific area of experience, there is a dual task to be performed. First a philosophical analysis must be undertaken in order to identify the formal question that is appropriate to this specific area of experience; then the various disciplines of scientific research must apply these questions to the given material and interpret the answers contained in man's experience in their light. For example, in the area of theoretical knowledge epistemology undertakes the philosophical analysis designed to uncover the presuppositions for answering the formal question, "Is it true?", in a meaningful way. The various forms of knowledge given in the experience of men are then studied by several specific disciplines, such as psychology, pedagogics, and others doing research in the dynamics of learning, in the light of epistemological theory. In similar ways, Nygren sketches the specific kinds of philosophical analysis that are concerned with the formal presuppositions lying at the base of the experience of the beautiful and the good, describing in each case also the particular brands of scientific research responsible for the examination of actual experiences of this nature. Finally, applying the same perspective to the religious area of experience, Nygren proceeds to assign the analytical task to the philosophy of religion. This discipline must be primarily concerned to understand the experience of the eternal and identify the unique principle of validity behind it, namely the formal presupposition for meaningful religious experience: the religious *a priori*. The religious category must be defined as a formal or "empty" principle, capable of serving as presupposition for meaningful experience in all the varieties of human religion.[2] Philosophy of

---

[1] *Filosofi och motivforskning*, 1940, p. 41.

[2] Gustaf Wingren, *Theology in Conflict*, 1958, has criticized Nygren on this point. "If the historical material gives (even) an oblique answer to the philosophically defined question, it would (according to Nygren) show only that the question was not completely formal. Formality means void of content; a condition which implies that the question does not clash with anything in the concrete material. All the historical material flows without friction into the form, provided that

religion must, therefore, be a critical discipline, objective, inclusive, non-normative. Subsequent to the philosophical analysis, the different disciplines of theology take over. These sciences have the task of studying the various manifestations of religious experience that are given in history, in sources of many sorts—events, records, beliefs, creeds, propositions, symbols, and many more. Their function is to describe and interpret these historical sources on the basis of the presuppositions basic to religious experience.

The following statement by Nygren can serve to sum up what in all of his philosophical considerations has been the main aim and purpose:

> "If it is true that religion is a necessary and inevitable spiritual form of life, which no one can or has the right to reject, but which can exist nowhere except in a positive historical 'Gestalt', and that Christianity is such a realization of the religious category—the only realization which in any way can come into consideration for us—then, at the same time, the scientific foundation is laid for dogmatics." [1]

Our task, next, is to examine the general form of the methodological framework which Nygren raises on these foundations.

NYGREN'S METHODOLOGICAL FRAMEWORK

We have already referred to Nygren's assumption of a certain "connection" between empirical reality and the transcendent principles that serve as presuppositions for meaningful experience. These

---

form is empty." *Ibid.*, p. 16. Such an approach to theology, argues Wingren, cannot but distort the interpretation of the Christian message. Bernhard Erling, *Nature and history*, 1960, offers the same criticism, in more direct language. To him, "categorical questions which made no resistance whatsoever to answers which might be given them would be meaningless." *Ibid.*, pp. 141 f. According to Erling, the questions applied to the material shall have to place certain limitations on it in order to be useful. Both these men seem to forget that *at this point* in Nygren's discussions, the task is simply one of analyzing human experiences for the purpose of showing that there are several distinct and independent areas within it, each ruled by a formal category, and that the mass of experiential material, if it is to be understood at all, must be understood in relation to these presuppositional categories. One should note that although in Nygren's view the categories are empty, *they are not formless*. In regard to the religious category, specifically, the category does not predefine the content of religion; it simply functions to outline its principal or presuppositional form. To say, then, as von Engeström quips, "I do not dare to say whether one who has a positive religious faith of some sort is thereby more legitimately committed to the category of the eternal than one who only believes in the multiplication table" ("Arvet från Albrecht Ritschl...," *Nordisk teologi...*, 1955, p. 195), is in one sense quite according to Nygren's intentions at this point. That Nygren goes on to analyze the different kinds of religion, and undoubtedly would find the *grundmotiv* of this mathematical "religion" somewhat lacking, is another matter altogether.

[1] *Dogmatikens vetenskapliga grundläggning*, 1922, p. 54.

presuppositional principles, the formal *a priori* categories, are related to the content of man's actual experience much in the manner of questions and answers, and on the surface the relationship seems direct. When Nygren analyzes the various areas of experience, however, he discovers that there are significant variations in the way this relationship functions. Particularly important are the differences that appear if one compares the theoretical area of experience, including commonsense knowledge, science, mathematics and logic, with the "a-theoretical" areas of experience, specifically aesthetic, ethic, and religion. In the theoretical area, the relationship between the actualities of experience and the categorical presuppositions of meaningfulness is immediate and direct. Men have reached general agreements as to how these presuppositions are to be understood, and the given experiential material can therefore be considered and interpreted with clear reference to these commonly accepted presuppositions, *i.e.* with theoretical consistency. In the a-theoretical areas of experience, however, the case is different. Ethical experience, for example, does not have a unified and consistent meaning. Here, the relationship between the formal category and the experiential content is not an immediate one; there is a "distance" introduced into the picture, an element of discontinuity set between reality and meaning. This is caused by a variety of ethical ideals or commitmental traditions which, in a sense, override the ethical experiences of men and organize them into several different systems of ethical interpretation. In studying the meaning of ethical propositions, therefore, one must not only consider them in the context of the formal *a priori* of the good; one must also observe them in light of the particular ethical system to which they belong.

The same is the case in the religious area of meaning. Between the pure category and the actual experiences of men, certain "secondary contexts of meaning" are introduced, each characterized by certain *grundsvar* (basic answers) or *grundmotiv* (basic motifs). These represent various religious "types" or different historical religions, each organized around its own characteristic motif. A religious proposition can only be understood consistently if it is understood both in its primary and in its secondary contexts of meaning, *i.e.* both within the religious area of meaning and in the particular motif-structure to which it belongs. Thus, in Ferré's words:

> "All the positive historical religions are...the realization of religion and the object for theological investigation. All the religions are to be

treated in the same manner, from the point of view of their own organic centers. Religion, in other words, has *centra* but no *centrum*." [1]

It is against this background one must see Nygren's descriptions of the problems and the possibilities of systematic theology:

"The most important task of those engaged in the modern scientific study of religion and in theological research is to reach an inner understanding of the different forms of religion in the light of their different fundamental motifs. For a long time they have been chiefly occupied in collecting a vast mass of material drawn from different religious sources for the purpose of comparison. But when the comparison actually comes to be made, the uncertainty of it immediately becomes apparent; for it is plain that no conclusion can be drawn from the mere fact that one and the same idea or belief occurs in different religious contexts. The idea or belief may have exactly the same form without having at all the same meaning, if in one case it is a basic conception, while in the other it is more loosely attached. Its meaning cannot be the same if—as is naturally most often the case—its setting is different in the different religions. What such an idea, or belief, or sentiment really means, can only be decided in the light of its own natural context. In other words, we must try to see what is the basic idea or the driving power in the religion concerned, or what it is that gives it its character as a whole and communicates to all its parts their special content and color. It is the attempt to carry out such structural analysis, whether in the sphere of religion or elsewhere, that we describe as motif-research." [2]

Nygren's theological method is described as the science of motif-research. He defines it in *Filosofi och motivforskning* as "an investigation which sets out to penetrate to the basic motif that rules a certain viewpoint or proposition." [3] A basic motif (*grundmotiv*) is defined as "the answer, given from some particular outlook, to a question (that is) of such a fundamental nature that it can be described —in a categorical sense—as a fundamental question." [4] As a scientific method, motif-research stands, in Nygren's terms, in a position of "double conditioning": [5] The question it asks is a philosophical question; the answer it seeks is a historical answer. Motif-research stands on the boundary between them, conditioned both by philosophy and by history. It participates, in a sense, in the philosophical problems

---

[1] Ferré, *op. cit.*, p. 60.
[2] *Agape and Eros*, 1953, p. 35.
[3] *Filosofi och motivforskning*, 1940, p. 44.
[4] *Agape and Eros*, 1953, p. 42.
[5] *Filosofi och motivforskning*, 1940, p. 44.

involved in the analysis of religious conceptions and the transcendental deduction of the religious category; it is involved also in the technical problems of establishing the confrontation between the categorical question and the historical answers in such a way that the basic religious motifs can be properly identified and clearly understood.

Nygren discusses the latter problems most explicitly in answering certain objections to his method of motif-research. In *Agape and Eros*, for example, he raises a question that is often asked by those who regard the historic-genetic analysis of religious ideas as the more scientific approach: whether motif-research is a method of synthesis rather than analysis. Is it not built on intuition instead of scientific investigation?[1] Nygren answers that the identification of basic motifs does not represent a subjective or arbitrary judgment at all; the interconnections that exist between religious ideas or propositions are identifiable in terms of fundamental, unifying motif-structures that are as much historically given as are the ideas and propositions themselves. Moreover, although the scholar may discern the shape of the basic motifs by way of sheer intuition to begin with, this intuition serves only as a working hypothesis which is subject to subsequent verification and therefore subordinate to the continuing scientific investigation of the historical material.[2] Says Nygren:

> "It cannot, of couse, be denied that the underlying idea or funda-mental motif of a religion may be intuitively discerned, or that such an intuition is of inestimable value for motif-research. But intuition alone does not constitute research; and if we are to speak of research in this connection, the gains of intuition must be subjected to scientific analysis and verification. The question we have to answer here, therefore, is whether it is at all possible by means of scientific analysis to determine the fundamental motif of any given form of religion. The answer can only be an unqualified affirmative (one)." [3]

A more serious challenge to the method of motif-research comes from the ranks of positivistic empiricists, who regard it as an illegit-imate overpowering of the historical material when categorical

---

[1] *Agape and Eros*, 1953, pp. 35 f.

[2] Cf. below, on "the resistance of the material," pp. 65 f.

[3] *Ibid.*, p. 37. Interesting parallels can be drawn at this point between Nygren and Michael Polanyi, *Personal Knowledge. Towards a Post-Critical Philosophy*, Chicago: University of Chicago Press (1958), who argues that intuition, commitment, and other "tacit components" enter into all forms of human knowledge, even in the work of the so-called "objective" sciences. The fact that one starts off with an intuition and follows it in the manner of a working hypothesis does not dis-qualify the investigation from a scientific point of view, then.

questions are "thrown over it" and fundamental motif structures are "strapped to it". In their view, the historical material must be taken as it is, *i.e.* on its own presuppositions. Nygren's answer is in the form of an extensive discussion of motif-research as a scientific method for the study of history.[1] His principal argument is that the formal categories and the basic motifs are never imposed on the experience of man from without; they are, instead, the basic presuppositions of meaningfulness that are integral to the validity of experience itself. As a matter of fact, historical research without a clear recognition of these presuppositions of meaning is, in Nygren's view, an impossibility. No material is "historical" unless it is incorporated into a context of meaning. All history stands within some sort of systematic "order", recognized with some degree of clarity. Without such contexts of meaning, experience would dissolve into an atomistic multitude of unrelated events. Thus, when the theologian approaches the historical material in terms of its primary and secondary contexts of meaning he is not doing anything that jeopardizes his scientific objectivity. On the contrary, his principles of interpretation are less subjective and less arbitrary "than any other viewpoint that may be taken." [2] They rise out of the material itself; they are the material's own bases of meaning.

In the same connection, Nygren takes up the question concerning the procedure for determining basic motifs: What is the criterion by which one identifies the particular concept that serves as *grundmotiv*? Can this decision be anything but subjective and arbitrary? We have already noted that Nygren strongly objects to the idea that the analysis of the contexts of meaning, or the identification of categorical presuppositions and basic motifs, constitute an imposition on the historical experience of men. Again, we have found Nygren arguing that although the fundamental motif may be intuitively perceived to begin with it is nothing more than a working hypothesis, subject to subsequent scientific verification. It is Nygren's delineation of the nature of this verification that concerns us here.

Clearly, Nygren is working to establish an objective criterion for testing the hypothetical *grundmotiv*. He describes the practical procedure in the matter in terms of what he calls "the resistance of the material." [3] He says, "In the greater or lesser resistance or pliancy of the material

---

[1] Cf. *Filosofi och motivforskning*, 1940, pp. 45-62. See below, pp. 168 ff.
[2] *Ibid.*, p. 47.
[3] *Ibid.*, p. 86.

in relation to the various interpretive theories...lies the possibility
of an objective evaluation of them." [1] Simply put, that *grundmotiv*
proves preferable which stands in least tension to the given material.
The material is always stronger than the hypothesis. Only by a
continuing process of verification in reference to the empirical-
historical material is the hypothesis validated as in any sense an
objective foundation for investigation and interpretation. Not at any
point does it gain the right to claim absoluteness and finality of truth.
Such claims are not scientific; they are expressions of metaphysical
speculation and arbitrary subjectivism, and therefore methodologically illegitimate. The validation of basic motifs is a strictly scientific
procedure. All that a scientist is concerned with is whether his hypothesis holds in so far as it has been tested; its truth, in other words,
is always tentative, always relative.

An interesting consequence of Nygren's concern to establish motif-
research as an objective science is that he has been forced to open
up a chasm between religion as a subjective experience of faith and
theology as an objective analysis of faith, or between the realm of
faith and the realm of science. The distinction is, perhaps, especially
evident with reference to the concept of truth: Religion, in the form
of a personal commitment to a context of meaning that presupposes
the category of the eternal, gives a peculiar assurance of absolute
truth; theology, in the form of an objective analysis of the nature
and meaning of such religious experience, gives only the relative
certainty which is a part of all science. For this reason, theology can
never become normative for faith. Life always comes before its
description, and description does not have the right to shape or
control the reality which it is only supposed to explicate. Neither
can theology take upon itself the task of evaluating the various
grundmotiv or forms of religion, declaring one more valid or true
than another. [2] It simply approaches its object of study, the various

---

[1] *Ibid.*, p. 88.

[2] One should remember that when Nygren delimits the Christian *agape* motif
so sharply from the Greek *eros* motif, cf. *Agape and Eros*, 1953, his primary
intention is to set the two motifs in direct contrast to one another in order to
understand the characteristic quality of each, not to prove *agape*'s superiority
as a religious motif. One may have divided opinions regarding this kind of
procedure; cf. below, pp. 190 ff. In itself, it need not be inconsistent with Nygren's
emphasis on non-evaluational theology. However, when Nygren presses his
analysis of the religious category beyond the formal reference to the category of
"eternity" and defines religion in terms of "God-relationship", and "God-
relationship" in terms of "theocentricity", it is difficult to avoid the conclusion

organic unities of religious experience and meaning, for the purpose of investigating their place in human history and their role in human life, seeking to understand their essential nature in terms of their basic motifs. This way, theology "accomplishes its systematic task, namely the discovery and systematic exposition of each religion in accordance with its own organic distinctiveness." [1]

The problem of subjectivity in theology is still not quite resolved, however. Although one separates scientific theology from the personal experience of religious meaning, the discipline nevertheless deals with religious experience, and religious experience is meaningful only as a conscious relationship between a decision-making subject and his highest values. Religion is fundamentally a subjective experience; theology, which studies this experience, is thereby subjectively conditioned also.

We are touching what Nygren calls "the sore spot" of his methodology.[2] He cannot deny the subjectivity of the material with which theology concerns itself. What possibility is there, then, for reaching scientific objectivity in the study of this material? Nygren answers with a logical *tour de force*, claiming that our concepts of subjectivity and objectivity need to be sharpened.[3] In what amounts to a basic logical analysis of the two concepts, Nygren finds that their meaning is thoroughly relative, capable of being understood in terms of polarities such as "experience-content vs. thing in itself", "psychical vs. physical", "value-conscious vs. value-free", or "arbitrary vs. necessary". When one charges theology with being involved in "subjectiv-

---

that Nygren has closed the door on "egocentricity" and that the *eros* motif is thereby disqualified as a true form of religion. Cf. "Egoism och religion," *STK*, 3, 1927, pp. 127-150. Nygren is here revealing a tendency, which we shall discover also in Ragnar Bring, to allow the assumption of a dialectic contrast between theocentricity and egocentricity to invade the formal framework of his philosophy of religion, while its proper function is simply as a working hypothesis in the objective investigation of historical forms of religion. Cf. below, pp. 192 ff. For a similar analysis of the tendency to compromize the critical philosophical perspective, this in reference to the ethical category, see my essay "Nygren's Ethics," *The Philosophy and Theology of Anders Nygren* (forthcoming).

[1] Ferré, *op. cit.*, p. 59.

[2] *Filosofi och motivforskning*, 1940, p. 180. We shall have occasion to observe how Bring attempts to overcome this difficulty by de-emphasizing the subjective and experiential nature of faith, stressing instead its "givenness" in history, and claiming that scientific status is a matter of having an object of study which is unique, a purpose for research which is distinctive, and a method of investigation which is appropriate to the material. Cf. below, pp. 153 ff.

[3] *Ibid.*, pp. 181 f.

ity", therefore, one should make perfectly clear which of these polarity structures one is working with; otherwise the argument will easily slip from one frame of reference to another under cover of the general ambiguity of the concept. Nygren describes this kind of argumentation as resting on logical equivocation;[1] it has its basis in a mistaken identification of one subjectivity/objectivity polarity with another, and it results in the total confusion of the issue. For Nygren, the first two polarity structures mentioned have no relevance to the problem of theology. The charge against theology is usually made in terms of the third polarity: theology is value-conscious, ergo subjective. However, on closer examination it is clear that scientific theology, as Nygren has defined it, is not value-conscious in the sense religion is. It simply concerns itself with a value-conscious material. Consequently, the only charge that can be made to stick against motif-research has to do with the type of subjectivity that is involved in the dialectic contrast between arbitrariness and necessity.[2] To answer the charge of subjectivity, then, theology needs to show that it has freed itself of all arbitrariness in regard to the object of study or methods of research, and that it belongs within an unbroken continuum of logical necessity.

The first of these Nygren has partly accomplished; the second he proceeds to undertake.[3] Theology, he claims, belongs as clearly as any other respectable science to a "chain of necessity" that interlocks at every link without break or contingency. The continuum in which Christian theology stands is this:

1. Philosophy of religion analyzes the historical content of human religion; it undertakes the transcendental deduction of the formal religious category and presents it as the necessary presupposition for a meaningful understanding of man's spiritual life.

2. Christian theology investigates the content of the Christian interpretation of religious experience; it seeks to identify the basic motifs that characterize the Christian understanding of spiritual life and to explicate their essential meaning.

3. Specific theological disciplines examine the various manifestations of Christian spiritual life; they are concerned with understanding these

---

[1] *Ibid.*, p. 182.
[2] *Ibid.*, p. 181.
[3] *Ibid.*, p. 183.

historical sources in the light of essential Christian faith and interpreting their meaning.

As one can see, the only possible break that can occur in this continuum is at the point where Christian theology shows partiality to the Christian form of religious experience. However, this gap is bridged before it is formed by Nygren's insistence that Christian theology is relative and non-normative, fully informed of the illegitimacy of claiming absoluteness in a pluralistic situation. Christianity represents one faith among many; it does not refuse other religions the right to build their own systems of faith and theology.

We shall not engage in critical evaluations of Nygren's methodological framework here. There is no doubt that he has developed a significant understanding of the nature and task of systematic theology, a methodology which—at least in theory—avoids the charges directed against traditional Christian dogmatics. Dogmatics has commonly taken one of two forms: It has either appeared as a speculative-metaphysical endeavor, an attempt to develop an eternally valid system of true faith on the basis of Scripture and logic; or it has been an ecclesiastical-confessional enterprise, designed to define the particular commitments that are normative for a certain group of believers in a certain place and at a certain time. Nygren rejects both of these approaches to theology: [1] first, because they make claims to be normative; second, because the scientific concern in the first instance is absent, and in the second only secondary. In contrast, Nygren defines Christian dogmatics as follows: It is "the attempt that has arisen within Christendom to investigate Christianity in its historical beginnings and developments and by scientific means to seek to understand the *egenart* (characteristic nature) of Christian faith and life." [2] Obviously, Nygren understands theology as a discipline with two main focalpoints: It is concerned with the essential meaning of Christian faith, and it is concerned with the scientific respectability of its methodology. As a scientific discipline, theology is historically oriented, critical in perspective, and relative in value. As a dogmatic discipline, it is an ecumenical enterprise, a continuing task, a never-ending process.

Nygren's rethinking of the nature and task of Christian theology may well be described as radical. He has laid the foundations for a

---

[1] *Ibid.*, p. 75.
[2] *Ibid.*, p. 168.

theological methodology that has direct address and relevance to the present. But his work in this area is far from completed. With his work alone, the Lundensian methodology is not established. The full shape of the Lundensian thoughtworld can only be understood by way of a close analysis of Ragnar Bring's contributions.

PART TWO

BRING'S THOUGHT

CHAPTER FOUR

PHILOSOPHICAL COMMITMENTS

Anders Nygren's closest follower, philosophically and methodologically, is Ragnar Bring.

> "Other disciples there are, and many, but none who has mastered to the same extent as Bring the essentials both of methodology and content, and endeavored skillfully to complete the system or to remedy insufficiencies in its original structure." [1]

Nygren and Bring found each other early. They had both felt the pressures of the modern critique of theology, and both respected the honesty with which Hägerström and Phalén expressed the mindset of the modern intellectual community. Both were interested in the philosophical problems of the day,[2] particularly as they influence the understanding of religion and the practice of Christian theology, and both decided there was no way back to the safe, untouchable circles of traditional dogmatics. The problem they shared was how to find a way forward without actually slipping backward, or—in demythologized sense—how to establish a way to do theology that would assure its intellectual respectability in the modern age while at the same time guaranteeing the authenticity of its Christian character.

When Gustaf Aulén in 1954 attempted to summarize Nygren's and Bring's contributions to the Lundensian philosophy of religion, he noted two main points by which to describe their primary concerns: a) the attempt to formulate a formal religious category and define its place within the totality of human experience, and b) the endeavor to free theology from any material influence of speculative metaphysics.[3] While Aulén is undoubtedly correct in indicating that the two men have shared these concerns through the years, it is only fair to note that the creative initiative in both directions is Nygren's. Bring openly and gratefully recognizes this. In his estimation, Nygren's work is of "classical" importance, so "fundamental for the methodology of theology" that since its publication it is

---

[1] Ferré, *op. cit.*, p. 33.

[2] "In my view, the responsible working through of the philosophical problems is one of our most important tasks." *STK*, 26, 1950, p. 163.

[3] Aulén, "Lundensisk teologisk tradition," *STK*, 30, 1954, p. 238.

"impossible" to continue the discussion in terms of the "old problematics".[1] In Nygren's thought, says Bring, are the rudiments of a
philosophy of religion which is "of highly important dimensions".[2]
By posing the problems in new ways, Nygren has laid the foundations
for a theology which "belongs to the future".[3]

If we should attempt, at this early point, to focus the attention on
Bring's particular contributions to the Lundensian methodology,
it would be sufficient to say that he has extended Nygren's philosophical perspective in two directions: inwardly, in reference to the
problems of elementary epistemology, and outwardly, in the direction
of the practical consequences for theology. It is significant, perhaps,
that as we come to analyze Bring's philosophical commitments we
find it necessary to reverse the order of Aulén's two points. Bring's
considerations of the actualities of human experience, including the
analysis of the essential nature of religious meaning and the deduction
of the categorical presupposition for it, are the consequential corollaries of that fundamental rethinking of the epistemological problems
which he undertakes in an attempt to solve the problem of metaphysics. Moreover, we could not study Bring's work without giving
considerable attention to the other side of his interest spectrum:
his consistent application of the results of philosophical analysis to
the understanding of the theological task. Bring's discussions of the
nature and task of theology, set as they are in sharp contrast to a
series of alternative methods past and present, help us to understand
the uniqueness of the Lundensian methodology in a way that Nygren
never managed to do. Therefore, while we maintain the opinion
that Nygren is the most original of the Lundensians, we must also
confess to the estimation of Bring as the more inclusive and complete
methodologian.

It was as a theologian Ragnar Bring found it necessary to take up
the basic philosophical problems. The nature of theology had become
a serious concern to him. Critical methods of biblical scholarship

---

[1] *STK*, 9, 1933, pp. 50 ff. This comment refers to Nygren's *Filosofisk och
kristen etik*, 1923, in particular. Bring's estimation of Nygren's *Dogmatikens
vetenskapliga grundläggning*, 1922, is no less glowing: not only does it represent a
new understanding of Schleiermacher's "grand attempt to solve the riddles
of systematic theology"—an attempt which nobody has tried seriously to complete—; it is also the starting point of a theology "which at one and the same
time fills the scientific demands for objectivity and the theological demands for
true explications of genuine Christian faith." *STK*, 12, 1936, pp. 288 ff.

[2] *STK*, 26, 1950, p. 163.

[3] *STK*, 16, 1940, p. 321.

had served notice long ago that literalistic biblicism is no longer a viable option for the theological community. Cultural developments had proved clearly that an isolationist ecclesiastical-pedagogical approach to theology, treating the Christian tradition of thought in complete diastase from contemporary intellectual problems, is utterly inadequate in the modern situation. And critical philosophy had made speculative theology, whether rationalistic or irrationalistic, meaningless and impossible.[1] As Nygren before him, Bring found himself inevitably drawn into the Kant-Schleiermacher problematics.[2] It was Kant who had forced the issue of an adequate methodology for modern theology by removing the basis for all metaphysically oriented theology, and Schleiermacher had suggested a way to take the Kantian criticism seriously while yet being concerned to establish an authentic Christian theology. Bring felt that the future belongs to a theology which finds its methodological foundations in the presuppositions of philosophical criticism itself.

In his study of Kant and Schleiermacher, however, Bring was led by force of logic to the realization that both of these men had failed to follow through on their critical presuppositions. Kant allowed for a second, "practical" principle of knowledge to stand beside "pure reason", thus opening the door to a new transcendentalism which is fully as metaphysical as the metaphysics he originally opposed.[3] Schleiermacher moved from the criticism of rationalistic metaphysics to a romantic identification of the essence of religion with certain "fromme Gemüthszustände", thus giving way to a psychologistic metaphysics that is as illegitimate as the speculative ontology he opposed.[4] Bring's own task was thereby clear. In seeking to formulate a theological methodology which could assure both intellectual respectability and theological responsibility, he would take his starting point in the Kantian-Schleiermacherian form of philosophical criticism but seek to develop the purest elements of this philosophy into a consistent system that would serve as basis for a scientific definition of theology. A scientific concept of theological methodol-

---

[1] Cf. *STU*, 1933, pp. 12 f.

[2] *Ibid.*, pp. 7 ff; cf. *ToR*, 1937, pp. 138 ff.

[3] *STU*, 1933, pp. 9, 25; cf. *ToR*, 1937, p. 165. Bring agrees with Phalén's critique of Kantian transcendentalism at this point; cf. Phalén, "Kritik av subjektivismen...", *Festskrift tillägnad E. O. Burman*, 1910.

[4] *STK*, 12, 1936, p. 289; cf. *ToR*, 1937, pp. 130, 143. See below, pp. 81 ff, 84 f, 92 ff, for further discussions of Bring's relationship to Kant and Schleiermacher; esp. pp. 112 ff.

ogy was, to Bring, the best guarantee for the authenticity of its Christian content.

THE STRUCTURE OF METAPHYSICAL PROBLEMATICS

The foremost expression of Bring's philosophical position [1] is his avowed opposition to all types of metaphysical speculation.[2] This does not, in Bring's case, constitute a capitulation to the positivistic perspective of the Uppsala philosophers.[3] Rather, he embarks

---

[1] Bring has never developed his philosophical views in any one major work or in any systematic manner. We shall therefore need to draw from a variety of sources spread throughout his total production. Most important in this connection are, of course, *NmPh*, 1940; *STU*, 1933; and *ToR*, 1937.

[2] One should note that metaphysics is a many-faceted concept in Lundensian thought. However, Hemberg's opinion that "the various constructions of the concept of metaphysics evident in Nygren's and Bring's writings are as good as incomprehensible," *op. cit.* p. 299, is vastly exaggerated. His judgment is the result of his misunderstanding of the framework of these men's philosophical position. There are, clearly, two different dimensions to the Lundensians' reaction to metaphysics. It represents, on the one hand, an illegitimate way of thinking which is to be rejected on rational and logical grounds (a reaction inspired by Kant's *Critique of Pure Reason*); it represents, on the other hand, a series of theoretical-religious world-views that challenge Christianity with their absolute claims to knowledge and truth. Cf. below, pp. 78 f. 88 f, 124, and pp. 142 ff.

[3] Jarl Hemberg, *op. cit.*, plainly overstresses Bring's dependence on Hägerström's philosophy while underemphasizing Kant's influence on his approach to philosophical analysis and theological methodology. Bring refers to various elements of Hägerströmian thought, as we shall observe, cf. below, pp. 98 ff., but these are more in the way of relating to categories that are relevant in the Swedish philosophical debate and do not signify a theoretical attachment to Hägerström's philosophy. Against the background of Hägerström's theory of reality, Bring's own "theory of reality" will, of course, seem "fragmentary"; *op. cit.*, p. 297. In fact, he does not develop one. He has, as we shall see, refused the epistemological perspective which makes "reality" or "knowledge" problematic. Instead, Bring simply assumes the validity of human experience and proceeds —in line with Schleiermacher and Nygren—to analyze its structure and its presuppositions. It is not, as Hemberg says, that Bring has failed to develop a theory of reality because he "so to speak glues the theory of the various areas of experience over his original conception of metaphysics (*sic!*)", *ibid.*; rather, it is Hemberg who glues Hägerström's theory of reality all over the picture so that he does not see Bring as Bring is. His criticism of this author, *ibid.*, pp. 287-295, based on the earlier edition of the present work, cf. *A Study of Lundensian Theological Methodology as Represented by Ragnar Bring*, 1962, suffers from the same malady. He says that "the error in Hall's analysis of Bring's theory is that he simplifies his exposition in much too high a degree. He seems prematurely to assume that one can know with certainty what role Hägerström's theories have played for Bring, what "metaphysics" means for him, and how the theory of the contexts of meaning functions and is to be interpreted. In general, Hall has probably represented Bring's theory correctly, but since he has been satisfied with Bring's own demands as to depth of intentions, he has not seen the difficulties of the theory." *Op. cit.*, p. 291. The difficulties of the theory are, of course, the ones that Hemberg sees

on an independent analysis of the fundamental structure of epistemological problematics, and he becomes convinced in the process that
metaphysics offers no solution. We shall need to examine Bring's
thinking in some detail at this point.

The most elementary of all philosophical problems has to do with
the development of a consistent theory of knowledge, *i.e.* with
epistemology. In the Western world, the epistemological problem
arose out of the conception—originally Greek—of a fundamental
separation between the beings and ideas which belong to an "absolute"
world and the sense perceptions and things which belong to the
relative and "contingent" realm.[1] In the course of time, this contrast
came to express itself in a sharp polarity between sense impressions
and substances, or between the knowing subject and the known
object. Thus the scene was set for the emergence of the problem
that has harassed Western philosophers since Plato: in Bring's
formulation, "How is knowledge of an object possible when the
object, by the very nature of perception, seems to be drawn into the
subjective sphere in the form of a subjective perception, although
by definition the object is at the same time the opposite of the subject,
i.e. that which is, independently of the subjective perception." [2]
Some philosophers have discussed this problem in the context of
the relationship between subjective sense perception and objective
facts within man's experience of the empirical world. Others have
drawn the consequences of this perspective for the relationship
between the realm of the finite and the realm of the infinite. In both
cases, however, the results are the same. As long as epistemology
remains within this setting, the attempts at solving the problem of
knowledge will inevitably end in one of two positions, both of which
are fraught with difficulties: On the one hand, one will argue that
the perception of an object in some ways captures the object and is
in some sense identical with it; on the other hand, one will claim that

---

from the perspective that Bring is, after all, a disciple of Hägerström. But the
burden of proof in regard to that question lies plainly with Hemberg. How
successful he has been in proving this assumption is revealed with devastating
clarity in his own admission of defeat: "It is precisely Bring's discipleship vis a
vis Hägerström which has created his problem: The situation in his case is that
the conception of metaphysics which he has taken over from Hägerström
seems to have landed in contradiction to the theory of the contexts of meaning
taken over from Nygren. What kind of contradiction, more closely determined,
this is *seems not to be establishable by means of Bring's writings.*" *Ibid.*, italics mine.

[1] *STU*, 1933, p. 25.

[2] *Ibid.*, p. 23.

the human perception has no way to get at the real object or the thing in itself. Jn either case, says Bring, the problem of knowledge is not solved. The first seeks to overcome the subject/object dichotomy by a logical *coup d'etat*; the other buckles under the pressure of the problem. The end result of the entire procedure is a frustrating choice between identity-philosophical metaphysics and absolute scepticism.[1]

Scepticism is not a viable epistemological option for Bring, but neither is metaphysics.[2] The problem that is raised by the subject/object polarity comes down to this: how to define an *a priori* concept of reality which can assure the validity of human experience and human knowledge. This, in fact, constitutes the essence of the metaphysical problematics, and the history of philosophy witnesses to the difficulties involved in solving it. The various traditions of ontological speculation seeking to develop a concept of the ultimate ground of being and reality—"being itself" or "reality itself"—continually found themselves in an untenable position, faced with the basic question: how is reality-as-we-know-it related to reality-in-itself?[3] And when philosophers sought to bridge the gap between the two realities by identifying a certain concept of reality with reality itself, there was no end to the disagreements which arose between them. One tradition, the idealistic philosophy originating with Plato and followed by

---

[1] Bring refers to Phalén, *op. cit.*, in support of this analysis; *ibid.*, pp. 25 f. It is interesting at this point to compare Bring's opposition to the subject/object problematics with similar notions in Michael Polanyi, *Personal Knowledge*, 1958, pp. 15, 17, 48. Bring argues that the result of the dichotomy has been a continuous clash between opposing metaphysical claims, a result which he would want to avoid. Polanyi shows that the disjunction of subject and object has resulted in a one-sided philosophical positivism or scientific "objectivism" which he would want to disclaim. Bring's opposition to the subject/object perspective thus emphasizes the dangers of absolutizing subjective notions, while Polanyi's opposition focuses on the illegitimacy of ontological objectivism. Bring could well learn something from Polanyi here. Positivistic theories of reality are troublesome to him, as we shall see; cf. below, pp. 146 f; Ch. IX. Under the pressure of the criticism against subjectivism in religious experience, Bring tends to buckle and begin to reconsider the concept of reality. Polanyi holds on to the critical perspective and simply turns the tables on the positivists, showing them deeply involved in commitmental, evaluational activities at all points.

[2] Bring is focusing on the first dimension of metaphysics here, cf. *supra*, p. 76, note 2, namely that which constitutes an illegitimate way of thinking. We shall soon discover that "metaphysical confusion" presents itself in two forms; cf. below, pp. 88 f, 124.

[3] *NmPh*, 1940, pp. 3 f. In this respect, Bring finds no real difference between Plato and the Atomists—or even Parmenides for that matter—; they all identify the concept of reality with a certain content-defined entity, though they define its nature somewhat differently. *Ibid.*, p. 5.

many Western schools of thought, defined the real in terms of an absolute ontological unity of substance, truth, goodness, beauty and value, all of which were considered predicates of the one "primal", "ultimate", "infinite" reality.[1] Another tradition, represented by the naturalistic-materialistic-positivistic philosophies of the scientific age, identified the categories of time, space, matter and causality as criteria for determining what is ultimately real and denied the validity of any other concepts of reality.[2] There is no solution to the conflict between these traditions. They follow essentially the same philosophical approach, solving the problem of validity by way of arbitrary decicions concerning the ontological content of the concept of reality.[3] Thus metaphysics stands against metaphysics, while the basic question concerning the validity of knowledge is begged.

It is important at this point to understand what Bring means by "validity". It is a central concept in Lundensian thought, as we have already observed in the study of Nygren,[4] but it contains a certain ambiguity of meaning. In its principal or "critical" sense, it refers to the existence of certain general or "formal" presuppositions for valid knowledge; but it may also be taken to mean that a definite idea or object is determined as valid in itself and therefore capable of guaranteeing knowledge as being true.[5] The second represents the way ontological speculation approaches the problem of knowledge; and it is illegitimate, in Brings estimation, because it is based on the arbitrary commitments of identity-philosophical metaphysics. Only the first is acceptable, and only on certain conditions. And the most important condition is the rejection of the Greek way of posing the epistemological problem.

In Bring's estimation, the most unfortunate effect of the Greek perspective is that it makes knowledge problematic. By separating between subject and object, or between the perceiver and the perceived, one is forced to introduce a distance also between the objects perceived (knowledge by perception) and the objects in themselves (the truth). Consequently, the definition of true knowledge becomes as difficult as the identification of the truly real. The problem of knowledge, if it is considered solvable at all, invites all

---

[1] *ToR*, 1937, pp. 162 f; *STU*, 1933, p. 218.

[2] *Ibid.*; cf. also "Kristen tro och vetenskaplig forskning," *STK*, 25, 1949, p. 207.

[3] *NmPh*, 1940, p. 6; *STU*, 1933, p. 26.

[4] Cf. *supra*, p. 57 (including note 1); also p. 59, note 1.

[5] *NmPh*, 1940, pp. 7 f.

sorts of identity-philosophical speculation to attempt a solution; and the result is a massive search for the real-in-itself or the true-in-itself for the purpose of identifying them as the valid-in-itself. Thus, in the context of the subject/object dichotomy the quest for the presuppositions of valid knowledge ends necessarily in metaphysics. Bring finds this illustrated in the case of Descartes, as well as in British empiricism and in Kant.[1]

Descartes' epistemology came to rest on the indubitability of the dictum, *cogito ergo sum*. The very formulation of the *cogito* shows not only that Descartes was concerned to establish the presuppositions for valid knowledge, but that he sought to do so in terms of a definite *"Dasein"*, an indubitable identity of being and knowledge. Thus both implications of the concept of validity were involved in the Cartesian form of indubitable knowledge; the search for the fundamental presuppositions of validity led him to the definition of one concrete point of valid knowledge, one definite indubitable truth, the true- in-itself. It was not sufficient for Descartes to speak of self-consciousness as the formal presupposition for the validity of knowledge. The subject/object polarity would not allow it. Self-consciousness had to be defined in such a way as to insure the unity of subject and object; *cogito* and *sum* were therefore identified by way of the *ergo*, and indubitability rested thereby on metaphysics.

The case was essentially the same in British empiricist epistemology, says Bring. Although these philosophers started out in explicit opposition to rationalistic metaphysics, their own psychologistic theory of knowledge proved them bound within the same problematics as the rationalists.[2] Intending to assert the validity of human experience, and to analyze the bases for it, they proceeded to tie the concept of validity to certain psychological processes of human understanding. Such a development is inevitable, says Bring, within the traditional epistemological perspective. One is forced to go beyond the general reference to experience and to identify a specific instance of experience that can be said to constitute an indubitable truth; otherwise one would be open to the untenable position of accepting the uncertainty of all understanding—which is scepticism. But the identification of a concrete instance of valid knowledge as valid-in-itself is essentially metaphysics. Bring illustrates the inevita-

---

[1] The following summarizes Bring's discussion, *ibid.*, pp. 9-38.
[2] Cf. *STU*, 1933, p. 219, note 11; *Förhållandet mellan tro och gärningar inom luthersk teologi (FTG)*, 1934, p. 254.

bility of such developments by reference to Berkeley, who disassociated himself from rationalistic metaphysics only to develop his own extreme brand of idealism, and to Hume, who consistently opposed such speculations only to find himself without any basis for speaking of valid knowledge at all.

Kant's epistemological position shows a similar double-sidedness in the concept of validity, says Bring. Although Kant pointed to a way of avoiding metaphysical speculation, he eventually fell back into it himself. In his analysis of Kant,[1] Bring is particularly interested in the elements which give promise of a breakthrough to non-metaphysical epistemology. These have to do primarily with Kant's theory that certain "synthetic judgments" function as presuppositions for human experience. But what did Kant mean? Did he desire to *establish* the validity of experience by reference to the *a priori* character of certain judgments, or did he *assume* the validity of experience, seeking only to identify the *a priori* presuppositions for its being so? In other words, did he want to identify concrete instances of valid experience, or did he think of the *a priori* categories of validity in purely formal and presuppositional ways?

In Bring's view, Kant did both; but the first, unfortunately, came to dominate his thought. He saw the dangers of his own position, however. The temptation to seek validity by reference to something valid-in-itself, which is by definition a metaphysical procedure, can only present itself in one form within a philosophy that endeavors to be a critical discipline of thought, namely in the claim that human self-consciousness or perception, the *"Ding-für-uns"*, is the sole principle of valid knowledge. This is Fichte's approach, but Kant was not willing to accept it; it was nothing but a subjectivistic form of metaphysics. Instead, he developed the theory that the de facto validity of human experience presupposes certain *a priori* categories or synthetic judgments functioning as transcendent principles of validity. So far, one may say, Kant's concept of validity appears "simple" and non-problematic. But here the problem appears: Kant had namely accepted the traditional way of posing the epistemological problem, including the subject/object dichotomy, and from this perspective

---

[1] Bring is, like Nygren, conscious of the fact that his relationship to Kant is not that of a historical-descriptive scholar. His approach, he says, is "philosophical-systematic". He is mainly interested in the elements of Kant's thought which in his own view are useful for the development of a consistent critical philosophy.

it now appeared that the critical epistemological structure would fall
on the basis of its subjectivity. The de facto validity of experience—
the *Ding-für-uns*—seemed in need of some objective confirmation and
verification—some connection with the *Ding-an-sich*—in order to be
fully valid. Kant's own critique of pure reason had shown, however,
that the access to this objective, "noumenal" verification was blocked.
So the verification of knowledge had to be done another way. Kant
proposed two: On the one hand, he made a fundamental distinction
between theoretical knowledge (pure reason) and phenomenological
knowledge (practical reason), describing the latter as having its
validity guaranteed by the indubitability of perception and by the
a priori categories. On the other hand, he developed a theory of a
highest principle of knowledge, a "transcendental unity of apperception", thus attempting to support the validity of the individual *a
priori* by reference to an ultimate principle of validity.[1] In Bring's
view, both of these procedures tend to compromize Kant's basic
position; they show that his concept of validity was such as to make
knowledge problematic and metaphysics inevitable. The validity
of experience had to be guaranteed by reference to an indubitable
transcendent principle, *i.e.* by something valid-in-itself. Thus it
appears that although Kant explicitly denied pure reason the access
to an objective, metaphysical verification of knowledge, he was still
working within a framework of thought which made such a verification
necessary. Kant was, in fact, deeply involved in the metaphysical
problematics.

FOUNDATIONS FOR A NON-METAPHYSICAL PHILOSOPHY

At the beginning of his little book *Wie ist nicht-metaphysische
Philosophie möglich?*, Ragnar Bring asked the fundamental question
which set the stage for all his epistemological analyses: "Kann der

---

[1] It is interesting to note that Bring finds in Kant's thought two different
concepts of the "transcendental", functioning parallel to the two concepts of
validity that are intertwined in his philosophy; *NmPh*, 1940, p. 32. "Transcendental
in the usual sense" describes the formal principles or presuppositions which lie
behind the validity of experience and which can be deduced by way of transcendental analytic; "transcendental in the psychological sense" refers to the
subsidiary Kantian idea that the validity of experience is proven on the basis of
the presuppositions at work, and that since psychological presuppositions are
subjective and arbitrary, they must in turn be proven by reference to other, higher,
"transcendental" presuppositions. In Bring's view, Kant's thought came to be
dominated by the second, subsidiary problematics, and it is at this point that critical
philosophy must turn back on its master in critique.

Gültigkeitsfrage eine Bedeutung beigelegt werden, wenn es sich gezeigt hat, dass es zu Unmöglichkeiten führt, von einem an sich Gültigen oder einem an sich Wirklichen zu sprechen?" [1] Following the discussion of these *Unmöglichkeiten*, Bring's question had narrowed somewhat. Kant had shown him a way to avoid the dead end streets of epistemological scepticism and speculative metaphysics, and now Bring was concerned to know whether it was possible to follow the Kantian suggestions consistently and thus find a way to solve the epistemological problem without depending on the particular *Durchführung* that Kant himself proposed. Bring's discussion limits itself to certain *Andeutungen* at this point,[2] but he has returned to the matter repeatedly, and the direction of his thought is clear.

We have seen that Bring, like Nygren, rejects the ontological-speculative approach to the problem of knowledge, claiming that such procedures necessarily lead to the arbitrariness of identity-philosophical speculation and to metaphysical conflicts over ultimate reality, absolute ideas, or the *Ding-an-sich*.[3] In effect, this means that Bring has rejected the traditional Greek way of posing the epistemological question. He says, "If one places the question of reality at the center of the epistemological consideration, subject and object will inevitably come to stand over against one another." [4] Questions concerning the relationship between known reality and absolute reality will then immediately present themselves, and the answer has to be found by way of ontological speculation concerning the metaphysical unity of the two, or one will end in scepticism. Instead of operating with the concept of "reality" and its corollary, the subject/object scheme, Bring decides to define the epistemological question in terms of *validity*, specifying that in seeking the presuppositions for valid knowledge one must "abstract from both subjective references (in a psychological sense) and from objective references (in the ontological sense)." [5] One must, in fact, make one fundamental assumption—the one proposed by Nygren—: that human experience is significant and that valid judgments can be made, or in Bring's terminology, *that human experience is valid and that it is possible to undertake a transcendental deduction of the formal presuppositions underlying*

---

[1] *Ibid.*, p. 6.

[2] Cf. *ibid.*, pp. 40 f.

[3] See further *STU*, 1933, p. 227; "Teologi och religionsfilosofi," *STK*, 23, 1947, p. 68; "Kristen tro och vetenskaplig forskning," *STK*, 25, 1949, p. 208.

[4] *STU*, 1933, p. 222, note 14.

[5] *Ibid.*, p. 219, note 11.

valid experience. In Bring's view, the philosophical discipline of
epistemology does not undertake to prove the validity of experience;
it simply analyzes the categorical principles which must be at work,
seeing that human experience is in fact valid and significant.[1]

Having thus laid the foundations of his theory of knowledge in a
way that he considers true to the intentions of consistent criticism,
Bring goes on to associate himself with those elements in Kantian
epistemology which he deems true to the critical intentions.[2] He has
no need for Kant's distinction between theoretical and practical
knowledge. Neither is he interested in Kant's speculation concerning
a highest principle of apperceptive unity. Since he has assumed the
validity of human experience, knowledge does not constitute an
uncertain and dubitable part of life; it is there in the human awareness,
and it is valid, as all experience is. The task of epistemology is not
to prove the validity of knowledge, but simply to examine the principal
presuppositions on which the validity of man's experience and knowledge actually rests. These presuppositions need not be defined in terms
of an indubitable content—in fact, they ought not to be, for this
would only prove that one considers knowledge problematic, in
need of external validation; and it would inevitably result in new
forms of identity-speculation and metaphysics. Instead, critical
epistemology engages its efforts in the interest of analysis: first
the analysis of experience, by which one identifies the various areas of
life to which independent validity and authentic meaning cannot be
denied; second, *the analysis of presuppositions*, by which one makes
deductions of the "pure", "formal", "transcendental" (in the critical
sense) [3] categories that are the bases of validity and meaning in the
various areas of experience.

Bring has thereby answered his own question in the affirmative.
By starting the epistemological reconstruction without the subject/
object problematics, he has been able to keep the concept of validity
purged of all metaphysical tendencies; and by following consistently
the non-metaphysical elements in Kantian criticism, he has succeeded
in developing a critical epistemology which is free of the difficulties of
the Kantian *Durchführung*. He comes out, in fact, with a concept of
philosophy similar to Nygren's, only more sharply defined. Allowing
human reason its full capacities within the limits of its competence,

---

[1] *NmPh*, 1940, pp. 40, 42.
[2] *Ibid.*, p. 44 f.
[3] Cf. *supra*, p. 81, note 1.

i.e., within the limits of human experience, namely the capacities to investigate experience, to understand its meaning, and to analyze its presuppositions, Bring has given his epistemology a "scienctific" grounding which in turn forms the basis of a scientific approach to the philosophy of religion and to systematic theology. And that, after all, was his primary concern.

AN ATTEMPT AT CONSISTENT CRITICISM

We have arrived at the point where a second major area of Bring's philosophical interests comes into focus: the philosophy of religion. With Nygren, Bring defines the discipline as a critical analysis of the nature of religious experience, the meaning of religious life, and the presuppositions for its validity and authenticity. Like Nygren, he finds Schleiermacher's approach to these matters especially promising —if not so much in content as in method. But again Bring reveals his characteristic capacity for thorough-going application of the critical perspective. Attaching himself closely to the work of Nygren, Bring takes upon himself the task of strengthening the inner logic of Nygren's thought and sharpening the awareness of its practical consequences. We shall focus, in the immediately following, on what appears to be Bring's particular contributions to the Lundensian philosophy of religion.

It is clear to Bring that when an analytical philosopher surveys human experience as a whole, he is immediately struck by the great multiplicity of the experiential material. Life is magnificently many-faceted—even confusing—in its unending variety and change. But it is valid, all the same; and it is meaningful, not nonsensical. Some form of meaning is there in all the varieties of human experience; that is the fundamental assumption which a critical philosopher must make. He is not a judge of experience. Life, instead, is the judge of philosophy. If life is meaningless, it is so only to philosophy, and the fault is to be laid to philosophy, not to life. Surveying human experience, the critical philosopher must not introduce a preconceived norm of meaningfulness by which he evaluates the material and sorts out its various facets, some of which are considered valid, others not. Rather, he must observe, listen, inquire, dissect and analyze human experience in order to understand the various dimensions of meaning which are there, integral to the very awareness of life itself.

By this process, the philosopher will find rising out of the experience of man a number of major "areas" or "contexts" or "connections" of meaning, each one presupposing a different category of meaning and each one having a definite, autonomous validity. Says Bring, "As we look over the spiritual life of man, we find certain general questions returning again and again...the questions of the true, the beautiful, the good. A unified answer to all these questions can never be found; answering all of them at one and the same time would be impossible." [1] Rather, the various categorical "questions" correspond to different clusters of historical-empirical "answers", each of which forms an independent area of experience which is made up of all the material that is releveant to a certain question and that can only be understood in connection with that question. Human experience reveals itself, therefore, not as a disorganized maze of disjunctive and fluctuating experiences, but as an ordered system of separate and distinct *meningssammanhang* (literally meaning-connections). Each of these is an authentic area of experience in the sense that "the validity and meaning of individual experiences and judgments (belonging to one area) cannot be understood in reference to the presuppositions of another area." [2] A philosophy which is to be critical in perspective must, in fact, recognize and respect the autonomy of each *meningssammanhang*.

We should note at this point that although Bring uses the term *meningssammanhang* in close correspondence to Nygren's concepts "areas of experience" or "contexts of meaning", there is a certain ambiguity involved. Bring employs the same word to denote both what Nygren describes as the "primary" and the "secondary" contexts of meaning.[3] On the one hand, it refers to the various areas of human experience, generally delimited by reference to the basic presuppositional categories and thus divided into different *sammanhang* of meaning. On the other hand, the word is used also to refer to the inner core or "connection" around which the various types of world interpretation or selfunderstanding that appear within each *sammanhang* appear to be organized—that which Nygren prefers to call the *grundmotiv*. There is no ambiguity in Bring's thinking, only in terminology. His double use of the term makes *meningssam-*

---

[1] *ToR*, 1937, p. 162. Cf. Nygren's maxim for clarifying the relationship between the empirical-historical realities of man's existence and the categorical presuppositions for their meaningfulness, *supra*, p. 60.

[2] *NmPh*, 1940, p. 40.

[3] Cf. *supra*, p. 62.

manhang a description of both the "formal" and the "material" contexts of meaning, *i.e.* it refers to both the formal category of meaning and to the specific structure of motifs. Bring could have dissolved this ambiguity simply by referring to the first as the *meningssammanhang* and the second as the *motivsammanhang*.

Our consideration of Bring's philosophy has so far brought only the first of these *sammanhang* into view. In taking over Nygren's practice of distinguishing between several different areas of experience, Bring's intentions are clear: He found here the basis for claiming that the ethical and religious experience of man possess independent validity and autonomous meaning, regardless of their noncompliance with the criteria of validity that apply to other areas, particularly the theoretical area of experience.[1] This is an important point to Bring, as we shall see. He considers Nygren's view of the differentiated categories of human experience a major step toward a consistent critical philosophy. It is especially important for securing a basis for a "religious" understanding of religion and an "ethical" approach to ethic.

But the philosopher has more to do. As Bring sees it, the modern philosopher of religion must seek to develop the analytic approach so that the study of the religious area of experience and meaning ties in with an inclusive view of the autonomous categories and results in a clear grasp of their mutual relationships.[2] The aim must be to understand all facets of man's life, religion among them. One cannot understand one area of human experience without an overview of the logical presuppositions at work in experience as a whole. Neither can one reach a consistent and integrated concept of experience without a conscious concern for the interaction and interdependencies involved in the relationship between categorical presuppositions. Philosophy must proceed, therefore, beyond the analysis of the areas of experience, beyond the deduction of the categorical presuppositions, to the analysis of the interlocking

---

[1] Cf. "Kristen tro och vetenskaplig forskning," *STK*, 25, 1949, p. 205.

[2] One of the most persistent criticisms against Nygren's theory of the areas of experience is that it tends to isolate religion from the other areas of life. Bring himself has been sharply criticized by Sven E. Rodhe on the same basis; *STK*, 15, 1939, pp. 92 ff. Bring does show definite interest in the relationships between the different *sammanhang*, however, and he has come to balance the emphasis on autonomy more and more with a stress on mutual interconnections and interdependencies. Cf. "Anders Nygren's teologiska gärning," *STK*, 16, 1940, pp. 317 ff; *NmPh*, 1940, pp. 34, 40.

structure of all the presuppositions for meaningful life. Human life, after all, is a unity; and "the loss of validity in one area of experience would ultimately lead to the loss of all meaning whatever." [1]

Bring has thereby identified a third task for philosophical analysis. The first two, the analysis of experience and the analysis of presuppositions, are to be complemented by the analysis of the total framework of meaning. This is, to Bring, the growing edge of philosophical criticism at the moment.[2] However, he does not himself endeavor to take up this task; quite disappointingly, in view of the importance that he ascribes to it, Bring leaves aside the task of analyzing experience as a whole and attempting an overall integration of the categorical presuppositions. Having identified the need for such an endeavor, he returns quickly to his own main interest, namely the autonomy of the various *meningssammanhang*. Bring is intensely concerned with this subject, for two reasons: He sees in it the key to the defense of theology against the pressures of the scientific worldview; and he finds in it, also, the solution to the logical confusion caused by mixing the categories of meaning.

At this point, a second definition of metaphysics comes to the forefront of Bring's thought. His first definition, as we have seen,[3] describes metaphysics as a speculative attempt to identify the real-in-itself or the true-in-itself in order to claim indubitable knowledge of the valid-in-itself. His second definition has to do with the tendency to disregard the categorical autonomy of the different areas of meaning and the subsequent confusion of experiential "answers" that are relevant to one fundamental "question" with material that belongs within an entirely different *meningssammanhang*.[4] One common error of this kind is evident in what appears to be a theological predisposition to absolutize ethical and religious answers and to set these judgments in

---

[1] *Ibid.*, pp. 42, 44.

[2] Bring has not done much to develop this concept. One should note, explicitly, that he does not here intend to return to the earlier interests of Nygren, seeking to "broaden" the transcendental analytic. The function of the analysis of the total framework of meaning is not to define an ultimate unity which will incorporate each of the independent areas of experience as parts of a single, absolute truth. Yet, the nature of this third analytical task is not clear. Bring has challenged Nygren to take up this concern, but so far no clear signs of an integrated view of man's experience have appeared among the Lundensians. One wonders, in fact, whether they are capable of producing such a view, since their main emphasis for so long has been on the "independent validity" and the "autonomous meaning" of each individual category of experience.

[3] Cf. *supra*, p. 78.

[4] *ToR*, 1937, pp. 168 f, 178; *STU*, 1933, pp. 199 ff.

direct contrast to the theoretical inquiries of the natural sciences. And the opposite error frequently occurs, also. The natural sciences tend to make the particular presuppositions on which their theoretical inquiries are based the norm of truth and validity within all of human experience, and to conclude that religious and ethical judgments are valid only in so far as they conform to the standards of verifiability that are presupposed by the sciences. In Bring's view, these and similar examples of categorical transgression and confusion of *meningssammanhang* must be opposed, on two counts: They are clear signs of massive conceptual disorder; and they represent presumptuous attempts at forcing all of life into one single form. In either case, the procedure is illegitimate; the logic is false, and the results are arbitrary. In short, it is nothing but metaphysics.[1]

There is a way to avoid the confusion of *meningssammanhang*, says Bring, namely by scrupulous *logical analysis*. What is needed is a clear conception of the context of meaning to which a particular concept or judgment or utterance belongs, a sure grasp of the dialectic at work in each area of meaning, and a keen awareness of the significant differences in the function of words within the various areas of experience.[2]

Bring has never developed fully his references to logical or conceptual analysis; neither has he worked his way through to the practical consequences of his philosophical criticism for the understanding of the nature and meaning of theological language. This is, as we shall see, one point at which his thought needs contact with later developments in logic, and especially with linguistic analysis.[3] As it stands, Bring's reference to conceptual analysis at this point functions simply to strengthen his hand in seeking a clear delineation of the autonomous validity of religious truth and in forcing the natural sciences to recognize the limitations of their own claims. It is, in a way, an apologetic move on Bring's part. Characteristically, he argues that to approach a religious utterance, which belongs to the *meningssammanhang* that presupposes the formal category of "eternity" and thus answers "the question of salvation",[4] and interpret it as a statement containing theoretical notions of scientific or metaphysical significance, is wrong, whether one is on the side that does theology

---

[1] *Ibid.*
[2] *Ibid.*, p. 202.
[3] Cf. below, pp. 140, 177; also Ch. IX.
[4] Bring's favorite term for the religious category.

this way or on the side that criticizes theology on this basis.[1] Thus, the brunt of Bring's argument falls with equal weight against his colleagues in the theological community and against representatives of the so-called "scientific worldview". Whenever one jumps the fences between the categorical fields and shows forgetfulness of the limitations of a specific area of meaning, one is guilty of disregarding the autonomous validity of all the areas of meaning; one is guilty of metaphysical confusion.[2]

What, then, is the essential nature and autonomous meaning of religious experience? One is surprised to find that Bring does not have much to say about this question. He points out in several places that Nygren has never actually undertaken what he called the "transcendental deduction of the religious category". But Bring does not attempt to remedy the situation. He gives the impression that he is waiting for Nygren to do this work. He is not satisfied with Nygren's choice of the concept "eternity" for describing the categorical presupposition of religious meaningfulness; it is too close to the particular commitments of Christian faith to be able to serve as a formal, "open" presupposition lying behind all religious types. Nor is he comfortable with Schleiermacher's concept "the feeling of absolute dependence". Although there are clear indications that Schleiermacher conceived of this formulation as a designation for the general attitude of religion, and not as a definition of a specific "ideal religion", the concept is easily taken as a description of the psychological essence of true religion, and thus as a material norm for evaluating historical religion, or as an ontological starting point for developing a faith by way of speculation.[3] Bring has suggested,

---

[1] *Ibid.*, p. 203.

[2] Cf. below, pp. 142 ff. Bring has shown that the "scientific worldview" is essentially an absolutization of certain tenets resulting from the scientific investigation of the world; "Kristen tro och vetenskaplig forskning," *STK*, 25, 1949, pp. 222 ff. See also *STK*, 9, 1933, p. 61, for a delineation of the various ways to deal with metaphysics—when it comes in the form of logical confusion, and when it appears in the form of a religiously functioning world-view. Metaphysical confusion, he says, must be countered by logical analysis.

[3] Significantly, Bring does not criticize Schleiermacher's philosophy of religion on account of psychologism or subjectivism as such; he is sharply critical of Brunner who in his analysis of Schleiermacher focuses on such features in the picture. Cf. *STU*, 1933, pp. 61-68. In his own critique, Bring centers on the fact that Schleiermacher did not allow the religious *a priori* to remain a formal category, but went on to define its content and use it as a criterion of evaluation, thus compromising the critical approach to the philosophy of religion. *ToR*, 1937, pp. 122, 123, 141.

rather timidly, that the concept "salvation" might serve as the presuppositional category of religion, but the suggestion suffers from
the same weaknesses as Nygren's "eternity".

Before one criticizes Bring and Nygren for their failure to provide
a positive identification of the religious category, one might consider
several items: First, recent philosophical and theological developments
have combined to cause a general disenchantment with the Kantian
approach to experience, and especially with the practice of defining
the categorical *a priori* or the transcendent presuppositions of meaning
in terms of constant or static forms. Post-Kantian philosophy, on
its side, has become convinced of the fluid and dynamic nature of
reality; and the new theory of relativity, the advances in nuclear
physics, and the progress of space exploration have combined to
break wide open the traditional understanding of the categorical
presuppositions, including time, space, and causality. Similarly,
though not for identical reasons, modern theology has become increasingly unwilling to accept the notion of a religious *a priori*; it carries
with it the idea of an essential religiosity in man, so offensive to a
theology that seeks to avoid anthropocentrism and humanism and
locate the source of faith in the divine initiative and in revelation.
In short, the market for a transcendental deduction of the religious
a priori has been very slim recently.

Secondly, Bring has been particularly concerned to emphasize
that any definition of the religious *a priori* or the general category of
religious meaning must be done in terms of a pure and empty form.
This is, of course, a consequence of his refutation of identity-philosophical speculation and ontological metaphysics. Says Bring. "It
seems generally accepted these days that we cannot count on finding
Truth with a capital T. It does not seem quite as clear that we cannot
define Religion with a capital R." [1] In his own view, the traditional
quest for a definitive description of "the essence of religion" is
suspect from the start, for "even the assumption that there is a Religion with a capital R, and that to know it is to understand true religion, is metaphysical." [2] The religious category—or the formal
presupposition for religious experience, to Bring—has no content or
substance or shape in itself. In this respect, there is no religion, only
different religions. Neither is there any value in searching all the
historical religions for a common element; all one has left when that

---

[1] *Ibid.*, p. 170.
[2] *Ibid.*, p. 171.

is done is a common feature of historical religion, not a concept of the essential nature of religious experience. The religious category does not define absolute religion; nor does it identify the least common denominator in religious experience. It simply functions as the formal presupposition upon which the actual meaningfulness of all human religion is based.[1] Obviously, Bring's concern to remain consistent with philosophical critisicm makes it difficult to speak with more specificity than that.

Finally, we should note that Bring's philosophy of religion is designed not to stand alone, and thus complete in itself, but to serve as groundwork for the scientific discipline of historical-systematic theology. In practice, this means that the philosophical task is carried no further than is necessary for the methodological interests to be served. More basic yet, perhaps, the philosophical foundations of Lundensian theology are constructed so that the interest is not focused there but is drawn, instead, to the theological superstructure. Thus, when Bring refuses to talk about Religion with a capital R, or when he shrinks from making positive identification of the religious category, the reason may well lie in his desire to deal objectively with all historical religion and his intention to study scientifically the characteristic features of each religious type. In Bring's view, the essence of religion is not found by way of philosophy, but by systematic theological investigation of historical religions; it is not a metaphysical entity but an empirical one. The religious *a priori* is nothing but an empty form that is filled with a variety of historical religious content. The essence of religion is represented by the *centra* of the historical religions of man, and these are the objects of study for scientific systematic theology.

CONSEQUENCES OF THE CRITICAL COMMITMENT

It is clearly evident that although Bring is concerned to establish the autonomy of religious experience, he is not prepared to do so in a way that might jeopardize his critical philosophy or endanger the scientific objectivity of systematic theology. In this respect, he has learned much from Nygren, and from Schleiermacher. As a matter of fact, Bring sees himself—along with Nygren—as the heir to the best tendencies in Schleiermacher's methodology. These are two, in particular: By arguing for the independent validity of religious

---

[1] *Ibid.*, p. 171 f.

experience as an experience *sui generis*, Schleiermacher pointed to the way by which philosophy of religion can avoid metaphysics while securing the autonomous meaning of religion; and by defining theology as a study of historical faith, he laid the corner stone of modern systematic theology. In Bring's view, Schleiermacher is to theology what Kant is to philosophy.[1] Before him, only occasionally did anyone think of theology as a scientific discipline engaged in objective research into the experiential and propositional material that is given in the history of man's religion. Schleiermacher's work has since been largely misunderstood or misappropriated—a fact which is partly due to the ambiguities of Schleiermacher's own thought. Nevertheless, his importance for the methodological renewal of theology cannot be over-emphasized, and Bring is determined to follow Schleiermacher's lead—only so that he avoids the methodological inconsistencies of the German master and draws the radical consequences of the critical philosophical commitment in full.[2]

Bring's consistent emphasis that *the religious category must be understood as a pure and empty form* is clear evidence of this determination.[3] His philosophical analyses had convinced him that to talk about the religious category in any other way would reveal the arbitrariness of metaphysical speculation and render the religious *a priori* useless as a tool for understanding the meaning of religious experience. For Bring, the deduction of the formal category of religion, the presupposition for the autonomous validity of religious experience, does not give as result a definition of ultimate and essential religion; neither does it give a criterion by which one may evaluate the religions of men. It provides a perspective by which to understand and interpret these religions. The question of the essence of religion can only be answered in an empirical way.[4] One must identify the "individualities" of the various historical religions or religious interpretations and investigate their particular answers to the general question of

---

[1] *STK*, 12, 1936, p. 288; *ToR*, 1937, p. 138; *STU*, 1933, p. 10.

[2] We shall not include any extensive analysis of Bring's interpretation of Schleiermacher here; only certain basic emphases are relevant. The questions whether Bring interprets Schleiermacher right or whether he is justified in drawing out a few elements of Schleiermacher's system and for the rest leaving his thought alone are, of course, interesting and important, but they cannot be considered here. Ragnar Bring does not see himself as a Schleiermacher interpreter; he is simply a philosopher-theologian who has learned certain basic things from Schleiermacher.

[3] Cf. *STU*, 1933, pp. 126; 223, note 14.

[4] *ToR*, 1937, pp. 125, 127.

religion; one must seek to understand what *in their view* the essence of religious life is all about.[1] All religious types or individualities are equally valid. They are different, because they are formed by way of personal or corporate commitments and value judgments, but they all have meaning—even when they are diametrically opposite one another—as answers to the formal question of religion.[2]

Bring has here drawn out the consequences of the critical philosophy of religion in a radical and consistent manner. By *recognizing explicitly the relativity of religious commitments and the pluralism of human religious experience*, he has, in fact, laid a methodological groundwork for religious tolerance and interfaith dialogue, while retaining the full value of doctrinal particularity and religious individuality. The various religious types represent different ways of shaping the meaning of religious experience. The fact that each type ultimately rests on the subjective decisions of individuals or groups of people means that there is no way to prove any one religion to be the "best" or the "right" one. But one can still be concerned to understand that which in the estimation of the various religions is considered best or right, and so proceed to compare the deepest intentions within the many types of religious concepts, interpretations, and ideals that are propounded among men.[3] By such procedures will emerge not a watered down syncretism based on general religious ideas, not a graded scale of more or less valid religious forms, but a deeper understanding of all religion and a greater appreciation for the characteristics of ones own faith.

Acknowledging the subjectivity and the relativity of historical religion, Bring has avoided the entire complex of problems involved in the metaphysical speculation concerning essential religion. However, as with Nygren, the problem of methodological subjectivity still remains to be taken care of, especially since it bears upon the scientific status of theology. The fundamental presupposition for a general acceptance of systematic theology among the sciences of man is that it be shown that its methods are scientific, objective, and not arbitrary. Thus the subjectivity of religious commitments—theology's object of study—is potentially an embarassment to the methodologian. In Bring's view, however, the problem is easily solved. The subjectiv-

---

[1] *Ibid.*, p. 172.

[2] *Ibid.*, pp. 147, 172.

[3] Cf. "Kristen tro och vetenskaplig forskning," *STK*, 25, 1949, pp. 212 ff, on the so-called "objective argumentation" within law and ethics.

ity of religious commitments is an epistemological observation of significance for the philosophy of religion, but it does not in any way jeopardize the scientific objectivity of systematic theology. *Religion is a subjective experience which manifests itself in objective historical materials of many sorts, all of them capable of being investigated. Systematic theology undertakes this investigation, and it does so by way of historical-critical methods of research.* Clearly, then, religion and theology belong to two entirely different categorical contexts: The first is part of an a-theoretical area of experience in which personal decisions and value judgments must be allowed to play their roles; the second is a theoretical exercise in which value judgments are illegitimate and decisions are tentative, always subject to the scientific requirements of evidence and the logical criteria of verification. Religion and theology are related to each other only in the sense that the fruits of the first become the objects of study for the second.

We shall return to Bring's discussion of the nature of scientific theology below. At this point we shall take note of a further item that exemplifies his discipleship to Schleiermacher and Nygren in regard to the fundamental bases of theological methodology, namely the explicit commitment to the presupposition that *there is within each individual religious type an inner connection or s a m m a n h a n g, a "motif" which serves as the organic center by which the many elements of a historical faith are held together and in view of which its concept of religious meaning is to be interpreted.*[1] Bring is here working with the second of the two senses of *sammanhang* referred to above, namely the unifying or connectional core that gives shape and character to each religious individuality and informs every facet of its understanding of religious experience.[2] The assumption of such a *motivsammanhang* serves a double function in Bring's thought. In the first place, it forms the basis for claiming that systematic theology, the study of the motif structure of a particular religious type, far from imposing external and arbitrary perspectives on the historical material which it investigates actually has its function as a science determined by the nature of the material itself.[3] Secondly, it also functions to indicate what sort of science systematic theology must be. There are three alternative approaches to the study of religion, according to Bring: One may undertake some form of historical-genetic analysis of religious

---

[1] Cf. *STU*, 1933, p. 197; *ToR*, 1937, p. 173.
[2] Cf. *supra*, pp. 86-87.
[3] *STU*, 1933, pp. 207, 229, 146.

ideas, aiming to reveal a maximum of logical interconnections between concepts that occur in a variety of religious types. Secondly, one may approach the task by way of psychological-descriptive investigations of religious experience, the purpose being to identity similarities and catalogue varieties in the interest of gaining an overall understanding of the dynamics of human religiosity. None of these alternatives is adequate, in Bring's view, to describe the nature and task of systematic theology.[1] In fact, if it is to be established as an independent scientific discipline, systematic theology must focus its efforts on a task that is different from those of the history of religion (or comparative religion) and the psychology of religion. It must establish itself as a critical analysis of particular historical religions, undertaking to search for the *motivsammanhang* that characterize the various conceptions of the God-relationship or that serve as their principle of unity, their *grundmotiv*.[2] Systematic theology is, in short, motif-research; it cannot be otherwise. Bring's assumption that there is within each religious type a unifying or connecting core, given in the historical material that is relevant to each type, means that theology by definition must be engaged in an objective, scientific study of religious motifs.

Another consequence of Bring's critical commitment should be mentioned at this point, one which shows that Bring is prepared to break with the Kantian-Schleiermacherian form of criticism, if that is necessary in order to defend systematic theology against the charge of subjectivism or arbitrariness: *his explicit rejection of a special religious epistemology*. Bring refers to certain "tendencies" in the works of Kant and Schleiermacher which prove these men unable to follow through on their own radical critique of knowledge. Kant's so-called "practical" philosophy is a case in point. Not only does Kant employ the metaphysics of identity-philosophical speculation in suggesting that the "categorical imperative" is identical with the absolute and unconditional will of God; he is also guilty of metaphysical confusion, proposing that ethical experience constitutes, in Bring's terms, "a second way of knowledge." [3] Such an auxiliary method of knowledge, superceding in certain respects the limits of human reason, may also be involved, says Bring, in Schleiermacher's use of the concept

---

[1] *Ibid.*, pp. 17, 215 f; cf. below, Ch. VII.

[2] *Ibid.*, pp. 220, note 11; 229.

[3] *Ibid.*, pp. 140 ff; *ToR*, 1937, p. 145.

"self-consciousness".[1] At any rate, certain of his followers, the proponents of the so-called "theology of experience", have taken Schleiermacher to mean this; they claim Schleiermacher as authority for the view that religious experience represents a superior way to knowledge.[2]

In Bring's estimation, such ideas are nothing but a reiteration of the scholastic practice of explicating the relation of reason and revelation in terms of a two-storey division of a "lower" and a "higher" knowledge.[3] Whether scholastic or Kantian or Schleiermacherian, such a bifurcation of knowledge is *ohållbar* (impossible, absurd).[4] All human science—theology included—works with the same presuppositions of knowledge; it is all "theoretical". If any discipline claims to have knowledge, it must be knowledge of something real, something that has reality to all men. To speak of reason and revelation as having reference to two different divisions of reality, one theoretical and another "practical"—*i.e.* one kind of reality which can be known scientifically and another which can only be gotten at in a practical, experiential, or "personal" way—leads to all sorts of difficulties, ontological as well as epistemological.[5] Theology, if it wishes to gain status as a scientific discipline, cannot claim for itself a special way of knowledge or define an object of study that would require such an approach.[6] It must understand itself simply as a critical investigation of the historical material that is relevant to a particular religious type, the purpose being to understand and explicate the central motifs which give character and personality to it.

While rejecting a special religious epistemology, Bring does talk about certain "psychological presuppositions" that are prerequisites for doing theological research. These are, in his own words: "interest" in the material, "involvement", "openness of understanding", "ability to identify oneself with the object of research" or "to stand inside of historical Christianity", and appreciation of "the Christian

---

[1] *STU*, 1933, pp. 214 f.

[2] *Ibid.*, pp. 29 f; *ToR*, 1937, pp. 139, 144 f.

[3] Cf. "Kristen tro och vetenskaplig forskning," *STK*, 25, 1949, pp. 217 f.

[4] *STU*, 1933, pp. 193.

[5] *Ibid.*, pp. 209 f.

[6] This is Bring's way of accepting the categorical restrictions of human knowledge, and it shows the influence of Kantian criticism as well as Hägerströmian positivism. His rejection of a special religious epistemology marks a clear break with the thought of Söderblom and Billing and with the views of their disciples, Runestam, Bohlin, and Lindroth. Cf. below, Ch. VI.

attitude to life".[1] Bring goes so far as to suggest that there is a certain psychological affinity between the religious attitude and the scientific mood; both are characterized by what he calls *saklighet* (matter-of-factness, unbiased objectivity) and *verklighetstrogenhet* (true-to-lifeness, realism).[2] However, none of these are said to be special qualities, belonging to the theologian by virtue of some peculiar epistemological endowment that is not available outside of the theological circle. In fact, any such claims would prevent the theologian from finding and sharing significant insights into the meaning of Christian faith; theology would then be a subjective and arbitrary exercise, totally cut off from dialogue with other disciplines of knowledge.[3] It would have lost its scientific status.

In the interest of guarding the scientific objectivity of theology, Bring makes explicit one or two further methodological commitments. The question had been raised by Hägerström and Phalén whether it is possible to make an investigation of a subjective, a-theoretical, non-material area of experience such as religious value judgments on a strictly scientific basis.[4] Bring answers by rejecting the basic assumption underlying the question: *he refuses to separate between the immediate experience of religious meaning and the reflective formulation of religious faith.* Faith, to Bring, does not consist of a primary, inarticulate awareness which is subsequently reflected upon and expressed in secondary religious propositions: ". . . The reflective aspect of faith—the theoretical element within faith—is not something extraneous to faith, but is a legitimate and integral part of it, given in and with the religious experience or attitude itself." [5] There

---

[1] *Ibid.*, pp. 92 f, 128, 169 f, 193; *ToR*, 1937, pp. 149 f, 150; "Kristen tro och vetenskaplig forskning," *STK*, 25, 1949, pp. 202 ff.

[2] *ToR*, 1937, pp. 181 f; cf. also *STK*, 25, 1949, pp. 237, 243.

[3] *ToR*, 1937, pp. 151 f.

[4] Hägerström's sharp separation of science and value judgments has been a two-edged sword for the Lundensians. The notion was valuable, when combined with the Ritschlian understanding of faith, in undergirding the emphasis on the autonomy of the religious area of experience, but it threatened at the same time to extricate theology from the ranks of the theoretical sciences. Cf. Hägerström, "Kritiska punkter till värdepsykologien," *Festskrift tillägnad E. O. Burman*, 1910. The positivistic trends in Hägerström's thought come to full expression in G. Wetter, *Tro och vetande*, Stockholm: Bonnier, 1915. In Wetter's view, religious propositions are valid as subjective value judgments, but from the point of view of rational and objective knowledge they are mere illlusions. Bring makes a rather jittery defense against Wetter; cf. *STU*, 1933, pp. 206 ff. We shall return to the question of Bring's fear of the illusionistic theory of religion below; cf. pp. 146 ff; also Ch. IX.

[5] *Ibid.*, p. 14.

is no legitimate way by which the experience of a faith commitment can be divided into an initial, non-rational (emotional) stirring and a subsequent theoretical post-script. "Faith is a unity, a concrete form of the religious attitude. Between faith and the faith-content there is no possible differentiation that can be made." [1] Thus, according to Bring, the problems involved in the traditional separation of *fides qua* (faith itself) and *fides quae* (that which faith believes) can simply be laid aside.[2] Religious experience is not, to use Hägerström's terminology, "non-material" experience; it is "a-theoretical", but it is not without actuality. The relation of rational reflection and elementary awareness is as close in religion as in any other area of experience.

In addition to his modification of Hägerström's understanding of religious experience, Bring explicitly *refuses to accept the idea*, proposed by the positivists, *that any scientific investigation of faith must presuppose the theoretical criteria of truth or it loses the right to declare itself a scientific undertaking*.[3] It is obvious to Bring that science must be guided by the criteria of logical consistency, inductive reasoning, or objective verification when dealing with questions of a theoretical nature. When one is concerned to understand a religious commitment or an ethical posture, however, other criteria of meaningfulness and sense may well be required. To investigate religious propositions as if they were theoretical conceptions, thus making faith answerable before the court of science or logic, is clearly a result of metaphysical confusion; in fact, it is plainly unscientific. It is to take statements that are meaningful in one context of human experience and evaluate them on the basis of criteria drawn from another area of meaning. One considers faith in God, for example, a rational theory expressing theoretical intentions; and then one proceeds to argue that such a faith is impossible to hold.[4] The procedure is altogether wrong, says Bring; ethical and religious judgments must be interpreted in terms of their own authentic context of meaning and must not be pressed into conformity with the standards of theoretical truth.[5]

In utilizing the categorical distinction between the theoretical and religious areas of experience in this manner, it is not Bring's intention

---

[1] *Ibid.*, p. 196.
[2] *ToR*, 1937, p. 146.
[3] *STU*, 1933, pp. 210 f.
[4] Cf. "Kristen tro och vetenskaplig forskning," *STK*, 25, 1949, p. 239.
[5] *STU*, 1933, p. 100.

to force the issue to a head and perpetrate a choice between science and religion. Rather, the intention is simply to take the issue to the opponents' home court and remind the positivists that since science and evaluation are two entirely different things, science should never involve itself in value judgments, but should restrict itself to the task of investigating the material at hand, value judgments included. Furthermore, Bring argues—on Hägerström's own premises—that science cannot ignore the ethical or religious material simply because it does not conform to the theoretical criteria of truth.[1] He shows that Hägerström should not have accepted the thought that something which *is* could be described as "inaccessible" to science. That value judgments *are*, even in Hägerström's world, is shown by the fact that he analyzes their character and finds them to be conceptions that are associated with certain emotional affections like hopes or wishes. To say that such conceptions, the reality of which has not been canceled by the fact that they are considered of special value, are not accessible to the tools of scienctific investigation is, in Bring's view, plainly absurd. The scientific approach to things is fully warranted, regardless of the nature of the sources, provided one focuses on objectively given historical material and recognizes the distinctive character of the area of meaning to which the material is related. Value judgments do not constitute exceptions to this rule; they can be scientifically investigated by means of "the question whether or not a unified motif is present in them." [2]

We shall consider only one other explicit consequence of Bring's critical-philosophical commitment, namely *his strong opposition to irrationalism*. This is, once more, a point at which Hägerström's challenges have been accepted and countered by Bring on the presuppositions of Hägerström's own reasoning. The fundamental assumption of Hägerström—which Bring accepts—is that reality is logical *sui generis* and does not first become so by way of an activity of the human consciousness. Logical inconsistencies, when they appear, must be charged to judgments and propositions, never to reality itself.[3] In Bring's words, it "does not make sense to say that anything real is absurd." [4] As a matter of fact, any statement to that effect is nonsensical by definition; one makes the "rational" judgment that

---

[1] *Ibid.*, pp. 97 ff.
[2] *Ibid.*, pp. 101 f.
[3] *Ibid.*, p. 201, note 12.
[4] *Ibid.*, p. 53.

reality is irrational. Critical philosophy, in approaching experience by way of the double methodology of conceptual and presuppositional analysis, can never accept the judgment that reality itself is absurd. Instead,

> "...its starting point is the assumption that an absurdity must mean that something has been thought in two ways that do not logically belong together. The task, then, is to resolve such absurdities and think consistently...; the contradictions must be analyzed in logical ways and eliminated—not set up as inevitable paradoxes." [1]

Applied to theology, this means that irrationality is inadmissible and that paradoxality is unacceptable. The idea that human reason is necessarily involved in logical conflict is an abomination to the critical mind. The same is the case with the thought that Christian faith cannot be understood by way of common sense. If Christian faith is not made to make sense by way of clear rational explication, theology has not fulfilled its task. In fact,

> "it will never fulfill its task if it acquiesces in the general tendency to accept the irrational and claims that Christianity cannot be contained in our common categories of understanding. Instead, theology must define, as clearly and concretely as possible, the precise nature of the 'paradoxality' of Christian faith." [2]

Thus, if paradoxality arises in the configuration of faith motifs, the theologian's task is to analyze the nature of the doublesidedness involved, to explain the intentions of each element in it, and to explicate the function of such a combination of motifs within the total "system" of Christian faith. If paradoxality appears in the correlation of religious statements and the propositions of theoretical knowledge, such difficulties can be resolved by a clarification of the nature and intentions of each of the statements involved.

In the chapters to follow, we shall observe in some detail how the various elements of Bring's critical philosophical commitment influence his approach to systematic theology. At this point, a summary may be useful. The following represents, in propositional form, the essence of Bring's philosophical framework:

1. In order to avoid the modes of thought that inevitably lead to metaphysical speculation, the consideration of epistemology should be kept clear of the traditional philosophical problematics, particularly the subject/object dicthomy; it should be approached, instead,

---

[1] *Ibid.*, p. 51, note 30.
[2] *Ibid.*, p. 210. Cf. *ToR*, 1937, pp. 213 f.

on the basis of the assumption of the validity of human experience.

2. In approaching the experiential material by means of analysis, the critical philosopher is made aware of certain basic distinctions between several areas or *sammanhang* of experience. These areas constitute so many independent and autonomous contexts of meaning, each of them valid and meaningful on its own particular presuppositions; and the material is properly understood only as it is interpreted in the light of the particular context to which it belongs.

3. The presuppositions of validity and meaning, the *a priori* categories, must be understood as formal and empty principles, not as content-defined concepts. The categories do not function to define the essence of the true, the beautiful, the good, or the religious; they do not define the content of experience, only the forms for its understanding.

4. In the a-theoretical areas of experience, including religion, the content of experience is influenced by a series of subjective value judgments, each type of standpoint constituting a distinct *sammanhang* that can be identified and described by reference to a characteristic *grundmotiv*. If a religious type is consistent, all its value judgments will appear to form an organic unity, all its material content is informed by one central motif, and all its manifestations are part of a recognizable individuality.

5. All investigations of the given empirical-historical material, religion included, must be undertaken by way of scientific methods of inquiry. All such scientific endeavors are subject to the same criteria of rationality; there is no special religious *episteme*.

6. Religious experience manifests itself historically in a series of objectively given sources for study—documents, symbols, or propositions; it can be fully understood and exhaustively interpreted on the basis of the material at hand.

7. The investigation of value judgments, including religious standpoints, represents a scientifically responsible investigation in so far as it aims to understand the religious material in the light of its own criteria of meaningfulness, *i.e.* in its *meningssammanhang* as well as its *motivsammanhang*.

8. The logical nature of reality must be assumed, regardless of which aspect of human experience one is studying. By way of conceptual and presuppositional analysis, the human reason is fully capable of understanding and explicating the various elements of experience in a rational and consistent manner.

It is on the basis of these fundamental commitments, epistemological, philosophical and logical, that Ragnar Bring endeavors to
establish a modern concept of the nature and task, the purpose and
procedures of systematic theology, the science of faith. Our next
concern is to seek a clear view of his thought on such matters.

CHAPTER FIVE

SYSTEMATIC THEOLOGY — PAST PROBLEMS AND PRESENT POSSIBILITIES

The primary interest underlying Ragnar Bring's epistemological and philosophical discussions is, as we have observed, to find a way to hold together two basic elements of theology, each of which is essential to the renewal of a meaningful and respectable theology in our time; namely, the development of a method which is "strictly scientific", and the recovery of a content which is "genuinely Christian".

In taking up this double concern, Bring—together with many colleagues in Swedish theological circles—openly confesses that he considers theology, especially systematic theology, to be in serious trouble at the present time.[1] Not only has theology lost the privileged position and high ranking among the sciences; the concept of theology as the queen of the sciences, in whose court all other disciplines of knowledge are but subordinate servants, is now an utterly nostalgic idea, he says.[2] The scientific status of theology is itself being questioned. This is particularly the case with dogmatics, or systematic theology. While many theological disciplines—the historical-critical or text-critical study of the Scriptures, the history of the church or of doctrine, and the psychology or sociology of religion—have already reached some sort of understanding in relation to the secular disciplines whose methods they have, to a large extent, taken over, systematic theology is still considered so closely identified with subjective value judgments and Christian faith commitments that any claims to presuppositionless objectivity and scientific impartiality is out of the question.[3]

Systematic theology is, for this reason, faced with a difficult dilemma. It seems as if the only alternatives available are that theology on the one hand present itself as a science of a higher order, thus showing the supreme audacity to claim objective validity for its value judgments quite apart from the strict demands of proof and verification that rest upon the empirical sciences; or, on the other hand, it may relinquish

---

[1] *STU*, 1933, p. 3.
[2] *ToR*, 1937, p. 156.
[3] *STU*, 1933, p. 3.

all special privilege and be incorporated into the ranks of the idea-historical or psychological disciplines of study. Both these alternatives are, of course, being tried. There are those who take a defensive stand against the critics of theology, rejecting the idea that theology requires the ratification of the scientific community in order to be recognized as intellectually acceptable. Faith, in their view, has its basis in revelation; and revelation constitutes the foundation of a "science" beyond science. There are those, also, who see no other way to securing the scientific status of systematic theology than to reduce it to—or dissolve it into—a general *religionsvetenskap* (literally, science of religion), in which those events, experiences, and propositions that are relevant to Christianity are investigated together with all other religious materials by means of historical-genetic, psychological, sociological, or idea-historical methods. This way, systematic theology is simply another name for the comparative study of religions.

Bring rejects both alternatives.[1] Neither of them is capable of taking systematic theology out of methodological trouble. The first leaves it wide open to the charges of speculative metaphysics and subjective arbitrariness; the second lets go of the autonomous purpose and methodological distinctness—and therewith the justification—of systematic theology. Bring denies, in fact, the proposition that these alternatives represent the only solutions to the methodological dilemma of systematic theology. There must be a possibility to avoid having to choose between a theology based on the subjective presuppositions of faith and a theology that is reduced to the ranks of historiography, psychology, anthropology, sociology, or philology and to transcend the old polarity of metaphysics versus objective recording of positive facts. In Bring's view, the effort to find an alternative by which systematic theology can both establish its place among the sciences and gain clarity in regard to its authentic nature requires that the methodologian is willing to take up a struggle on two fronts: On the one hand, systematic theology shall have to be disassociated from its traditional anchoring in the presuppositions

[1] *Ibid.* Cf. Bring's review of Nygren's *Dogmatikens vetenskapliga grundläggning*, *STK*, 12, 1936, pp. 287 f, where he points out that the problem of the scientific nature of theology is not extraneous to the understanding of religion. Rather, it arises from the situation of religion itself. Science "means quite simply to present something truthfully," says Bring. When the "thing" to be presented is something so complicated as religious events or experiences or propositions, it immediately becomes problematical how a true presentation can be made.

of Christian faith and experience; it must stand "presuppositionless" and "objective" in relation to its historical object of study, in the same way as any other science. On the other hand, it shall have to provide justification for its existence as a science by establishing the necessity of its task and the autonomy of its purpose in distinction from all the other disciplines already recognized as sciences of religion.[1]

Bring's own methodological discussions, though rather wide-ranging, are clearly organized in reference to these two foci. He faces opponents on two fronts and seeks laboriously to carve out a middle position—a place for a genuinely Christian, strictly scientific systematic theology. Because of the polemic setting of the majority of his methodological works, Brings' argumentation tends to run in somewhat negative, if not dialectic patterns. The ultimate outcome, however, is positive. In his discussions with one group of opponents, one finds explicated in considerable detail a view of the nature and task of systematic theology that has deep roots in his critical epistemological and philosophical commitments; and as a result of his confrontations with another set of adversaries we have in his writings rich resources for a positive delineation of the purposes and procedures of scientific systematic theology. The first of these areas is the topic for this chapter and the next; the second will be analyzed in Chapters VII and VIII. The difficulty of selecting, out of Bring's multifaceted discussions, what are the important issues—those that are essential to the development of Bring's methodology—and of organizing his *ad hoc* arguments in a logical or progressive order is indeed considerable. One can only hope that the finished product will prove the insights and abilities required for such an endeavor to have been present.[2]

The Metaphysical Approach to the Essence of Christianity

The most elementary delimitations of the nature and task of systematic theology are found, in Bring's works, in his argumentation against theologians who construct their methodology within a framework which is by definition metaphysical—especially those who do not distinguish sharply enough between the theoretical character of scientific theology and the religious character of Christian faith.[3] Bring's position at this point is in many ways similar to his

[1] *STU*, 1933, p. 5.
[2] Our sources here are mainly *STU*, 1933, and *ToR*, 1937.
[3] *STU*, 1933, p. 33.

emphases in regard to scientific philosophy; the basic philosophical commitments which we have observed operating in his thought clearly inform his views even here. He says:

> "Just as a scientific philosophy stands in contrast to a metaphysical philosophy, so does a scientific theology stand in contrast to metaphysical theology. No science, be it philosophy or theology, can accept any element of metaphysical thought without at the same time losing its scientific character." [1]

Stated positively, one may say that if there is a way to do philosophy—"pursue the philosophical interests", as Bring puts it—in a non-metaphysical way, there must also be a possibility of pursuing the theological interests without falling prey to the influence of metaphysics. Bring makes it his purpose to find that way. In fact, it is precisely for the purpose of avoiding the problems of metaphysics that Bring has dug so deeply into philosophical and epistemological matters. Only by way of a thorough understanding of the fundamental dynamics of knowledge and the basic presuppositions for rational thought can one hope to find a solution to the methodological problems with which systematic theology is faced in our time. These problems are not only connected with the presence of certain material evidence of metaphysical speculation in the traditional forms of systematic theology; they have to do also—and more crucially—with the tendency of all theology to accept as necessary a formal involvement in metaphysical ways of thinking. As we have seen, in his critical philosophy Bring has undertaken to lay the groundwork for a theological method that avoids the formal involvement in metaphysical problematics. He claims that by developing consistently the critical approach to religious experience, one may even come so far as to be able to free theology of the material impact of metaphysical ideas. Building his methodology with this in mind, Bring undertakes to show, by reference to the systematic theology of the modern period, how various forms of metaphysics have tended to influence the pursuit of "the theological interest" and how, by means of the critical approach, systematic theology can free itself of the burden of such associations.

If one should ask, by way of clarification, what specifically constitutes a legitimate "interest" for systematic theology, Bring would answer that it has to do with identifying and explicating "the character-

---

[1] *Ibid.*, p. 74.

istic content of Christian faith" or, as he also describes it, the "typical"
or "unifying" or *bestående* (lasting, unchanging) elements within
Christianity: that which makes it what it is.[1] Many systematic theologians have defined their task in similar ways. One definition of
theology that has come to the forefront in the modern period centers
the theological interest on the quest for "the essence of Christianity".[2]
Thus, on the surface, one may speak of a general consensus regarding
the purposes of systematic theology. Yet the history of the discipline
reveals that the quest for the essence of the faith may be undertaken
from many different perspectives and with widely varying methods.
When one asks about the "essence" of something, one can obviously
mean by that concept several different things.

In an interesting essay in his book *Teologi och religion* entitled
"Diskussionen om kristendomens väsen inom upplysningsteologien"
(literally, the discussion concerning the essence of Christianity within
Enlightenment theology),[3] Bring considers the influence of the
metaphysical concept of essence—Greek in origin—on the historical
development of Christian theology. Basically, the Greek philosophical
perspective presupposes a sharp distinction between essence (*essentia*)
and existence (*existentia*); it considers the former a higher form of
being or reality, entirely separate from the latter, more contingent and
changing reality. The question of essence is thus by definition
contrasted to everything historical and empirical; essence cannot be
the object of historical-critical investigation the way finite existence
is. Essence is absolute, not dependent; ultimate, not derivative—
as the things of experience. For that reason, the search for the foundations of things—reality, validity, knowledge, and meaning—must
focus on the realm of essences, and not on the realm of the relative
or the historical. Theology, if it is to be concerned with the ultimate
essence of religion, cannot possibly be a historical or empirical science.

According to Bring, when the nature of theology is considered on
the presuppositions of the dichotomy between essence and existence,

---

[1] *ToR*, 1937, p. 51.

[2] According to Bring, the expression "the essence of Christianity" began to
be used only during the Enlightenment. Older Protestantism did not ask for
the "essence", but looked instead for the propositions of doctrine that were
considered "necessary for salvation". Through Schleiermacher's influence, the
question of "essence" came into a different light altogether, and Harnack, more
than any other theologian, exemplifies the new empirical-historical approach to
its answer.

[3] *Ibid.*, pp. 51-127.

it will by necessity be defined in terms of metaphysical speculation. Moreover, the pronouncements of theology—its presentation of the essence of religion or the content of Christian faith—cannot then be considered the result of a responsible scientific discipline of study. Bring finds evidence to support this judgment both in the Enlightenment's approach to the essence of religion and in the orthodox Protestant interpretation of the Christian faith.[1] Based on a combination of the Greek two-storey structure of reality and the corresponding two-storey structure of knowledge taken over from Medieval scholasticism—"reason" and "revelation" being the epistemological correlatives of the ontological polarities "existence" and "essence"—most theology during these periods assumed a speculative and metaphysical character.

There were significant differences between Orthodox and Enlightenment thought, of course—principal contrasts in commitment as well as in concepts. Orthodoxy, on its side, interpreted the essential aspects of Christianity in terms of an absolute system of supernatural-revelational truths. Enlightenment thinkers, on the other side, turned against such dogmatic systems and developed instead a core of general ideas which were considered essential to all religion, the assumption being that absolute truth is revealed in human reason and that Christianity is the most reasonable of all religions.[2] In spite of their differences, however, it is obvious that both Orthodox and Enlightenment theology were caught in speculative thoughtforms—and therefore in metaphysics: Reason was understood as a "natural" light by which man has access to a storehouse of common, natural truths; revelation was considered a "supernatural" light by which truths of a higher order become available to those who are receptive. It makes little difference whether one asserts the dogmas of revelation

---

[1] Bring's discussions of pre-Schleiermacher theology are held in rather broad lines; his purposes are to illustrate certain methodological characteristics. *Ibid.* pp. 69 ff, 114 f.

[2] Bring finds that the Enlightenment's interest in the question of the essence of religion was partly a reaction to the supernaturalistic systems of dogmas characteristic of Orthodoxy, and partly an apologetic move toward a biblicistic concept of original Christianity. Cf. *ibid.*, pp. 56, 74, 86 f, 96 f, 99 f. The approach was a double-barreled one, with a reference to reason and natural religion, on the one hand, and a reference to the New Testament and the "simple religion of Jesus", on the other. Any discrepancy between the two did not seem to appear to the Enlightenment theologians. This, says Bring, has to do with the fact that their conception of the nature of Christianity was consistently based on reason and nature; their biblical orientation functioned simply to give their speculation a Christian aura. Their exegetical methods were far from critical.

—the supernatural light—or chooses to spin a network of truth out of man's natural resources, one is still bound within the metaphysical problematics; the concept of essence is in both cases speculative, non-historical, and unscientific. The perspective itself is an invitation to metaphysics. If one moves into the two-storey structure of thought, be it philosophical or theological, ontological or epistemological, and expects to find the essence of Christianity within this framework, apart from the world of historical facts outside, it does not matter much whether one claims the first or the second floor as one's own particular apartment; one has preempted the possibility of pursuing truth in a scientific manner. [1]

Bring finds further evidence to support his judgment that Enlightenment theology was thoroughly metaphysical and unscientific in the fact that the concept of reason on which this theology was based is not a formal, theoretical principle of logic or a value-free, historical-critical method of investigation. It functions, rather, as the source, the method, and the content of theology wrapped into one package. It is a rational principle which includes both truth and value; in it, formal and material considerations are joined together in a confusing mixture. In the Enlightenment perspective, "reason" beame synonymous with "religion"; and the theologian's task was understood to be the deduction of a set of basic religious ideas that could be demonstrated as valid simply by reference to their rationality. "Reasonable religion" became the trademark of "essential religion", and Christianity was considered the purest form of rationality.

The unscientific and metaphysical character of Enlightenment theology became evident, also, as it proceeded to criticize a number of alternative interpretations of Christianity, particularly the Orthodox systems of dogma. The criticism of Orthodoxy was in some respects the presupposition for the emergence of a modern theology, and as such it served an important theological function. However, the Enlightenment's approach to the critique of Orthodoxy was in no

---

[1] Bring's critique of the deists—from Herbert of Cherbury to Thomas Chubb, with Locke, Tindal and Toland as connecting links—is held on the level of methodology, not theological opinions. He focuses on the fact that these men were all confident that the essence of religion could be formulated in terms of an absolute ideal, either natural or supernatural, and that Christianity could be proven to be the ultimate manifestation of this religious ideal. The error of Deism, in Bring's view, was not in its rationalism, but rather that rationality here moved to metaphysics, and not to criticism. *Ibid.*, pp. 80 ff.

ways based on historical-critical or objective-scientific criteria. Instead, the various theological propositions of Orthodoxy were evaluated against the background of the Enlightenment's own definition of reasonable religion, and what was not in full accord with this norm—that is, anything the Enlightenment considered unreasonable—was summarily discarded as having nothing to do with essential Christianity. A typical example of such methodological arbitrariness can be drawn, according to Bring, from the so-called Neological school in Germany, the movement that arose in reaction to the conservative supernaturalism of Wolff and whose most mature proponents were Reimarus, Lessing and Semler.[1] In their criticism of traditional Christian doctrine as developed by the speculative dogmatists of Orthodoxy and their conservative successors, the representatives of Neological thinking [2] clearly presupposed the ultimacy of their own concept of reason, so much so that they made it the criterion for the evaluation of historical Christianity and the norm for the interpretation of New Testament faith. Anything that did not seem entirely "simple" or "practical" or "reasonable" was regarded as a consequence of the "Hellenization" of Christianity. And whenever they discovered a lack of correspondence between the simple religion of Jesus—essential Christianity as defined by Neology—and the biblical material, the Neological theologians were always able to develop plausible theories for the purpose of explaining away the discrepancies.[3] In short, reason prevailed.

Bring explains that as a consequence of the Enlightenment's approach to the definition of essence, the ideal and the historical fall inevitably apart. The essence of Christianity is formulated by way of reason, speculatively, and this formulation is considered the

---

[1] *Ibid.*, pp. 100 f.

[2] F. ex. Gruner, Starck, Arnold, Spittler, Löffler, et. al.

[3] Semler, for instance, developed the so-called "accomodation-theory" (an early form of demythologizing). Those aspects of the New Testament which seemed unacceptable were explained by reference to the theory that Jesus and the apostles accomodated themselves to the thoughtforms of their day. Thus, the eternal truths in Jesus' message are hidden behind a *tidshistorisk* (contemporary-historical) veil; in order to get at these eternal truths, it is necessary to strip them of the crude first century garbs. Teller and others used the "reduction-" or "subtraction-method" to lift out of primitive Christianity that which seemed essential. As the next logical step, Lessing formulated the "perfectibility principle", according to which Christianity must move away from its original attachment to contingent historical facts and go on to consecutively higher stages of enlightenment and insight. Cf. *Ibid.*, pp. 55, 107 f, 110 ff, 137.

final—or at least the most advanced—manifestation of religious truth and meaning. In contrast to reason, the given historical material gives only knowledge of the finite or contingent forms of Christian faith, and it has therefore little or no value for the higher understanding of Christianity. Lessing expressed the mind of the time clearly in his famous dictum, "Contingent historical facts cannot contain eternal spiritual meaning." Says Bring: "Any attempt to define the essence of Christianity by separating the eternal from the finite must of necessity lead to the dissolution of the history of Christianity."[1] He might have added, it leads to the dissolution of theology as a scientific discipline as well.

Generally, systematic theology as understood traditionally—or before Schleiermacher, as Bring speaks of it—includes two definitive factors, both of which are closely intertwined in and inseparable from the content of theology, and both are clearly metaphysical in nature:[2] In the first place, there is the tendency to identify the principle of knowledge (revelation or reason) with the essential content of religion (or the essence of Christianity, which is considered the same thing), which means that the theological method is also the norm of faith and the criterion of religious truth. This is metaphysics of the first degree—or what we described in an earlier chapter as identity-speculation: the attempt to identify, by way of an inclusive definition, the religious category and the religious content, material and form, the answer and the question. In the second place, there is the tendency to extend the function of the concept of religious essence (be it the result of a rational or a revelational concept of religion) and to consider it a system of absolute truth, normative not only within the religious context of meaning, but in the theoretical area of experience as well. This is metaphysics of the second degree—or that which Bring defines as the confusion of *meningssammanhang*: the interpretation of the answer to one categorical question as if it were the answer to another, or every other, question. We have seen how eager Bring is to avoid all tendencies in these two directions. It is obvious that his pursuit of the theological interest—the study of the essence of Christianity—shall have to be approached in a way that is radically different from what he has observed among the theologians of Orthodoxy or the Enlightenment.

---

[1] *Ibid.*, p. 113.
[2] *STU*, 1933, p. 13.

THE TURNING POINT FOR MODERN THEOLOGY

We have already observed that Bring considers Kant and Schleiermacher as representing the decisive turning point in the development of modern theology. They are, in a sense, the fathers of the scientific approach to the theological interest, and therefore of a new brand of systematic theology. Kant revealed, in his analyses of the metaphysical problem, how utterly unwarranted it is to consider the human intellect capable of identifying, defining, or investigating in an objective way that which is true-in-itself or valid-in-itself; there is no way by which pure reason can get at the transcendent essence of things. As a result of Kant's demolition of metaphysical speculation, says Bring, modern theology must rid itself of the traditional concept of essence. After Kant, it is entirely anachronistic, for example, to speak of Christian dogmatics as the "science of God".[1]

This does not mean, however, that the science of theology is assigned to oblivion or that the question of the essence of Christianity is ruled out. Schleiermacher was able to define, within the presuppositions of the Kantian critique of reason, a new way of doing theology, a method which assures the scientific status of systematic theology while still leaving the question of the essence of Christianity at the center of interest. Schleiermacher's understanding of the nature and place, the purpose and procedures of systematic theology is, to Bring, a master-stroke of methodological genius; although only a few of this successors in the theological community have managed to survey the consequences and follow the implications of Schleiermacher's work,[2] it is clearly the way forward.

Two aspects of Schleiermacher's methodology are particularly relevant to Bring at this point. In the first place, Schleiermacher *resolved*, at least in one facet of his thought, *the traditional identification of the questions concerning the essence of religion and the essence of Christianity*.[3] Schleiermacher assigned the first question to the philosophy of religion, defining the task of this discipline as the critical analysis of religious experience, and designating the result—the religious category—as a pure, transcendent form, open to and accepting of all the historical material that is relevant to it. The second question he

---

[1] *Ibid.*, pp. 6, 9; cf. *ToR*, 1937, p. 117.

[2] "Scarcely anyone before Schleiermacher spoke of theology in terms of a presuppositionless, scientific discipline; and after him, it is only to a small degree that these tendencies in his thought have been continued." *STU*, 1933, p. 13.

[3] *ToR*, 1937, p. 125.

assigned to the science of systematic theology, identifying the purpose of this discipline as the critical investigation of religious types, and describing its object of study—historical religion—as characterized by a variety of content-defined typological traits.

In the second place, Bring notes that according to Schleiermacher *the essence of Christianity must be sought in the historical manifestations of Christendom, where it is operative as the organic center of faith and the organizing principle of thought.*[1] By means of this specification, Schleiermacher was able to cut through the traditional dilemma of the bifurcation of *essentia* and *existentia*, the absolute and the relative.[2] The essence of Christianity is not found by formulating a metaphysical concept of faith in abstraction from the historical manifestations of faith; it is found, instead, within the manifold and often incongruous historical material. The investigation of this material and the identification of its essential and characteristic elements—the basic motifs functioning as the unifying and connectional principles within it— is an entirely scientific task, theoretical, objective, historical-critical.[3]

Thus, two features emerge as fundamental to Schleiermacher's way of doing theology: the historical-critical perspective, and the interest in the characteristic motifs of Christian faith.[4] In Bring's view, it was precisely the combination of these two methodological elements that gave birth to modern systematic theology; and it is by developing this understanding of theology further—and particularly by devising appropriate procedures of historical-critical research—that contemporary systematic theology will have the means to its present renewal: a method which establishes it at one and the same time as strictly scientific and genuinely Christian.[5]

Schleiermacher's methodological principles provide Bring with a

---

[1] *Ibid.*, p. 140.

[2] "Enlightenment theology can be said to have fallen into a situation like the one Kant found in philosophy: Empiricism stood before a mass of materials without any principle of unity; philosophical rationalism ended up with a construed unity that had no relation to the experienced manifold." *Ibid.*, p. 138.

[3] Once more we emphasize that a detailed discussion of Bring's interpretation of Schleiermacher is irrelevant to our purposes here. Neither do we need to analyze Bring's critique of Schleiermacher. His relationship to the German master is at all points quite eclectic; he speaks of *uppslag* (proposals) and "tendencies" in Schleiermacher's methodology which are of fundamental importance for a modern systematic theology. His source is primarily Schleiermacher's *Reden. Ibid.* pp. 122 f.

[4] Cf. *ibid.*, pp. 52, 53, 56, 124.

[5] *Ibid.*, p. 154.

perspective from which to study the history of systematic theology and evaluate its status in various periods, also. To the systematic theologian, such a study of the history of the discipline is instructive.

In retrospect, one can understand, for example, why seventeenth century theology took the form that it did; it did not have the presuppositions for establishing itself as an historical-critical discipline of study.[1] Under the heavy impact of the long years of religiously inspired wars, leading theologians at the time attempted to reverse the former trends toward confessionalism and religious absolutism, seeking to find a common basis for the several contending factions. In the process, Christianity was reduced to a series of basic theological theses and propositions, but the procedures were non-critical, non-historical, and non-scientific. They could not be otherwise; the historical manifestations of Christian faith which the theologians were attempting to synthesize were not considered finite and relative, subject to historical criticism or evaluation. The creeds were absolute and ultimate.

Again, during the eighteenth century, when occidental Orthodoxy took up the struggle against religious syncretism, spiritualism, Arminianism and Latitudinarianism, there was once more a need for giving expression to the essential and characteristic elements of Christian faith. But, without a historical perspective, Orthodoxy fell back into metaphysics.[2] The opponents of Orthodoxy fared no better. In their criticism of confessionalism, the non-conformists did, of course, make the point that since confessions are historically conditioned, they are of relative and limited value. Thus they did apply a historical perspective on the confessions, at least laying the groundwork for asking the historical-critical question, "What in all of these confessions is characteristically and authentically Christian?" But since the methodology for seeking the answer in a scientific way was not developed, the non-conformists were left stranded with a non-historical and speculative approach to theology; they proceeded to answer the systematic-theological question by way of a rational construct called "common Christianity". Eighteenth century theology points, in fact, toward the Enlightenment's concept of "natural religion" rather than in the direction of scientific investigation of historical Christian faith.

There were strong tendencies toward historical criticism in Enlight-

---

[1] *Ibid.*, p. 59.
[2] *Ibid.*, pp. 66 f.

enment theology, especially in German Neology; [1] and the emphasis on the organic unity of the Christian faith came now also to the forefront. However, the two presuppositions for scientific systematic theology fell apart in these traditions, mainly because of the disparate and disjunctive ways in which they were understood. Historical criticism was not able to de-metaphysicalize the Enlightenment's concept of the essence of Christianity. The speculative understanding of essential Christianity was, in fact, set over against historical research as a guarantee against the disintegration of the faith—which was considered the inevitable result of historical relativity. Consequently, scientific systematic theology became an impossibility. This is particularly evident in Semler, who in spite of a strong leaning toward historical-critical investigations found no other principles of unity within the contingent and changing forms of Christian faith than those that he identified as expressions of the moral and rational nature of man. As a whole, the Enlightenment's approach to theology consisted in making metaphysical deductions, not in seeking the essential characteristics of Christianity by way of scientific historical investigation.

Bring not only analyzes pre-Schleiermacher theology from the perspective of Schleiermacher's methodological presuppositions; he considers representatives of post-Schleiermacher theology as well. In an essay in *Teologi och religion*, he scrutinizes Harnack's understanding of the early Christian community's soteriology,[2] pointing out that in spite of Harnack's express intention to work in a "purely historical manner" there is evidence of rather definite preconceptions of what essential Christianity must be. Such discrepancies between explicit intentions and implicit notions are not, of course, uncommon in historical study, but one would have expected Harnack to be on guard against them. As it is, Harnack's approach is not purely historical. He does define a historical criterion for determining the essential elements of Christian faith, namely "the religion of Jesus"; but when one analyzes the central motifs in Harnack's delineation of essential

---

[1] When Bring, at the beginning of *STU*, 1933, sums up the various factors that lie at the basis of a modern conception of systematic theology, he mentions —together with the influence of Kant and Schleiermacher—the methodological breakthrough in the area of historical research that occurred in the latter part of the eighteenth century and continued in the nineteenth century, particularly in the work of Strauss and his disciples. Cf. *ToR*, 1937, pp. 124 f.

[2] The chapter is entitled "Till kritiken av Harnack's syn på den gammalkyrkliga frälsningsuppfattningen," *ibid.*, pp. 183-208.

Christianity, one is struck by its close correspondence to the general ideas of God, virtue, and immortality that are typical of Enlightenment thought.[1] Similar tendencies are found, says Bring, in the works of Wobbermin and Troeltsch, and as a result the scientific intentions of their theology are compromized.[2]

THEOLOGY AS FAITH-REFLECTION AND AS SCIENCE

Having come to consider Schleiermacher's methodological contributions as fundamental for the establishment of a scientific systematic theology, Bring is immediately aware that this represents a somewhat unorthodox definition of the discipline. "Scientific theology", he says, "is in itself something different from what historically and traditionally was called theology." [3] In common thought, "theology" most often refers to "the authoritative definition of the dogmatic content of the Christian faith." [4] As such, it has—by its very definition —an intimate relationship to the faith; it is, in fact, an expression of faith, an immediate corollary to the Christian religious commitment.[5] Bring calls it *trosteologi* (faith-theology) or *trosreflektion* (faith-reflection).[6] Scientific theology, in contrast, does not produce dogmas; it simply studies them. Its task is "to investigate the historical expressions of faith, including the dogmatic formulations of its content, and to clarify their intentions. . . . The purpose of (scientific) theology is the identification and analysis of the religious motifs to which the various dogmas give expression." [7] Its function, in other words, is entirely theoretical.

One should note here that although Bring speaks about a "theoretical" element in faith-reflection, this does not mean that such theology can also claim scientific status. "Theoretical", in this context, refers to the reflective aspect of religious experience; it is theoretical

---

[1] *Ibid.*, pp. 191, 193. Another point is that Harnack was at a disadvantage from the start. The investigation of the historical Jesus was becoming increasingly questionable during his time. Not willing to submit to the historical scepticism which seemed to grow out of the text-critical study of the biblical sources, Harnack naturally took refuge in the more speculative definitions of essential Christianity.

[2] *Ibid.*, p. 54.

[3] *STU*, 1933, p. 18.

[4] *ToR*, 1937, p. 154.

[5] "In earlier days, it was not usual to distinguish between theology and religion; the two belonged together in logical identity." *Ibid.*, p. 128.

[6] *STU*, 1933, p. 16.

[7] *ToR*, 1937, pp. 154 f.

in a psychological sense, but not in the sense that it is based on the
presuppositions for meaningfulness that apply within the theoretical
category of experience. Faith-reflection, even though it represents a
rational endeavor and is theoretical in the psychological sense, is an
exercise entirely within the religious category of experience. It is, as
we have seen, part and parcel of religious experience,[1] and as such it
belongs to the subjective or a-theoretical sphere. "It is a part of the
subjective religious commitment." [2] Scientific theology is not. It is
theoretical in the categorical sense, *i.e.* it operates on the basis of
generally accepted rules of objective investigation and empirical
verification. Thus, "scientific theology and the reflection which belongs
to faith stand identified with completely different areas of experience."[3]
They answer entirely different types of questions, and they should,
for that reason, be kept apart. Says Bring:

> "The thoughts which arise out of the faith commitment itself
> have...no validity from an intellectual standpoint. They do not
> belong to the theoretical area of experience and meaning; they do
> not answer the question of theoretical truth, but develop instead the
> religious faith commitment in various ways. They belong, in fact,
> within the faith commitment." [4]

We have already in several places referred to the Lundensian
tendency to open up a chasm between the subjective experience of
faith and the objective study of faith, and to identify the latter as
theology proper, while the former is quietly expelled from the ranks.[5]
Bring is not unequivocally guilty of this tendency. He does allow
for the term "theology" to be used in two ways, denoting two brands
of theology: one religious, another theoretical; one reflective, the
other analytical; one value conscious, the other scientific. He calls them
"faith-reflection" and "scientific theology". Bring ascribes to faith-
reflection autonomous validity within its own category of meaning, *i.e.*
within the cirle of faith to which it belongs. Its function is a necessary
one. It serves to explicate and expound the various aspects of Christian
faith and experience in so far as the individual theologian has reached
maturity of understanding. There are, of course, vast differences in
quality among these faith-reflective theologies. Some spring from the
religious genius of men like Paul or Luther. Others represent the

---

[1] Cf. *supra*, pp. 98 f.
[2] *ToR*, 1937, p. 149.
[3] *STU*, 1933, p. 16.
[4] *Ibid.*, p. 172.
[5] Cf. *supra*, pp. 66, 47 f.

ingenious constructions of men more gifted with words than spirit. There are some theologies that take the form of complete systems of doctrine, exhibiting the inward strength of consistent argumentation and the outward beauty of structural unity. And there are others that are quite primitive and informal. Every single believer has some form of faith-reflective theology—even the scientific theologian, in so far as he is a religious man.

Bring does provide room for a theology of faith-reflection, then. Yet this is not the theology he is interested in. Methodologically speaking, it constitutes something of a liability to him, for it is not scientific, not theoretical, not historically oriented. It is, instead, wrought with elements that would invalidate any attempt at providing a place for it among the sciences of men. It can never become a scientific discipline. If it should ever claim to be scientific, it would not only lose all respect in the intellectual community; it would also lose its character as religious reflection, for it would have transgressed the limits of its applicability and proven itself a victim of metaphysical confusion. Bring puts faith-reflection in its place, therefore, and goes on to develop his methodological framework so as to establish *scientific systematic theology*—not this theology—in a position of intellectual respectability. Intellectual respectability, to Bring, spells scientific status. Thus, the Lundensian tendency to open up a chasm between religion and theology and to consider the methodological foundations of scientific systematic theology in abstraction from the concerns of faith-reflection is clearly present even in Bring's work.

We shall not stop to analyze the deeper causes or the methodological consequences of this tendency at this point. These are complicated questions, and they have to do with basic assumptions as well as contextual concerns that combine to give shape to the Lundensian methodology. Our critique must take these into consideration, and so we must hold it for a later context.[1] But we must register our disappointment over Bring's unwillingness—or inability—to give further methodological clarity to that kind of theology which characterizes the Christian community corporately and Christian persons individually. He has laid the roundwork for such an endeavor. His philosophy of religion creates the presuppositions for it. The emphasis on the autonomous validity of the religious area of experience clearly demands to be carried through to a principal examination of the

---

[1] Cf. below, Ch. IX.

peculiar character of religious reflection and to a full clarification of
its authentic meaning. To point out that there is an element of religious experience called faith-reflection, that it is valid as such but not
as a science, since it is subjective and a-theoretical, and that it should
for that reason be kept strictly separated from scientific theology, is
significant as far as it goes. But is it not adequate to give intellectual
respectability to faith-reflection or to explain to the modern mind the
peculiar meaning of such thought processes. A methodology which
ignores the methodological problems of faith-reflection while giving
all its attention to securing the scientific status of the academic disciplines of theological research has left a gaping hole in the framework of faith. It has freed the professional theologian from the criticisms of the scientific community, but it has left the church and the
individual Christian without an equally secure methodological basis.

The extent to which Bring abstracts his theological methodology
from any serious involvement in the methodological problems of
faith-reflection is evident in his use of the term "theology". Though
principally it refers to both kinds of theology, the reference to faith-
reflection is so peripheral and tenuous that it seems at times virtually
irrelevant. The concept stands most often for scientific theology,
uniquely.[1] Faith-reflection appears simply as the historical-empirical
material which theology investigates, *i.e.* the theological "object of
study". Theology proper is defined as a theoretical activity, the study
of faith. To secure its intellectual respectability and good standing
among the sciences, theology must relate to its object of study in an
objective and presuppositionless way. Thus, the only kind of theology
that is intellectually defensible in Bring's view is a scientific-systematic,
historical-critical investigation of the various sources in which Christian faith expresses itself. Christian theology is simply research aimed
at uncovering the essential characteristics and basic motifs of
historical Christian faith.

One might ask, perhaps, what the scientific study of historical
Christian faith has to do with *theology*—except that such a question
proves that one is still interested in the non-scientific, a-theoretical,
and religious kind of theology. Yet the question is fully valid. Must
not systematic theology as defined by Bring more appropriately be

---

[1] "Theology is science, but faith is not science; it is not a form of knowledge
at all." *STU*, 1933, p. 232. "Theology's task is not to evaluate, but to *konstatera*
(state, record), to describe and to analyze the views of faith. However, it cannot
itself be an expression of faith." *Ibid.*, p. 58.

called *fidelogy*? Is motif-research, strictly speaking, a way *to do theology*, or is it simply a way to study *the theology that is being done*? Even guarding against the traditional misconceptions of theology, is not *Christian theology* necessarily a function of Christian faith? And is it not necessary, therefore, besides developing a scientific method for the investigation of historical Christian faith, to rescue the subjective, value-conscious, religious thoughtform described as faith-reflection from intellectual obscurity and cultural ghettoism by a thorough ana-lysis of the nature of its function and the basis of its meaning?

These are questions we shall have to raise again; they point to the fact that Lundensian methodology, for all its accomplishments, has not completed its task. Nevertheless, it has begun well, and we fully acknowledge the importance of its contributions. With dramatic strength, these theologians have set the stage for the appearance of a new type of play: a theology that claims to be strictly scientific while yet representing essential Christian faith; a theology that avoids the traditional traps of metaphysical speculation and categorical confusion by defining itself as a theoretical discipline and its object of study as a historical religious type. The original play is Schleiermacher's, but Bring, the director, is intent upon giving the new production a modern form and contemporaty relevance. He is especially anxious to explain his own conception of the plot and to set it in contrast to other interpretations of the role of theology in the scientific age. In order to understand what the director intends with the play, we shall proceed to listen next as he articulates, at length, what he does not intend.

CHAPTER SIX

SYSTEMATIC THEOLOGY — CURRENT CONFLICTS AND CRITICAL CLARIFICATIONS

Ragnar Bring's methodological stance became, with unavoidable logic, a polemic one. Against the background of his philosophical commitments, his methodological presuppositions, and his general definition of systematic theology, it is only natural that he should acknowledge the presence of various alternative approaches to theology in the contemporary theological community; it is plainly necessary that he do so. His own approach to theological methodology is in many ways so "new" and "different" that its author is obligated to clarify its implications and set it in contrast to other conceptions of the theological task.[1]

Bring's polemics does not consist in frontal attacks on the theology of colleagues and competitors, however. His primary purpose is not to establish theological contrasts or prove the superiority of his own method. He is not out to form a "school" or to rally a party. Quietly and responsibly, he sets out instead to analyze the methodological character—the philosophical *frågeställning* (problematics) and the conceptual presuppositions—of a variety of theological standpoints. His aim is simply to discover any tendencies that are liable to discredit theology in the eyes of the contemporary intellectual community or cause its methods to be considered theoretically and scientifically suspect. His approach, therefore, is not dogmatic, not evaluational. But neither is it purely encyclopedic. He does not attempt to describe in inclusive fashion all the alternative methods that are in evidence in the theological community. His intentions are strictly methodological, so he examines primarily those trends within contemporary theology which in his view constitute a threat to the scientific respectability of the discipline. He shows sure instinct and keen sensitivity in selecting issues and opponents—though he draws these mostly from among his colleagues, the twentieth century Swedish theologians—and with his own methodological presuppositions clearly in

---

[1] The larger part of Bring's main methodological work, *STU*, 1933, is given to such a discussion.

mind he lays bare those tendencies in contemporary thought which theology, in his view, ought to guard against.

One does not find in Bring's works extended reportorial or critical analyses of the wider circles of twentieth century theology. Except for some passing references to the methodology of Wilhelm Herrmann and a few pages devoted to Emil Brunner's approach to theology, his discussions focus mainly on the thought of Einar Billing, Arvid Runestam, and Hjalmar Lindroth. These are men of no small stature, but they are not by any means the major lights within the twentieth century world-wide community of scholars. One may ask what value there may be in analyzing Bring's controversies which these men. Are they not simply local squabbles? The answer, of course, is yes; but they are not therefore the type of squabbles which have only local applicability. On the contrary, the Swedish debate has focused on important methodological issues, and the differences that are evident here are representative of larger controversies, on a world-wide scale. Bring's contributions to this debate are methodologically interesting, therefore, even though the occasions or the contexts of their appearance are not so. It is as methodological acts that we shall consider them here.[1]

The problem which is foremost in Bring's mind throughout all of his methodological discussions is how to keep the relationship between the religious commitment or value judgment and the investigation of historical faith so structured that the two are understood as belonging to separate categories of meaning while yet not being allowed to drift apart as though they had nothing to do with one another.[2] This is indeed a formidable problem. Bring finds himself

---

[1] In line with this perspective, we shall not in the following attempt to describe fully all facets of Bring's theological controversies; neither shall we engage in critical analyses of his interpretations of the opponents. Bring's own approach to methodology will be followed here: certain basic elements in these discussions will be incorporated into the framework of our own development of Bring's methodology. The structure of our argument is not, therefore, given in Bring's works; the logic of methodological understanding is not coincidental with the chronology of Bring's theological controversies.

[2] "How is faith in God related to the logically ordered thinking about God, and how is theology related to these?" *Ibid.*, p. 5. We should observe that in Bring's thought the distinction between faith (or religion) and theology is not defined in the way of the Enlightenment or of Semler; neither is it that of mysticism or of Ritschl. Usually in the history of theology, when a distinction of this nature was made, it meant that religion was considered valuable, while theology was judged worthless. Both rationalism and mysticism show tendencies to defining Christianity in terms of "life", not "doctrine". Semler, f. ex., reacted to the

up against violations of both sides of the dictum: There are those
who tend to identify faith and theology, considering them necessarily
one and the same; and there are those who tend to separate faith and
science, considering them absolutely incompatible. Both types of
distortions appear in several different editions, and the consequences
for the understanding of theology are many and varied. In Bring's
view, they can all be ascribed to one common cause, however: the
influence of the metaphysical problematics.

As we have observed, Bring defines metaphysics in several different
ways, and every form of it is set in direct conflict with the critical-
analytical approach to philosophy and thereby with the methodological respectability of theology. The first has to do with the
tendency to confuse the formal, categorical presuppositions of
validity with some arbitrarily chosen ontological entity; Bring
describes it as identity-philosophical speculation, or the attempt to
define the essence of things in terms of some specific empirical or
transcendent reality. The second is a form of confusion that results
from disregarding the autonomy of the several areas of experience
and misunderstanding the peculiar kind of meaning that characterizes
each one: in short, logical equivocation. These two forms of metaphysical confusion, one epistemological, the other conceptual, can
be found operative in much of contemporary theology, says Bring;
and the effects are fateful for the discipline, particularly for its status
in the estimation of a science-oriented culture. It is in order to reveal
these effects and point out the dangerous impact of metaphysical
confusion on theology itself and on its external situation that Bring
goes hunting for the methodological presuppositions of his colleagues.

---

theological dogmatism of Orthodoxy with such fervor that theology itself
became a synonym for something complicated and unnecessary, while "religion"
symbolized something simple and valuable. Cf. *ToR*, 1937, pp. v ff, 7 ff, 95,
104, 130 ff. In Ritschlian theology, also, the real meaning of religion was found
within personal religious experience. In the psychological scheme that characterized experience-centered theology, meaning was considered given in the emotional
aspects of the human *psyche* rather than in the theoretical aspect of it. Thus "life",
or *fides qua creditur*, was distinguished from "theology", or *fides quae creditur*,
and the experience of an immediate religious consciousness was judged to be of
primary religious value, while the theoretical understanding of it was
considered secondary. Cf. *ibid.*, pp. 18 f, note 1. Bring's distinction of theology
and religion is different from both of these predecessors; it has to do
with his analyses of the scientific nature of theology and the religious nature of
faith, and it rests upon the categorical distinction between the theoretical and
the religious areas of meaning. Cf. *STU*, 1933, pp. 4 f, note 1.

FAITH AS THE IMPLICIT PRESUPPOSITION OF THEOLOGY

Already in his discussion of the relationship between faith-reflection and scientific theology, Bring is concerned to identify what is perhaps the most common manifestation of metaphysical confusion, namely the tendency to consider faith the necessary presupposition of theology. Scientific theology must, of necessity, be on guard against the introduction of any subjective elements in its presuppositional foundations. Christian motifs of faith are valid within the context of faith-reflection, but if transferred to the methodological framework of scientific systematic theology they immediately discredit the objectivity of the discipline. Such theology is a victim of metaphysical confusion.

Bring charges Einar Billing with such confusion.[1] His use of the so-called "dramatic perspective" is a case in point. Originally identified as a characteristic feature in the Christian view of things, the dramatic symbolism is subsequently widened by Billing so as to serve as a general description of the religious category and as the normative definition of essential religion. While Bring can accept the original, more limited application of the dramatic perspective, he finds it necessary to protest against the direct correlation of positive Christian faith content and principal epistemological or ontological delimitations. Not only does this represent an illegitimate extension of a specific religious concept, in open disregard of its categorical limitations; it represents also a philosophical leap from theological particularity to identity-philosophical speculation.

It is, in a sense, fully legitimate to say—as Billing does—that the difference between the Greek type of religion and the Christian faith lies in the way they ask the religious question. In this case "the religious

---

[1] Bring does not stand in opposition to all facets of Billing's thought. As we have observed above, cf. pp. 39 ff, Billing has contributed in several ways to the development of twentieth century Swedish theology. The Lundensians in general —and Bring in particular—have learned much from Billing's approach. Especially significant, to them, was Billing's emphasis on the "dramatic perspective", and his typological approach to the historical investigation of the constitutive elements of religious faith. In the opinion of the Lundensians, however, Billing had compromised his original methodology by identifying himself openly with metaphysical purposes. He sought to widen the application of the "dramatic perspective" so as to make it synonymous with the religious perspective itself; he attempted also to enlarge the purposes of theology and include not only the descriptive-analytic task, but an evaluational-normative task as well. These are the two points at which Bring attacks the *"Billingska frågeställningen"*. Cf. *ibid.*, pp. 109-158. We shall discuss Bring's critique of Billing's use of the "dramatic perspective" here, returning to the question of normative theology below. See pp. 135 ff.

question" serves as a general description of the categorical form into which the different formulations of the question so to speak fill the particular content of the individual religious types.[1] But if a particular formulation of the religious question—for instance the Christian, characterized by dramatic theocentricity—is considered methodologically superior or especially capable of calling forth the right kind of answer, then the perspective is distorted and the method is a product of metaphysical confusion, epistemological and conceptual.

Bring illustrates the confusion in Billing's methodology by asking what the dramatic perspective actually entails. Granted that the prophetic-Christian type of religion can be considered organized around the unifying motif-symbol of "the active God"; is this also a fundamental characteristic of all religion whatever? What does Billing mean? When referring to the active God, does he intend simply the general idea "*that* God acts" or does he also include a particular conception of "*how* God acts"?[2] Bring's reason for asking is clear: He could accept the dramatic perspective as methodologically significant in the first sense, although the definition of the religious category in terms of God's action would exclude all non-theistic types of religious commitment. The category of religion would still have a certain amount of openness, allowing the various religious types to specify the nature of their faith by reference to their particular conception of *how* God acts.[3] But in the second sense, describing a definite conception of the nature of God's action, the dramatic symbolism clearly represents a type-oriented theological motif which is

---

[1] Bring does not prefer this formulation, of course; he uses the symbolism of the categorical "question" in referring to the open, formal, or presuppositional category which must be capable of accomodating a variety of possible "answers", namely the various religious types. Cf. *supra*, pp. 86, 93 f.

[2] *STU*, 1933, pp. 146 f; 150, note 35.

[3] According to Bring, the philosopher of religion may ask the question of religion in a variety of ways, if he makes sure that the question is open and does not contain the criteria of a correct answer. If, as Billing evidently does, one should decide that the dramatic perspective represents the best way to ask the religious question, then the answer must be sought in terms of the dramatic formulation both when one speaks of Christianity and when one studies other religions, otherwise one would be guilty of comparing religions on the basis of inconsistent perspectives. If one formulates the religious question in terms of "God's action", then both Greek and Hebrew-Christian religion must be considered under this perspective, and as a consequence, the difference between these religions appears simply as a contrast between two interpretations of *how* God acts. For Christian faith, the typical answer would be that God acts "in love"; for other religions, the answer might be that he acts "arbitrarily", "in fury", etc. Cf. *ibid.*, p. 147, note 32.

without general methodological applicability; it would have to be excluded from the presuppositional framework of scientific theology.

In the analysis of Billing, Bring does find that the dramatic perspective is described in terms of the general idea *that* God acts. This would indicate that Billing avoids epistemological confusion and leaves the religious category open and formal, free of the material peculiarities of Christian faith. However, this is not so. Although Billing speaks in terms that seem free of the particular Christian interpretation of how God acts, he does not observe the fundamental distinction between a content-defined religious commitment and the formal categorical presuppositions for religious meaning; he uses the dramatic concepts interchangeably for describing the best way to ask the religious question and for summarizing the essential content of the Christian faith. According to Billing, the Christian understanding of the God-relationship is characterized by what he calls "the unique insight *that God acts*". This unique insight —the essence of religion— has come into the Christian faith and confession only by way of the unique perspective from which the Christian asks the religious question: the dramatic perspective. Thus, there is no openness in Billing's method; both the perspective and the content of theology are given within the Christian faith itself. On Bring's presuppositions, such a theology can never claim to be scientific. It is defined in a way which implies faith.[1]

FAITH AS STARTING POINT FOR TRANSCENDENT KNOWLEDGE

Billing's tendency to identify the Christian revelation with the dramatic perspective, and the dramatic perspective with essential religion, points in the direction of a second manifestation of metaphysical confusion which is evident in his own works as well as in the thought of Wilhelm Herrmann, namely the assumption of a close correlation between the shape of the Christian perspective and the content of ultimate religious truth. This is a common assumption in circles that seek to take seriously the revelational character of Christian faith, and it gives rise to the claim that true knowledge of God presupposes the Christian perspective. From Bring's point of view, all such claims are, of course, intellectually suspect.

Looking a little closer at Billing's way of contrasting Greek religion and Christian faith, Bring discovers that it is not simply a

---

[1] *Ibid.*, pp. 90 f, 153 f.

matter of comparing two different formulations of the religious
question—*i.e.* analytically contrasting the motif structures or symbolic
frameworks of two types of faith. The contrast, rather, is set up in
terms of two ways of answering the religious question, one that has
its grounding in revelation and therefore in "the reality of the acts
of God", and another that is grounded in human speculation and
therefore considered inferior or incapable of containing transcendent
truth. It is, in fact, a contrast between religious truth and theoretical
speculation; Billing even considers it a contrast between "divine
action" and "the cycles of nature." But his entire argument is circular:
He defines religion in such a way that it presupposes the dramatic
perspective, and on this premise he proceeds to prove that Christian
revelation is the only valid principle of religious knowledge.[1] Thus,
by reference to the singular validity of the way Christian answers the
religious question, Billing hopes to show that the only valid way to
ask the religious question is the Christian way.

It is clear to Bring that the entire procedure is full of metaphysial
confusion. He finds further examples of this. Billing was concerned
to avoid the ontological speculation of Greek metaphysics, and
he attempted therefore to define the God-concept not in terms
of "being", but in dramatic-dynamic images such as "will to create" or "will to redeem". This could signify a significant reorientation. However, in attempting to solve the problem of the knowledge
of God, Billing came to use his dynamic concepts in ways that are
strikingly similar to the identity-speculations of old-line ontological
metaphysics. The only difference is that "substance-speculation" is
here exchanged for a new "will-metaphysics".[2] Billing's thinking
is in reality little different from those procedures that Kant proposed
in his practical philosophy and that were followed to a great extent by
the nineteenth century "theology of experience"—and particularly
by Herrmann.[3]

Bring's reference to Kant is particularly directed to *Grundlegung
zur Metaphysik der Sitten*. Here, says Bring, the concept of "will"
functions in what are clearly identity-philosophical ways: The
categorical imperative is defined in terms of "absolute will", and

---

[1] *Ibid.*, p. 150.

[2] The title of Ch. 5 in *STU*, 1933, is, in translation, "The will-metaphysical
background of the unity of theology and faith."

[3] For a reference to Bring's interpretation of the role of will-metaphysics in
Kant, cf. *supra*. pp. 81 f.

the presence of "the good will" in man is said to be established by the presence within of the absolute will. The good will is a unified will, a "whole" or a "true" will; the true will is "one", "unconditioned", a will which wills one thing, namely itself. Thus, the quality of will is identical with the concept of will; the good will is the only real will; and all good will springs from absolute will.[1]

Similar procedures can be found in Herrmann, says Bring.[2] For Herrmann, religion represents the realization of the good will, and Christianity is the ultimate form of it. Herrmann claims, in fact, that the Christian realization of the good will corresponds directly to the ultimate concept of will, *i.e.* to the "true", the "real" or "essential" will. Thus Christian experience and absolute truth are closely related, so closely that the knowledge of truth is simply "a process of self-realization in which the theologian undertakes essentially the same task that any ethical personality is called upon to assume," [3] namely the realization of the good will. To Bring, of course, this process of self-realization is clearly a metaphysical epistemological variant. It rests on the assumption that form and content are one.[4] Self-realization is an act of will which presupposes that the absolute will is already known; it consists simply in calling to consciousness an immediate experience within which both the form and content of ultimate truth are given.[5]

In Bring's view, the dynamics of Billing's thinking is essentially the same as Kant's and Herrmann's. Billing determines arbitrarily that "the active God" can be known only through "the activity of God", and God's activity is his will: the will to create and the will to redeem. God's will is uniquely revealed in the Christian revelation. Outside of revelation God is not known; but in it he is known fully, since revelation is, in fact, God's own doing. Thus, in revelation both the method and the content of religious knowledge are given, and they are one. They are one because God is one and because God's will and his acts are one.

Bring finds the dramatic concept of the unity of faith and truth little different from the traditional ontological speculation concerning

---

[1] *Op. cit.*, pp. 138 ff, footnote.

[2] Bring relies in the main on Herrmann's *Ethik*, Tübingen & Leipzig: Mohr, 1901, and on Runestam's study of *Wilhelm Herrmann's teologi*, 1921, at this point.

[3] *Op. cit.*, pp. 136 f. Cf. *supra*, p. 42, for the distinction of "self-realization" and "self-reflection" in Billing's method.

[4] *Ibid.*, p. 144.

[5] *Ibid.*, p. 145.

the ultimately real or the absolutely true. Both are premised on the definition of a specific entity—substantial or dynamic—within which being and knowledge are united into one. Thus, despite Billing's attempts at ridding himself of the speculative perspective and proving that revelation provides a unique sort of grounding for theology, he has not managed to free himself from metaphysical thoughtforms. He still interprets revelation in a speculative manner, his theology continues to be caught in the metaphysical problematics, and he is unable to establish a theological method that is free of epistemological and logical confusion.

FAITH AS THE PSYCHOLOGICAL PRESUPPOSITION OF THEOLOGY

A third example of the methodological consequences of metaphysical confusion becomes evident when faith is considered the fundamental psychological ingredient of a superior scientific method such as the so-called "deeper psychological method" of Arvid Runestam.[1] A disciple of Herrmann and Billing, Runestam is the heir to several of the characteristic elements in these men's thought. His own contribution is that he seeks to lift Billing's emphases from the context of theological-epistemological speculation and apply them to the construction of a practical psychological method. In the process, he also seeks to give Herrmann's methodological principles a more thoroughly psychological application than Herrmann himself did. In spite of his practical methodological orientiation, Runestam does not manage to avoid his teachers' errors, however.

To Runestam, "self-reflection" and "self-realization" represent two separate and distinct ways of understanding. Both are psychological methods, functioning differently and in different contexts as channels by which we obtain knowledge. From Bring's perspective, there is nothing wrong with distinguishing between two such procedures, if the intention is simply to differentiate between various aspects of the psychological capacities of man. There is reason to believe that such a differentiation can be supported by an empirical study of the psychological endowments of persons. But when Runestam proceeds to make the two concepts signify two distinct methods of scientific investigation, and when he argues that the two are in principal opposition to one another, Bring cannot follow. Runestam's claim that self-realization—the theological method—is far superior to

---

[1] Bring's critique of Runestam is based mainly on Runestam's essay "Gudstro och självkännedom," in *Ordet och tron*, 1931. Cf. *STU*, 1933, pp. 159-175.

self-reflection in penetrating the deeper levels of reality and bringing insight into the true meaning of things is utterly unsupported by facts. It rests on metaphysical assumptions.

Bring proposes that Runestam, in attempting to gain scientific recognition for a special theological method, is seeking to hide his Christian faith commitments—his real methodological starting point— behind a cloak of scientific terminology. To argue that self-realization, "insight based on personal involvement with the object of knowledge," is a deeper psychological method than self-reflection, "insight formed by the logical organization of the material at hand," is perhaps possible even from a scientific point of view. The scientific value of such a deeper psychology can presumably be substantiated.[1] However, the argument must be kept free from the religious connotations with which Runestam connects it. Runestam claims that when the reality which is to be investigated lies "deeper" than the reality which can be logically ordered or analyzed—namely on the level of "experiential reality"—then there is need for a "deeper psychology" or a "more profound method of investigation", but this is clearly a metaphysical attempt to justify the existence of a peculiar religious science. The argument presupposes what it sets out to prove, namely the fundamental identity of the deeper reality and the deeper psychology. This becomes evident, for example, when Runestam applies his perspective to anthropology. He says:

> "Anthropology or psychology will never attain to knowledge of the real nature of man, regardless of how thoroughly he is turned inside out, unless he is understood in the context of his God-relationship. Man exists and is, in his innermost being, only as he exists in God and is encountered by him. It is in the knowledge of God that we know something essential about man also." [2]

In Bring's view, such procedures are definitely built on metaphysical confusion. The commitments of faith are allowed to serve as presuppositions for the consideration of method. This leads of necessity to epistemological-ontological problems and to identity-philosophical

---

[1] Bring has some appreciation for this element in Runestam's perspective; *ibid.*, pp. 182 f.

[2] Runestam, *op. cit.*, p. 132. "Man must be himself, must be realized, before he can know himself. . . . Man can get to know himself only in God." *Ibid.* Cf. also Runestam's *Psykoanalys och kristendom*, 2. rev. ed., Stockholm: Sveriges kristliga studentrörelse, 1931, pp. 68 f: "Nobody really knows himself, as he is in his innermost being, through self-reflective analysis. . . . To know oneself, in the full meaning of the word, is possible only in a unifying act of self-relinquishing commitment. . .to another unified personality."

answers that violate against the categorical autonomy of both the religious and the theoretical areas of experience. Furthermore, it makes impossible the development of a practical procedure for scientific investigation. Runestam's own attempts in this direction exemplify the difficulties abundantly. Forced to invent a method of research which corresponds to his psychological-theological principle of knowledge, Runestam cannot but perpetuate the confusion which is built into his perspective. His scientific method is described as follows:

> "The scientist...tries to place himself within the self-realizing individual's standpoint and to observe him, not as an object among other objects that may be analyzed and described, but as a living, willing, knowing and acting subject....He has, in a sense, a secondary involvement in the self-realizing individual's situation—a 'secondary self-realization'—while at the same time keeping himself in the primary self-realization's attitude." [1]

Obviously, Runestam's "secondary self-realization" shares completely "the primary self-realization's attitude"; the former is simply a form of the latter, and the latter—none other than the religious attitude itself—is the presupposition for the former.[2] Thus Runestam has allowed faith and science to mingle freely and condition each other mutually, and in the process both faith and science stand compromised. The metaphysical confusion is complete.

THEOLOGY AS THE RECEPTION OF DIVINE TRUTH

In Bring's catalogue of methodological vices, a fourth item has to do with the explicit rejection of the scientific perspective and the subsequent definition of theology as the opposite of science, or as the passive reception of divine truth. Bring discusses Emil Brunner's concept of theology as an example of this approach, describing it as "a metaphysical contrast between theology and metaphysics." [3]

There is little doubt in Bring's mind that Brunner is justified in reacting to the kind of theology which he describes as "scientific". His critique of the "psychological immanentism" and "subjectivistic mysticism" of nineteenth century theology is both necessary and wise.[4] There are strong tendencies in these directions both in Schleier-

---

[1] "Gudstro och självkännedom," *Ordet och tron*, 1931, pp. 138 f.

[2] *STU*, 1933, p. 171. According to Runestam, the "secondary self-realization" of the scientist is also intimately dependent upon the personal and ethical standards of the individual; if the moral integrity of the scientist is broken, so is his ability to enter into the "self-realization" of his subject—the self which he investigates. *Ibid.*, p. 169.

[3] *Ibid.*, pp. 35-68.

[4] Cf. *ibid.*, pp. 12 f.

macher's thought and among his followers. The Lundensians have themselves taken issue with these trends. However, Brunner's critique is not presented in such a way as to reveal the methodological inconsistencies of the so-called "scientific" theology. Neither do his arguments against what he calls "metaphysics" prove conclusively that Brunner is capable of avoiding the metaphysical problematics and establishing a more acceptable concept of the nature of theology. He tends, in fact, to be tied in with the perspectives that he opposes; and because of his propensity to operate with a dialectic of logical opposites, Brunner's own *frågeställning* tends to be metaphysical.

In an interesting analysis of Brunner's concept of metaphysics, Bring points out that Brunner provides no principal definition of the metaphysical thoughtforms except to say that they represent human "speculation", subjective preoccupation with the *"Diesseits"*, or "immanentism". In close conjunction with metaphysical speculation —and closely related to the immanentist perspective—is "science". Science, as Brunner sees it, is not simply a method which can be applied to all the areas of experience; it represents a definite philosophy, a world-view with a rational and inner-wordly bias. Therefore, any concept such as the "science of religion" is a contradiction in terms; it is neither true science nor true religion. A science of religion which does not give positive expression to the Christian faith is, in fact, another religion, for "voraussetzungslose, 'einfach wissenschaftliche' Religionswissenschaft gibt es nicht." [1]

Setting his own perspective in sharp contrast to all immanentist speculation—but without analyzing the dynamics of metaphysical logic—Brunner proceeds to develop what in Bring's estimation is a typical example of a transcendental-objectivistic concept of faith and theology. He lays the groundwork for his method by claiming that it is the nature of science that it can only deal with matters that are historically or psychologically given. What is "beyond" this realm of the given, belonging to the transcendent dimension of reality, is only revealed to faith; divine revelation is the source of theology. Bring takes note of the fact that although faith and theology are not quite the same in Brunner's thought, they are still very closely related. "Thinking about faith," says Brunner, "is something else than faith itself. Theology is not faith." Yet faith is not happening outside of our thinking, but "am Denken, und von diesem Werk Gottes an

---

[1] *Ibid.*, pp. 58 f.

unserem Denken kann unser Denken Zeugnis geben."[1] Faith, then, according to Brunner, is "a work of God on our thinking", and theology is "our thinking giving witness to faith".

Bring finds Brunner's thought infused with methaphysical confusion—it is a "metaphysical (in Bring's sense) contrast between theology and metaphysics (in Brunner's sense)". By presupposing an absolute contrast between the given realities of historical or psychological experience and the transcendent truths of revelation, Brunner has allowed the dialectic framework within which he operates to serve as substitute for a principal analysis of the errors of identity-philosophical speculation—of which historicistic or psychologistic positivism is only one form. Brunner's dialectic brings only a competing metaphysics into view. Instead of unveiling and avoiding the metaphysical problematics, Brunner is logically bound to it. In place of immanentism he puts the transcendent; in place of speculation, revelation; in place of science, faith. But the framework is the same.[2] The dialectic could not have functioned otherwise.

The methodological consequences of Brunner's perspective are serious, in Bring's estimation. By defining both science and faith in ways that confuse the religious and the theoretical categories,[3] Brunner has developed a confused concept of theology. Furthermore, he has explicitly excluded the possibility of defining theology as a science. It is defined instead as non-science or anti-science. Its task is exclusively to listen to faith, register the work of God on our thinking, and express the truth which is thus revealed. Strictly speaking, theology has nothing to do with theoretical analysis or rational explication. It does not exist outside of the positive witness to Christian values.[4] It contains in itself a complete world-view—the direct opposite of all human speculation. Theology has the singular responsibility to reflect on the meaning of faith from within the

---

[1] *Ibid.*, pp. 57 f, note 40. One can understand why Bring charges Brunner with having exchanged the subjectivism of psychologism for what he calls "objectivism". *Ibid.*, pp. 64 f.

[2] *Ibid.*, p. 67, note 53.

[3] There is a bit of surprise in Bring's mind in connection with Brunner's claim that empirical science is capable of understanding the "fact" that man is a sinner, while it cannot possibly get at the "fact" that man, through faith, is declared righteous. *Ibid.*, p. 65 f. In Bring's view, both of these "facts" belong to the same order of things, namely faith; and if one is available for investigation, so must the other be, also.

[4] *Ibid.*, p. 47.

Christian perspective and to proclaim the truth of faith in contrast to all science and reason.[1]

Here, then, lies the fundamental flaw in Brunner's methodology, according to Bring. He has identified science and speculation, on the one hand, and faith and theology, on the other. He excludes the possibility of thinking of science as a purely theoretical, non-evaluational, presuppositionless method of research, and he makes it impossible to think of theology as in any way abstracted from the presuppositions of faith and defined as a theoretical, scientific discipline. Theology, as Brunner defines it, has no scientific status and can never have one. It is determined, instead, from within a metaphysical framework of thought.[2]

THEOLOGY AS PROOF OF THE TRUTH OF FAITH

We have already observed in several places that it is quite typical for a theology that bases its methodology on faith and argues by way of epistemological and conceptual confusion to consider theology in possession of absolute truth and therefore responsible for proving to the scientific mind the ultimate validity of this truth. Bring gives considerable attention to such a concept of theology; he regards it as a transparent example of the effects of the metaphysical problematics. He uncovers it in many quarters, but his criticism falls again with the greatest weight on Billing and Runestam.

As we have seen, Billing develops a theological methodology which includes a double task, one scientific and another apologetic or demonstrative.[3] Theology, as Billing sees it, is partly type-description, partly value-demonstration; its procedures are partly a comparison of religious types, partly a confession of one of them.[4] The question is, of course, whether it is possible to bring two such concepts of theology together without in the process compromising both. Ragnar Bring raises this point in connection with Billing's comparison of Greek thought and prophetic-Christian faith: [5] If Billing had intended simply to analyze the two types of religious orientation and set them over against one another so as to illustrate the differences between them, then his procedures would have been

---

[1] *Ibid.*, p. 69.
[2] *Ibid.*, p. 67.
[3] Cf. *supra*, p. 42.
[4] *Op. cit.*, pp. 118 f, 120.
[5] *Ibid.*, pp. 112 f, 116 ff.

methodologically consistent and intellectually respectable. But he intended also to assert the superiority of prophetic-Christian religion —including its thought and ethic—and to defend this assertion by way of a "scientific demonstration" of the truth of faith; and this immediately involved him in logical inconsistencies and methodological confusion.

Within the presuppositions of the Christian faith itself it is, of course, fully legitimate to assert the conviction that Christianity is the only true view of reality. As Bring sees it, such statements are perfectly valid when functioning to express the Christian commitment; they are then a part of the confession of faith and express the characteristic absoluteness of the Christian consciousness of truth. But in the context of a scientific investigation of several religious types or in connection with an objective comparison of basic religious motifs, all such confessions of faith or subjective value judgments are entirely irrelevant and completely unwarranted.[1] Their presence signifies a fusion of faith and science which is logically illegitimate and methodologically incriminating.

To Bring, it is a clear sign of methodological inconsistency when Billing charges theology with the task of proving "scientifically" the truth or "reality" of religious propositions. Billing thought that the Christian faith could be proven true by "connecting" its propositions with the historical-empirical reality.[2] He claimed, in fact, that without the inclusion of "spiritual reality" our concepts of reality are not "true". As it is commonly understood or experienced by sense perception, our reality is not fully "real".[3] From Bring's perspective, all such claims belong within the Christian point of view. To the Christian believer, the connection of grace and history is a reality; but it does not constitute a scientific observation, and the connection that is asserted is not a fact that can be verified. By making theology responsible for demonstrating the truth value of Christian value judgments, Billing has not only robbed theology of scientific

---

[1] Ibid., p. 126.

[2] Gustaf Wingren, who is in fundamental agreement with Billing on this point, has given special emphasis to the recovery of this aspect of the theological task; cf. "Einar Billings teologiska metod," Nordisk teologi..., 1955. In his view, it is a more significant role for theology than that of "a systematic theology which can consider its task fulfilled simply through the reproduction of what, for example, Luther once thought and said." Ibid., p. 291. Cf. also Einar Billing. En studie i svensk teologi före 1920, 1968. We shall have occasion to consider Wingren's disenchantment with the Lundensian method below; cf. pp. 208 ff.

[3] STU, 1933, pp. 155 f.

objectivity; he has also robbed theology of its autonomous validity as faith-reflection. His theology is in reality neither true science nor true faith-reflection; it is built on metaphysical confusion.[1]

Billing's disciple Arvid Runestam, who once more takes his teacher's suggestions conscientiously, lays down as his own methodological dictum that "in order for systematic theology to attain scientific status, it is necessary that it be able to demonstrate the rightness of the Christian faith commitment." [2] In this statement, Bring finds Runestam concerned to combine the two features of Billing's methodology: the interest in the scientific respectability of systematic theology, and the interest in the demonstration of the truth value of Christian faith. Runestam goes so far as to claim that the scientific status of theology is directly dependent on the demonstration of its "rightness". Says Runestam:

> "The scientific status of theology is...dependent upon the rightness of the Christian faith and its world-view, and the rightness of the faith is dependent upon its natural—in a deeper sense—necessity.... By this term 'natural', I mean to say that theology is scientific in the degree to which it succeeds in demonstrating that the Christian faith is 'right', *i.e.* that it corresponds to the natural needs of human spiritual life and to the natural laws of personal development." [3]

Clearly, to Runestam the scientific foundation of systematic theology rests on the assumption that it is possible to prove the correspondence between the Christian view of life and the basic facts of life.[4] To Bring's way of thinking, this assumption is a product of categorical confusion and results in the discreditation of both faith and science. To the Christian believer, naturally, the Christian view of man is right. When Christianity claims, for example, that the health of the human soul depends on a faithful relationship to God who is the dynamic, creative, and continuingly active power behind all that lives, every Christian believer identifies himself with that claim and holds it for truth. But the statement presupposes a Christian faith commitment, and its truth value depends on the same commitment. To prove the rightness of the Christian view of life by scientific

---

[1] *Ibid.*, p. 119.

[2] *Ibid.*, p. 175. For Runestam's development of these views, cf. *STK*, 1, 1925, pp. 359 ff; 2, 1926, pp. 96 ff. Bring draws a parallel between Runestam and Troeltsch in this context; they both ascribe to theology the task of demonstrating that Christianity stands highest among man's religions. *Op. cit.*, p. 180, note 40.

[3] *STK*, 2, 1926, pp. 97, 96.

[4] Cf. "Naturligt och kristligt," *Till ärkebiskop Söderbloms sextioårsdag*, Stockholm: Diakonistyrelsen, 1926, pp. 431 ff.

means is logically impossible. In order to do so one would have to presuppose a commitment to its truth, and consequently the argument would fall under the ban against subjectivism and metaphysics.[1]

Bring argues also that the attempt to prove the truth of the Christian faith commitment would destroy the religious character of faith.[2] Christian assurance "is the assurance of faith..., not of science." [3] It is a personal type of assurance, not dependent upon ratification by way of "scienctific" argumentation; the assurance of faith is absolute. Bring's reaction to Runestam's methodological confusion is summarized as follows:

> "While a truly scientific theology has (the task) of describing Christian faith, understanding it, and defining its character, the theology which springs from faith—or from the self-realization that belongs to it—will make claim to scientific status while aiming to demonstrate the truth of faith or prove its (rational) justification. In this case, theology does not only aim to show how faith sees things or what faith entails; it attempts to show that this view of things is right and that the propositions of faith are scientifically verifiable. This is the brandmark of a theology that has assumed the character of metaphysics." [4]

THEORETICAL CONFLICT BETWEEN SCIENCE AND THEOLOGY

It is obvious to Bring that any attempt to define the functions of scientific theology in terms of a theoretical demonstration of the objective truth of Christian faith must be rejected on principal grounds. To consider faith and science related in such a way as to make possible this kind of demonstration is to disregard the autonomy of the various categories of experience and confuse the meaning of religious truth and theoretical knowledge. But the same is the case, according to Bring, when the relationship of science and faith is defined in terms of conflict. To consider faith and science so related that the propositions of the one stand in direct opposition to the statements of the other is again a grave misunderstanding of the categorical integrity of both religious experience and the theoretical area of meaning.

Bring returns to this problem again and again, attempting to iron out what has undoubtedly been the most persistent problem on the

---

[1] *STU*, 1933, p. 179, note 40.
[2] Cf. "Kristen tro och vetenskaplig forskning," *STK*, 25, 1949, pp. 210 f, where Bring argues that an ideal which is proven true is no longer an ideal.
[3] *STU*, 1933, p. 182.
[4] *Ibid.*, p. 172.

intellectual scene in Sweden.[1] Under the domination of empiricist and positivist thought, Swedish philosophy in the twentieth century has made frequent attacks on the truth value of faith propositions. Typical of the trend is Ingemar Hedenius, who in 1949 opened a new round of debate over the relationship of faith and knowledge with a book entitled *Tro och vetande*.[2] Here Hedenius undertakes to analyze the theoretical implications of a series of traditional Christian dogmas, at each point making counter-claims based on common-sense reasoning and modern scientific insight. In the process, Christian believers are made to appear rather simple-minded, superstitious, and hopelessly out of touch with modern culture. Bring's contribution to the so-called "Hedenius debate"—an article entitled "Kristen tro och vetenskaplig forskning" (Christian faith and scientific research) [3] —is a remarkably balanced presentation of the view that any conflict between the various areas of meaning is a manifestation of epistemological and conceptual confusion, and any absolutization of theoretical knowledge is as clearly an arbitrary metaphysical commitment as the theoretical extension of the meaning of faith statements. Both these points are important: The first expresses Bring's conviction that the relationship of faith and science is in reality a *Scheinproblem*; [4] the second indicates that the conflict of faith and science is often a struggle between two speculative metaphysical worldviews. We shall consider both these aspects of Bring's thought in turn.

First of all, Bring makes clear how easily conceptual confusion arises in the relationship between science and faith.[5] One reason lies in the dogmas of the church. Serving in a sense as the theoretical delimitation of Christian faith, they are often thought of as a separate superstructure on religious experience; and their meaning is often disassociated from the essential nature of religious experience itself. The essence of religion is described as "trust"; dogmas, on the other hand, have to do with "truth". Put together, trust and truth make up faith. The Christian faith is said to consist partly in a personal attitude of trust, partly in an assertion of certain dogmatic truths; it contains one religious element and one theoretical element. This distinction, which is equally common among those who look at faith from the

---

[1] Cf. *Ibid.*, pp. 5 f; *ToR*, 1937; "Teologi och religionsfilosofi," *STK*, 23, 1947.
[2] Stockholm: Bonnier, 1949.
[3] *STK*, 25, 1949, pp. 201 ff.
[4] Cf. *ToR*, 1937, p. 37.
[5] *Ibid.*, pp. 5 f.

standpoint of an "insider" as among those who approach it from the perspective of an "outsider", is attacked by Bring on two fronts.

In the first place, he refuses to separate —except in a psychological sense—between the immediate-experiential and the reflective-formulative elements of faith.[1] This means that all of faith—including the dogmatic formulation of its content—is united within a single *meningssammanhang*, namely the religious area of meaning. In the second place, Bring clarifies in what sense one may speak of a "theoretical" formulation of the content of faith.[2] Christian dogmas, which are theoretical in the sense that they express in logical formulations the thinking which belongs to Christian faith and experience, are not theoretical in the sense that they belong to the theoretical *meningssammanhang*. Says Bring:

> "If one will understand what Christian teachings or dogmas mean, one must learn to see that although they give expression to clear and concrete thought, they do not express anything theoretical in the sense that the *sammanhang*, or the intention, is theoretical." [3]

Bring's reference to the "intention" of faith statements is a pregnant methodological feature. It indicates a certain openness toward significant subsequent developments in the analysis of meaning and the understanding of religious language,[4] and it specifies somewhat the purposes of the logical or conceptual analysis which Bring considers indispensable for avoiding metaphysical confusion.[5] Bring has not himself developed this subject in detail, but he has staked out a course. He says, for example, that it is never the concrete content of propositions or concepts or acts in and of itself that decides whether

---

[1] Cf. *supra*, pp. 98 f.

[2] Cf. *supra*, pp. 117 f; *ToR*, 1937, p. 17.

[3] *Ibid.*, pp. 17 f.

[4] It is sufficient here only to refer to the influence of Ludwig Wittgenstein, the so-called "Vienna circle" under Rudolf Carnap's leadership, and the Cambridge philosophers John Wisdom, Gilbert Ryle, Antony Flew, *et. al.* Religious language has been analyzed with some intensity by Ian Ramsey in England and by Paul van Buren, William Hordern, and John Macquarrie in America. Bring has not taken account of these developments in the philosophy and analysis of language, though he has repeatedly indicated that theological methodology ought to do so. Curiously, Bring seems in a sense to have stopped in his methodological development, standing so to speak within view of the future fulfillment of his intentions, but unable to go forward and take possession. Anders Nygren shows more interest in the theological consequences of linguistic analysis; cf. "The Religious Realm of Meaning," *Christian Century* (July 16, 1958), pp. 823-826; "From Atomism to Contexts of Meaning in Philosophy," *Philosophical Essays dedicated to Gunnar Aspelin*, Lund: Gleerup, 1963, pp. 122-136.

[5] Cf. *supra*, pp. 89 f.

the meaning is religious or theoretical; it is the intentions which inform
them, the context within which they belong, and the "connection"
which unites them.[1] He also attempts to specify the kinds of intentions
which characterize religious statements in contrast to theoretical
propositions: The intention of a theoretical proposition is to describe
something real and true; a religious statement intends to express the
content of the God-relationship—particularly its soteriological
essence.[2] Bring's formulations are vague and unsatisfactory,[3] but
they do at least indicate that religious statements, regardless of their
form, are categorically different from theoretical or scientific propositions and that they must not, therefore, be considered as if they intended to pass on theoretical knowledge. They belong to a different
area of experience, and they express a different attitude or orientation
altogether.[4]

It is obvious to Bring that confusion on this score will have grave
consequences for the understanding of Christian dogmas:

> "...Every Christian doctrine, every attempt to formulate some
> aspect of the Christian faith, must become a meaningless metaphysical
> assertion if it is not understood as it is intended—namely as an answer
> to the religious question, the question of the nature of the God-
> relationship—but is considered as an expression of a theoretical
> standpoint." [5]

As theoretical statements the dogmas are absurd; from a rational
perspective the creeds fall to pieces and become nothing.[6] On such
presuppositions, the conflict between faith and knowledge is direct,
unavoidable, and insoluble. But the conflict is a child of metaphysical
confusion. It is a consequence of the fact that "one does not quite let

---

[1] *ToR*, 1937, pp. 19 f, note 1.

[2] *Ibid.*

[3] One is struck, once more, by the absence of a clearly defined concept of the
religious category in Bring's thought. He is using the rather general terms "God-
relationship" and "salvation"; but these concepts refer, after all, to the type of
content religious statements have, not to the nature of the intentions behind them.
Obviously, the failure to complete the critical deduction of the formal religious
category is haunting Bring throughout. Cf. *supra*, p. 90.

[4] *STU*, 1933, p. 196. "If the perspective to which a certain conception belongs
and in the context of which it is to be interpreted expresses the intentions of a
religious attitude and does not aim at expressing a theoretical truth but a certain
God-relationship, then it is clear that this conception belongs to the religious area
of experience and does not indicate a way of thinking which—from the standpoint
of validity—is equivalent to science". *Ibid.*, p. 15.

[5] *ToR*, pp. 178 f.

[6] *Ibid.*, p. 32.

this remain this, and that, that." [1] One makes the double mistake of thinking that faith contains a series of theoretical truths that are asserted metaphysically and held against the results of science, and that science represents a view of the world which is at the same time an adequate answer to the religious question. Thus faith is made halfway theoretical and knowledge halfway religious. Says Bring: "If science is able to disturb faith, the reason is that faith is understood metaphysically, as a piece of theoretical knowledge." [2] Likewise, when the scientifically minded criticize Christian dogmas, they either misunderstand the nature of religious affirmations or misappropriate the results of science. [3]

Bring's contribution to the Hedenius debate did not gain much attention. It fell, as it were, between two chairs. He criticized both the proponents of dogma and the opponents of theology and did not, therefore, take sides in the conflict. In his view, there was no necessary conflict; it had its roots in the fact that the problems had not been adequately thought through. [4] The warring factions did not see it that way. Battle lines were too clearly drawn, and a third party mediator had no place to stand.

We shall need to ask, of course, whether the mediator failed because of internal weaknesses in his own arguments. Such a possibility is always there. In Bring's case, the question is whether he managed to carry his methodological intentions through to their full consequences. We have expressed reservations in this regard at earlier points; [5] we shall have to return to this question again. [6]

RELIGIOUS CONFLICT BETWEEN FAITH AND REASON

The conflict between faith and science does not always take the form of a *Scheinproblem*. As a theoretical conflict, caused by a common disregard for the categorical autonomy of the religious and the theoretical areas of meaning, it could easily be resolved if the dogmatician and the scientist would agree to recognize the specific presuppositions for meaningful discourse upon which their respective utterances—in so far as they are logically consistent—are based. But the problem is not always that clear-cut. Conflicts and confusions do not only occur,

---

[1] *Ibid.*, p. 12.
[2] *STU*, 1933, p. 163, note 9.
[3] *ToR*, 1937, pp. 38 f.
[4] *Ibid.*, p. 37.
[5] Cf. *supra*, pp. 89 ff., 119 ff.
[6] Cf. below, Ch. IX.

in the relationship of faith and knowledge, by default; occasionally they appear by design. This happens, for example, when faith and knowledge, both, represent explicitly commitmental standpoints, *i.e.* when they are understood as conflicting world-views or contrasting conceptions of life—even as different ways of salvation. Here it is not just religious faith and theoretical knowledge that stand over against one another; "here religion stands against religion, faith against faith, one conception of salvation against another." [1]

This sort of conflict is illustrated by Bring in reference to the rationalistic opposition to Christian doctrine that has its roots in the absolutization of reason. It is not simply the demands of intellectual honesty, rational cogency, or theoretical knowledge which inform such an opponent's perspective; "reason", rather, represents a subjective value judgment, a life perspective which has its focus, one might say, in "natural" or "secular" man.[2] Bring calls it a "metaphysical world-view." This reference to metaphysics represents, in a way, a third manifestation of it, different from the confused thought-forms—identity-philosophical speculation and categorical equivocation—which we have identified as characteristic of the metaphysical way of thinking; and Bring emphasizes that it must be handled differently. In so far as metaphysics consists of bad logic, one can, of course, establish a critical position and marshal a rational argument in defense against it. But when metaphysics appears in the form of a value judgment or an ultimate commitment, it must be handled as another religious type or as a species of faith.

Bring emphasizes that the conflict between the Christian faith and the various metaphysical world-views must be approached in such a way that faith retains its character as faith and is not drawn into dialectic dependency upon the reasoning of the opponent.[3] This is at best a difficult task, requiring a sure grasp of the nature of faith and a clear understanding of the metaphysical dialectic. These are not always present, and the result is confusion.

Bring exemplifies this by reference to Brunner's critique of idealistic humanism and romantic mysticism.[4] Brunner is particularly critical

---

[1] *Op. cit.*, pp. 38 f.

[2] *Ibid.*, pp. 40 f.

[3] Cf. *STU*, 1933, pp. 29; 33, note 30.

[4] Bring's discussion of Brunner's methodological stance, *ibid.*, pp. 35 ff., represents an important chapter in the evaluation of dialectic thought; it focuses on the central affirmation of this theology, the assertion of an infinite qualitative distinction between God and man.

of the prevailing practice—taken over from Scholastic and Enlightenment thought—of relating nature and supernature in a synthetic
fashion, *i.e.* as realities that are in conjunction and continuation of
each other. In his own view, the relationship between the natural
and the transcendent is characterized by disjunction rather than
conjunction. In the Christian way of looking at it, says Brunner,
nature and supernature are dialectic opposites; there is an infinite
qualitative distinction between the two. On the surface, Brunner
appears to be engaged in an objective comparison of philosophical
idealism and Christian faith. The two perspectives are different, and
Brunner contrasts them. But the procedure is not quite that simple, says
Bring. Brunner does not, in fact, refuse the philosophical perspective
underlying the two-storey structure of the universe.[1] On the contrary,
he utilizes it, having sharpened its dialectic character by means of
the Christian theological perspective, and proceeds to prove that
idealism and mysticism are illegitimate forms of thought. This is
clear evidence, to Bring, that Brunner's confrontation with idealism
is infused with metaphysical confusion.[2]

Bring finds examples of Brunner's philosophical-theological
tangles at several points in the dialectic system.[3] In his discussion of
the nature of human knowledge, for example, Brunner operates on
the basis of theological concepts, but he switches freely between the
religious context of meaning and the theoretical consideration of
epistemology. Christian thought is described as "faith", while common
thought is termed "speculation". Faith and speculation are not two
forms of valid thought; they are dialectic opposites. According to
Brunner, speculation makes God the object of thought; faith makes
us the object of God's acts. Common thought is "es sich selbst

---

[1] *Ibid.*, p. 37.

[2] In his article on the critique of Harnack's interpretation of the soteriology
of the early church, *STK*, 9, 1933, later incorporated in *ToR*, 1937, Bring makes a
similar analysis of Brunner's desire to substitute the *"Gott-Kreatur"* contrast for
Harnack's polarity of the ethical and the physical. Bring wonders whether both
Harnack's and Brunner's contrasts are expressions of nineteenth century idealism:
"...Dialectic theology assumes that it can reject the metaphysics underlying
idealistic thought, as given form by Ritschl and Harnack, just by substituting the
contrast God/world for the polarity ethical/physical; but this means only that one
form of metaphysical thought has been replaced by another." *Ibid.*, p. 204. Bring
observes with a certain satisfaction that Aulén and Nygren, when setting idealistic
philosophy and Christian faith in contrast to one another, do so entirely within the
comparison of religious motifs, not for the purpose of proving faith to be the
better metaphysics. Cf. *STU*, 1933, pp. 71 ff.

[3] Cf. *supra*, pp. 133 f.

sagen"; Christian faith is "es sich selbst lassen". Such comparisons are not invalid, of course, if the intention is simply to set in perspective the essential character of two contrasting but equally valid religious motifs. However, Brunner intends more than that. He considers speculation an illegitimate form of human thought and faith the only valid alternative; and since speculation is identified with human thought at the outset, faith is actually set in opposition to rational activity *per se*. The end result is that faith alone stands validated—but within the framework of a logically indefensible epistemology.[1]

Brunner's anthropology, as Bring sees it, is structured in a similar way.[2] Man's situation is described by the theological concept *Widerspruch*. This concept is set in dialectical contrast to every view of man that defines the human situation in the world in terms of unity or harmony. But the contrast is not set up simply for the purpose of comparing two different—and equally valid—interpretations of man. Brunner feels obliged to invalidate his opponents' views, and he does so by manipulating the Christian theological concepts and proving their direct correspondence to the facts of life: There are conflicts and disharmonies in human life; conflict equals revolt equals sin; man, therefore, is a sinner. To deny the existence of conflict is to deny fact; to deny fact equals revolt equals sin; man is a sinner. Thus Brunner establishes the Christian view of man as "right"— but he is left with a concept of reality which is irrational and even incongruous.[3]

We shall return to the discussion of Bring's own procedures for comparing contrasting religious types or commitmental standpoints below.[4] Already it is clear that his perspective is helpful. Its strength, one might say, is in the consistency with which Bring guards against metaphysical procedures of thought and holds on to a purely religious concept of faith. He has suggested a logical way to resolve the conflict between the Christian faith and the various metaphysical world-views: it is simply a question of letting faith retain its character as faith and accepting the pluralism of religious experience and the relativity of religious types.

Against the background of Bring's sensitivity to the metaphysical problematics, one is surprised to discover that he does not feel

---

[1] *Ibid.*, p. 41.
[2] Cf. *ibid.*, pp. 48-52.
[3] *Ibid.*, p. 52.
[4] Cf. below, pp. 190 ff.

constrained to disclaim, on behalf of faith, all metaphysical interest. He seems to accept the idea which is propounded by Ingemar Hedenius and Martin Fries, a contemporary interpreter of Hägerström, that faith is inevitably metaphysical *in interest*.[1] Both these men launched their criticism of religious beliefs on the observation that faith is by definition concerned with realities that transcend space and time. The propositions of faith are therefore beyond scientific verification, beyond physics—metaphysical. One would have expected Bring to reject this premise. His own epistemology is an attempt to avoid the ontological perspective and refuse the question of *reality*. He says that the ontological approach to the problem of knowledge will inevitably lead to a choice between metaphysics and scepticism;[2] and since neither of these is acceptable to the critical mind, he proposes instead to structure his own thought on the concept of *validity*. Validity lies in experience; human experience is valid. Beyond our experience, there is nothing of interest except the formal, categorical presuppositions for understanding the various areas of meaning. From Bring's own perspective, then, *any interest* in realities which transcend space and time seems by definition out of the question. And yet we find Bring toying with a metaphysical interest.[3] How can he?

---

[1] Cf. Martin Fries, *Metafysiken i modern svensk teologi*, Stockholm: Natur och kultur, 1948; Ingemar Hedenius, *Tro och Livsåskådning*, Stockholm: Bonnier, 1958. In defense against the positivistic discreditation of religion, Bring is forced to specify his concept of metaphysics; cf. "Kristen tro och vetenskaplig forskning," *STK*, 25, 1949, 201-243. In this context, he reveals a tendency toward arguing against the particular theory of reality which lies behind positivism, saying that it is never an adequate definition of metaphysics to claim that it represents "an illegitimate interest in that which is beyond physical knowledge." To oppose metaphysics on such a basis would itself be metaphysics, in Bring's view; it means that physical reality is identified with reality itself. Cf. *ToR*, 1937, pp. 164 f. Bring has thereby returned to the question of „reality"—which on the presuppositional level he intended to reject. He is doing so in order to allow for a "legitimate" kind of metaphysics: the interest in a reality which of is a broader nature than that defined by the natural sciences—one which includes the reality, f. ex., of God. See note 3 below. On Bring's philosophical premises, however, these ideas are entirely foreign to his thought.

[2] Cf. *supra*, pp. 78 f.

[3] At various points, Bring raises the question concerning the "truth" of religious propositions, *i. e.* the relationship between their content and "reality"; cf. *STU*, 1933, p. 156; *ToR*, 1937, pp. 77 f; "Teologi och religionsfilosofi," *STK*, 23, 1947, pp. 45 f; and „Kristen tro och vetenskaplig forskning," *STK*, 25, 1949, pp. 208 ff. We note with some surprise that the answer is usually said to depend on the particular definition of "truth" or "reality". According to Bring, if one defines these concepts in a way which excludes religious realities to begin with, and then proceeds to evaluate the truth of religious propositions on that basis, one will naturally end up with an illusionistic conception of religion. Ethical and religious propo-

We shall hold our judgment for a later context.[1] It remains here only to point out that Bring claims to have avoided metaphysics in its most troublesome forms.[2] He has identified the cause of the metaphysical problem, unveiled the dynamics of the metaphysical dialectic, avoided the tendencies to identity-philosophical speculation, guarded against the confusion of concepts and categories, and he has explicitly refused to allow faith to be drawn into a metaphysical stance that would make the dialogue of faiths into a contest between absolutes. All this one must grant, even though one retains the suspicion that further clarifications of the meaning of faith are necessary.

Absolute Separation of Faith and Science

We come now to the last manifestation of metaphysical confusion in the relationship between faith and science which Bring takes account of and goes against. The problem at this point does not consist in mixing the religious and the theoretical categories and locking faith and science together in presuppositional unity or in bitter conflict. The issue, rather, is the opposite one. Faith and science are considered two entirely different and distinct entities—so different, in fact, that they are absolutely incompatible. One must therefore separate between them—even to the extent of distinguishing between two autonomous concepts of truth. In Bring's view, the end result for theology can be predetermined: theological methodology will be based on the presuppositions of faith, and the theologian will have no interest in gaining scientific recognition.

The example of this particular methodological distortion Bring finds —sadly— in a theologian who in some respects holds views that are similar to his own, his friend Hjalmar Lindroth.[3] Lindroth was under the influence of Hägerström's philosophical criticism. He was committed to freeing theology from metaphysical tendencies. He made an open rendezvous with the methodological principles of Schleiermacher. In formulations that are close to Bring's, Lindroth says that the only way to do theology scientifically is to realize that thought and science, on the one hand, and faith and religion, on the

---

sitions do not, however, represent illusions; they deal with truths and realities that lie "beyond" the limited realm of the positivist's vision.

[1] Cf. below, Ch. IX.

[2] *ToR*, 1937, p. 168.

[3] Cf. *STU*, 1933, p. 95, note 89, where Bring comments on Lindroth's essay "Om teologien såsom en positiv vetenskap," *Festskrift tillägnad Axel Hägerström*, 1928, saying that it expresses views he also could subscribe to.

other, "are best served by being allowed to remain what they are." [1]
However, it soon appeared that Lindroth meant by "letting them
remain what they are" something Bring was not ready to concede.[2]

Lindroth claims that Hägerström's criticism of subjectivism
demands that there be a complete separation of estates between
science and value judgments, or between the theoretical and the a-
theoretical dimensions of experience.[3] The "practical" areas of life—
aesthetic, ethic, and religion—are inaccessible to theoretical analysis.
They are the direct opposites of the theoretical orientation and
therefore completely incompatible to scientific investigation. The
perspective from which science approaches life is totally inadequate
for understanding the a-theoretical areas of life. Only "life" can
understand life. Only by personal commitment to and subjective
involvement in the value systems one sets out to investigate will
the material yield its secrets and submit to research. In regard to
religion, the traditional formula still stands: "Religion kann nur
durch Religion verstanden werden." [4]

We have already observed that Bring makes an entirely different
response to Hägerström's criticism of subjectivism.[5] As he sees it,
there is nothing in Hägerström's thought to suggest that the a-
theoretical areas of life are inaccessible to the empirical perspective
or to scientific investigation. Nothing that is real is inaccessible to
science; [6] nothing that is true in life can be withdrawn from logical
analysis. To conceive of life as inconceivable is obviously self-

---

[1] Lindroth, *op. cit.*, p. 197.

[2] Bring identifies this "unhappy tendency" primarily in Lindroth's major discussion of Hägerström's philosophy, *Verkligheten och vetenskapen*, Uppsala: Lindblad, 1929. Cf. *STU*, 1933, pp. 93 ff.

[3] Lindroth, *op. cit.*, pp. 68 f.

[4] Lindroth, "Logos—Ordet," *Ordet och tron*, 1931, p. 97.

[5] Cf. *supra*, pp. 98 ff. The question which of these represents a correct interpretation of Hägerström is not relevant here.

[6] Bring's reference, of course, is to the reality of the experiential material;
basically, this is the only "reality" there is. Lindroth is concerned with the reality
of the object of faith, namely that reality which is beyond space and time. Of this,
one cannot strictly speaking have "knowledge", he says; it is "the great *irrationale*
of God and life with which the theologian has to count, not *in line with* but *in
spite of* logic and culture and rational viewpoints...." "Religion och vetenskap en
sista gång," *STK*, 7, 1931, pp. 411 f. Bring is, as we have seen, also concerned with
this question; cf. above, p. 146, note 3. The difference between them comes down to
this: Lindroth defines theology as a religious exercise (non-scientific), with God as its
object; Bring defines theology as a theoretical investigation (scientific), with faith
as its object. The two methodologies clash at the point where Lindroth claims
that religious life is inaccessible to theoretical (scientific) investigation.

contradictory.[1] Bring must therefore disassociate himself from Lindroth's conception of the relation of religion and science.

It is one thing to say that scientific investigation is different from the value judgments of a-theoretical experience; it is another thing altogether to say that the a-theoretical areas of life are incomprehensible to the scientific mind.[2] It is one thing to say that science ought not to investigate religious experience or evaluate religious propositions on the basis of theoretical criteria of truth; it is a completely different thing to say that religious life does not submit to logical conceptualization. In Bring's own words,

> "It is self-contradictory and meaningless to say that science or logic cannot understand life or that such an approach to things would be to 'imprison life within scientific categories'....When science or logical perception seeks to understand life, it is not for the purpose of making life anything other than it is—not to 'throw a net of logic over life'. It simply records facts and observes relationships." [3]

A second aspect of Lindroth's separation of religion and science which Bring finds it necessary to challenge has to do with the way Lindroth explains the relationship between the religious and the theoretical concepts of truth.[4] The theoretical concept ("logos") is "philosophical", built on the principles of logical consistency and verifiable identity; the religious concept ("the Word") is a "practical" one and cannot therefore be defined by way of theoretical formulas or by reference to a system of criteria. Its approach to truth is simply through "participation in life".[5] While the theoretical principle of truth is operating in the impersonal, more objective contexts of experience, only the religious principle is adequate in the personal, subjective realm of religion. From Lindroth's point of view, one may even say—in a different use of terms—that the philosophical principle of truth is an "immanent-subjective" concept, while the religious

---

[1] *STU*, 1933, p. 22.

[2] *Ibid.*, pp. 96 f., note 94; p. 107.

[3] *Ibid.*, p. 28.

[4] Cf. *ibid.*, pp. 78-88. Here Bring discusses Lindroth's way of using the concepts *"logos"* and *"Ordet"* (the Word) to describe the basic distinction between Greek philosophy and Christian thought. Cf. Lindroth, *op. cit.* Lindroth apparently received his inspiration from Billing; however, he developed what were mere tendencies in Billing's thought into a full grown theory.

[5] Lindroth, *op. cit.*, pp. 96 ff. His comparison between the objective "spectator" and the subjective "participant" is strongly reminiscent of Henri Bergson, whose thought has had more influence on the Runestam-line of Swedish theology than on any other Scandinavian group.

(and particularly the prophetic-Christian) concept of truth refers to "transcendent-objective" facts.[1]

In the further delineation of these differences, Lindroth describes the two concepts of truth as different "in appearance". Theoretical truth is characterized by clarity and consistency; religious truth is ridden with paradoxes and antinomies—it is not at all reasonable or logical. From the point of view of reason, religious truth is irrational. This does not make it less important, however. On the contrary, the religious concept of truth manifests its superiority by "bending" all theoretical considerations into subjection under religious conviction.[2] Lindroth does not consider truth ultimately bifurcated, therefore. Christian truth is such that it overshadows the logical or theoretical truth. Under the influence of the Christian faith all of life is seen as the manifestation of one single ultimate truth.[3]

From Bring's perspective, the claim that Christianity represents the highest in a many-leveled system of truth is, of course, sheer presumption. Furthermore, it is clearly a result of metaphysical confusion. When religious truth claims superiority over theoretical truth, it is clearly guilty of overstepping its categorical boundaries. Even the idea that there are two principles of truth —one theoretical, one religious—which in some ways are in conflict with each other and therefore to be separated from one another is a sign of metaphysical confusion. Thus, from Bring's point of view even the attempt to separate science and faith in a radical way does not avoid confusing them.

Confusion is not inevitable, however. In Bring's view, one may well speak of a variety of concepts of truth if one makes clear at the same time what are the specific contexts of meaning to which they refer. It is not enough to point out that there is one "theoretical" and another "religious" concept of truth. One must explain the exact context and the appropriate function of each concept, and not allow the theoretical concept to assume the function of religious truth—or vice versa. One must, in other words, observe the autonomy of each area of experience, particularly the distinction between the theoretical and the a-theoretical categories of meaning. And if one compares two concepts of truth, one must make certain that they function

---

[1] *Ibid.*, p. 100.

[2] *Ibid.*, p. 98. Lindroth refers to Billing's method at this point. Cf. *supra*, pp. 42 f., 135 ff.

[3] *Ibid.*, p. 105.

within the same *meningssammanhang*; otherwise the comparison is illegitimate and meaningless.[1]

We should note that when he speaks of the theoretical area of experience Bring considers it a test of intellectual honesty to acknowledge only one principle of truth, namely that which is loosely defined in terms of "logical consistency" and "rational correspondence".[2] Such criteria do not, of course, determine truth as a static or closed system; truth is always dynamic and open-ended. One might say that theoretical truth develops, as do the tools for finding it. Yet a general agreement concerning truth is possible only if all men observe the same basic criteria of verification. This we do in the theoretical area of experience. In the a-theoretical areas of meaning the situation is different. Here "truth" is a function of subjective commitments and personal value judgments, and it appears in many forms. Presuppositions vary, perspectives differ, and convictions clash. There is no common convention on criteria, so a general agreement on truth cannot be reached. No common logic applies to all; no objective proofs of truth can be given. Since all convictions of truth are equally subjective, no impartial arbitrator can be found. One must accept the fact that truth in these areas of meaning is manifold and relative.

Thus Ragnar Bring distinguishes between a theoretical concept of truth and an a-theoretical type of "truth", but he does not force a choice between them. A man of faith can be both scientifically minded and a committed Christian. There is no conflict between the two which would make it necessary to take sides or hold on to the one and let go of the other.

We said above that Bring set out to find a way to hold together without confusion an authentic Christian faith and a strict scientific method. His conception of this methodological task has obviously been sharpened in the confrontation with colleagues who have a

---

[1] *STU*, 1933, p. 86. Bring gives an interesting analysis of the various heterogeneous elements which are included in Lindroth's comparison of "*logos*" and "*Ordet*"; *ibid.*, pp. 81 f. In Bring's view, Lindroth considers "*logos*" in such a way as to include references to both a logical principle of rationality and a philosophical world-view. But these two elements are categorically different and cannot without confusion be blended into a single concept. Furthermore, when Christianity is set in contrast to such a mixture of logic and metaphysics, the result will inevitably be a confusion of the nature of Christian faith; it makes faith appear as logical paradoxality, the antithesis to rational thought. Says Bring: "Any meaning or significant result that may be derived from such a comparison cannot easily be found." *Ibid.* p. 88.

[2] Cf. Bring's rejection of a special religious epistemology; *supra*, pp. 96 ff.

different understanding of faith and science and who therefore define the nature of theology differently. But his negative delimitations of the critical approach to theology that are evident in his methodological polemic are not adequate to describe the methodology he has developed. We must go on to his positive delineations of how the scientific study of Christian faith is to be understood and undertaken.

CHAPTER SEVEN

SYSTEMATIC THEOLOGY — THE SCIENCE OF FAITH

The scientific status of systematic theology, in Ragnar Bring's view, is dependent on two factors: In the first place, it must prove itself worthy to be included on the roster of scientific diciplines by avoiding all implications of metaphysical confusion and subjective value judgments; in the second place, it must be capable of justifying its inclusion on this roster by demonstrating its necessity as a separate science.

Obviously, the methodological troubles of systematic theology are not over once one has divorced the discipline from formal and material involvements in metaphysical problematics. Its epistemological perspectives and philosophical foundations may be sound. Its theoretical presuppositions and logical delimitations may be clear. Nevertheless, the scientific status of systematic theology is not secure unless one also has the wherewithals to support its claims to an independent place and an autonomous purpose, particularly in view of the fact that historical, psychological, anthropological, sociological, and philological disciplines dealing with religious materials are already well established. In short, systematic theology must be able to show that it has an object of study which is unique, a purpose for research which is distinctive, and a method of investigation which is appropriate.[1]

This is the task to which Bring addresses himself secondarily— but not less energetically—in his methodological works. He has no illusions of a general acceptance—or even understanding—of his endeavors to stake out the territory and mark the methodological *egenart* of systematic theology. The intellectual climate, for one thing, does not give much grounding for such hopes. On the contrary, there is considerable anti-theological bias abroad, expressing itself in prejudicial negations of any attempt to establish systematic theology among the sciences of men. The scientific world-view dominates

---

[1] This is the second main purpose in *STU*, 1933; cf. pp. 32, 193. Bring's considerations of these matters are spread throughout his works, however. We shall attempt to bring his views together in a systematic fashion.

the modern mind.[1] The secularist culture takes a dim view of any effort on behalf of something "religious". Moreover, among those who do systematic theology in the present, only a few have given much support to the radical methodological renewal of their discipline. The prevailing mood in the theological community is one of isolation and intra-discipline discussion. A new scholasticism threatens to capture the Christian mind.[2] Christian scholars tend to look askance at the attempt to do theology "scientifically". Thus science and theology still seem to belong to two different worlds; they continue to be so strange to each other that it is difficult for the one to understand the other—not to speak of the problems involved in bringing them to mutual recognition and respect.

Bring feels, however, that it is necessary to try to do just that. If theology is not able to break out of its isolation and gain recognition as an intellectually respectable and scientifically responsible discipline, Christian theologians will not be in the position to enter into dialogue with the modern mind or to communicate the meaning of the Christian faith in our age. The methodological concern has direct bearing on the situation of the faith at the present time and on the work of the church in the contemporary situation. Thus theological methodology has practical and pragmatic dimensions as well as principal and theoretical value.

The pragmatic dimension of the methodological concern is not,

---

[1] In some interesting paragraphs in *ToR*, 1937, Bring comments on the change that occurred in the general attitude to religion as a result of World War I. Earlier, culture-conscious people considered reason man's highest asset; now they were no longer sure of man's rationality. The estimation of philosophy had changed. No longer did reason seem to be the key to absolute truth; the question of truth could only be answered by science, in a relative way, or by the individual, existentially. The attitude to religion had become more positive; irrationalism was no longer laughed at. Bring is not sure that this was good for theology, though: "Perhaps...the demands for rational clarity and intellectual honesty that characterized the older culture-radicals were more profitable for theology than the easier cultural situation at the present...." *Ibid.*, pp. 3 f. These remarks, coming out of the 1930's, could not have been written in the Scandinavia of the 1950's and 1960's. Rationalism, technocracy, positivism and cultural radicalism have an overwhelming grip on these societies; and if theologians are looking for demands for intellectual honesty, they have certainly found them. Whether they measure up is another question. See f. ex. Philip Houm's evaluation of the intellectual honesty (he calls it *"den hellige alminnelige uredelighet"*, translated "the holy catholic dishonesty") of the theological community in Norway; *Mannen fra Nasaret og Den norske kirke*, Oslo: Aschehoug, 1965; *Hvem var han? På sporet etter mesteren fra Galilea*, Oslo: Aschehoug, 1968.

[2] Cf. "Teologi och religionsfilosofi," *STK*, 23, 1947, p. 38; also *STK*, 34, 1958, p. 55.

of course, the primary interest in Bring's work. In fact, he warns against the pragmatic tendency to sacrifice principle for the sake of expediency. Seeking to establish dialogue, one may, for example, proceed to synthesize Christian faith motifs and modern secular ideas—even elements of scientific knowledge. In the process, both essential Christianity and the modern mindset are approached eclectically, and the basis for synthesis is most often the least common denominator of the two. The end result, says Bring, is not scientific respectability, but compromise and confusion:

> "A theology which is in search of a synthesis between the motifs of faith and the concepts of a predominant philosophy can not do honor to the name of scientific theology. Such a synthesis is a product, partly of an exchange of genuine Christian motifs for certain religious elements belonging to this philosophy, partly of a confusion of religious propositions and intellectual theories. Furthermore, by seeking philosophical or rational support for the plausibility—or at least the possibility—of faith propositions, there arises a theology which claims to represent both a certain faith commitment and a philosophical argument for its truth. Such a theology is an attempt to demonstrate the value of faith by proving its superiority over other religious conceptions." [1]

Bring's hesitancy in regard to the pragmatic motivation for methodological reconsideration is caused also by the fear that the theological community might be tempted to give up the discipline of systematic theology and transfer its interests to disciplines that are more easily vindicated when challenged on the criteria of scientific respectability. To Bring's mind, it would be a disaster if the study of the Christian faith were reduced to a branch of the historical-descriptive or historical-genetic or historical-comparative sciences of religion. One could, perhaps, guarantee scientific status to doctrinal studies by such means, but one could not secure the second focus of the methodological ellipse, namely the authentic content and genuine meaning of Christian faith. No theological methodology is adequate which does not define systematic theology as an autonomous discipline whose procedures are strictly scientific and whose content is genuinely Christian.

The Object of Study

Bring has laid the methodological foundations for developing a scientific discipline of systematic theology concerned with investi-

---

[1] *STU*, 1933, pp. 20 f. Bring's critique hits all theology which is dependent in matters of content on the mind of the times, whether this dependency is direct, established by logical correlation, or it results from dialectic opposition.

gating and understanding the essential meaning of Christian faith
deep in the presuppositions of critical philosophy. To make clear
what this science of faith is, what it does, and how it operates, we
shall need to refer back to the philosophical foundations and draw
out the methodological consequences with specific reference to the
shaping of a modern discipline of study. The first element which
must be established is the object of study: It is necessary to show that
the discipline has an object of study which is historically-empirically
given, and that this object is unique.

We have already observed that Bring grants the premise that
only that which is given in history and experience is available for
scientific investigation. He explicitly rejects the notion that the
object of theology is inaccessible to science or incompatible to theoretical research.[1] Clearly, if systematic theology is to have even the most
elementary presupposition for claiming to be a science among the
sciences of men, it must concern itself with an object which is historically given, freely available to all men, and logically consistent so as to
make possible objective research, theoretical analysis, and logical
description.

Theology cannot, therefore, have God for its object. God is not
given within historical-empirical reality. He is not available for
scientific investigation; neither is his nature such as to warrant theoretical analysis or logical definition. Statements about God, affirmations of his existence, or descriptions of his nature, his character,
or his acts, cannot be considered theoretical in the sense that they
represent knowledge of a given object.[2] They are religious utterances,
meaningful only in the sense that they express a certain view of
reality or interpretation of life, a value judgment, a personal commitment—or in Christian terminology, a revelation through the Spirit
to faith. To make theoretical claims on behalf of religious propositions
is plainly absurd. A theology which has God for its object and claims
science for its method can only serve as fuel for those who are putting
metaphysics and subjectivism, confusion and arbitrariness—in short,
all un-scientific attitudes—to the stakes.

We have observed that Bring renounces all special ontological
or epistemological claims—at least on behalf of systematic theology.[3]

---

[1] Cf. *supra*, pp. 100 f., 134 f., 147 ff.

[2] Cf. *supra*, pp. 141 f.

[3] There remains, as we have noted, a certain hesitancy in regard to renouncing
all metaphysical *interest*; cf. *supra*, p. 146. However, this element belongs to Bring's

A discipline which claims to be scientific cannot arbitrarily change the common concept of reality and introduce an object of study which is of an entirely different—that is, transcendent or supernatural—constitution. Neither can it, on its own, widen the theoretical presuppositions of reason so as to allow for a special avenue of knowledge not available to common men. Theology—scientific systematic theology—must accept the necessity of finding its object within the given realities of human experience and its tools among the rational capacities of man.

Such statements must be understood within their appropriate context, of course. The context here is theoretical or methodological, not religious or theological. When Bring without hesitation declares that the object of systematic theology must be given within man's experience or history, he does not in any way intend to express the character and content of Christianity; the statement has, in fact, no theological significance whatever. Only methodologically is his framework experience-centered or anthropocentric. This methodological empiricism does not give grounds for charging Bring with a Cartesian interpretation of Christianity or a humanistic conception of the basic motifs of Christian faith.[1] The context is formal, not material; his statements describe the logical constitution of the object of systematic theology, not the content of theological motifs.

Bring describes the object of systematic theology simply as "faith" or "religion".[2] It is not the object of faith which is the object of the science of faith, but faith itself, the historical, empirical, existential fact of faith, which manifests itself in a wide variety of ways, but most clearly in the thoughts and propositions and documents that spring from faith and witness to it. Scientific theology stands in relation

---

discussions—spurious in nature—of faith-reflection or, as he also calls it, "Christian philosophy of religion". In the discussions of scientific systematic theology, the interest is entirely historical-empirical. Cf. below, Ch. IX.

[1] This, the favorite charge of dialectic theologians against theologies which in any way take a starting point other than a theocentric or revelational or kerygmatic one, is often misdirected. See f. ex. Regin Prenter, *Skabelse og genløsning*, *Köbenhavn*: Gad, 2nd ed., 1955, pp. 26 ff., who criticizes Anders Nygren on the grounds that Nygren's deduction of the religious category involves an inescapable tendency to regard religion as an aspect of human culture, *i.e.* anthropocentrism. Plainly, Prenter—and most Barthian theologians with him—fails to understand the difference between a theoretical approach to the problems of theological methodology and a religious commitment regarding the priorities of Christian values.

[2] *STU*, 1933, p. 73; *ToR*, 1937, pp. 120, 159. Cf. *supra*, Ch. IV, for the philosophical groundwork for this definition.

to religious existence much in the way the theory of art is related to the creative arts, or as the analysis of musical forms is related to the art of music-making.[1] The sciences are not themselves creative in the same sense as the different forms of artistic existence are; the task of the sciences is to observe, describe, investigate, and understand the meaning of the creative dimensions of life on the basis of the material through which they manifest themselves within historical-empirical reality.

When the object of theology is defined this way, however, a major methodological complication immediately appears. All the a-theoretical areas of experience depend ultimately on factors which are subjective and artibrary—and therefore inconstant. They are expressions of personal standpoints and individual commitments, functions of human decision-making or value jugdment. This subjectivism creates what seems to be an insurmountable obstacle for any sort of systematization of the material. It becomes a particularly serious problem in regard to religious experience, for here the subjective element is especially strong and the varieties of subjective commitments appear in great quantities.

A scientific investigation of faith can hardly describe itself as objective and systematic without indicating a basic incongruity between the method and the material. The only approach one can reasonably expect to be able to justify from a scientific point of view seems to be an objective description of the many varieties of religious experience, including their fleeting and disjunctive character, or a genetic analysis of the various factors that influence individual believers; and this task is already adequately covered by the history of religion and the psychology of religion.[2]

This is indeed a formidable problem, and Bring cannot ignore it. He does, in fact, grant the validity of the argument. If the object of study is entirely subjective, void of constancy or permanence, chang-

---

[1] *ToR*, 1937, p. 159.

[2] This is G. Wetter's view; cf. *Tro och vetande*, 1915. In his opinion, the task of theology should be taken over by a general philosophy of religion that would include the historical-genetic or psychological-genetic explanation of religious phenomena. The study of doctrine, if it is to be scientific, must be taken over by the history of religion or the psychology of religion; these should provide the material for a critical philosophy of religion whose function would be to evaluate the degree of rationality in dogmas and sort out the illusions that still prevail. Bring takes Wetter's challenge seriously; he seeks to counter it by deemphasizing the capriciousness of religious experience and arguing for the scientific autonomy of the systematic theological discipline. Cf. below, pp. 167 f.

ing character arbitrarily, and capriciously resisting connection and coherence, then there can be no room for any other type of investigation than that which is already undertaken by the general sciences of religion. The only way to approach such an object of study is to describe each single religious event and analyze its constitutive elements, psychological, ideological, or sociological—of whichever character they may be.

However, Bring is not willing to grant the premise of the argument. In his view, faith is not a disjunctive and formless entity, a circumstantial collection of atomistic, oscilating experiential units. We have observed—in the context of our discussions of Bring's philosophical commitments and his description of the theological interest—that he attributes to historical faith two specific qualities which function as presuppositions for the scientific concept of theology: In the first place, there is his view that each religious type has within it a principle of unity or a *motivsammanhang* which serves as the organic center in reference to which the many different elements that combine to make up a faith are held together and given a peculiar character.[1] In the second place, there is his view that the experience of faith is at one and the same time emotive and reflective, not first subjective feeling and then theoretical reflection; it is real only as it expresses itself in symbols or language, in acts or thoughts or propositions, *i.e.* in documents of one form or another.[2] In the light of these assumptions, faith, according to Bring, has a certain concreteness as well as a certain consistency; the many-faceted object of scientific theological research is of a subjective nature, but it is not inconstant; it is dynamic, but not arbitrary.[3] In short, it does not resist systematic study; it requires it.

Having explicitly disassociated the concept of faith, for purposes of scientific investigation, from its object, Bring proceeds to abstract it also, for purposes of systematic theological research, from its subject. Says Bring: "Neither the question of the reality of the object

---

[1] Cf. *supra*, pp. 95 f.

[2] Cf. *supra*, p. 99.

[3] Bring refuses principally—though not consistently—to approach the problems involved in the subjectivity of faith by giving faith objective reference; cf. his critique of John O. Cullberg, *Religion och vetenskap*, 1930, *STU*, 1933, pp. 216 ff. Cullberg considers faith as having reference to "another subject", a "thou"—an attempt, obviously, to avoid the old ontological references to transcendent substances. Bring says that even this approach will ultimately lead to the definition of the nature of this "subject", *i.e.* speculative metaphysics.

(of faith) nor the question of the nature of the subject stands for us at the center of theological interest so as to determine the nature of the theological method, but faith in abstraction from the believing subject." [1] The reason for this move is clear: The methodological dilemma of systematic theology is not overcome once it has been shown that the discipline has an object of study which is empirically-historically given. Neither is it, strictly speaking, an adequate basis for a separate scientific discipline simply to show that the object of study is such as to warrant the type of research which is being proposed. One must be able to demonstrate that the object in question requires precisely the type of approach which systematic theology represents, *i.e.* that faith is such an entity as to make necessary a separate discipline of systematic theology. At this particular point, the problem—in practical terms—is this: Since faith is an expression of a subjective religious commitment, must not the investigation of faith in practice be a study of the personal dimension of religious experience, *i.e.* an aspect of the psychology of religion? [2]

According to Bring, this is the question the so-called theologians of experience—the wayward disciples of Schleiermacher—had difficulties answering. [3] In their view, the personal and subjective character of religious faith immediately placed it in the psychological field of interest, and since the psychology of religion could reasonably claim that all aspects of personal experience belong most appropriately to its domain, these theologians had little basis for arguing the case for a separate systematic theology. The case was open and shut; the psychological methods already available seemed entirely appropriate for the investigation of religious experience and since systematic theology could prove no particular justification for its own existence as a science, it could be dismissed as superfluous.

Ragnar Bring, also a disciple of Schleiermacher, found this a most unsatisfactory answer, however. In his view, the subjectivity of religious experience does not mean that faith is to be considered exclusively as a psychological entity; neither does it mean that only psychological methods are adequate to uncover the nature and meaning of faith. [4] The historical-empirical fact of faith includes material which

---

[1] *Ibid.*, pp. 231 f.

[2] *Ibid.*, p. 192.

[3] Cf. *ibid.*, pp. 29 f., also *ToR*, 1937, pp. 144 f.

[4] "The fact that theology, the science of faith, has faith as its object does not in any way mean that faith must be understood psychologically." *STU*, 1933, p. 63.

is significant quite apart from the psychological dimensions of religious experience. The psychological perspective represents, in fact, an illegitimate restriction on the study of faith. According to Bring, it was not Schleiermacher's primary intention to promote a narrow psychological perspective on faith. His was a broader historical-empirical perspective. His methodology did not focus on the nature of the experience of faith, but on the nature of the faith itself. This is an important distinction as far as theological methodology is concerned.

The contrast between the psychological and the systematic concepts of the theological object of study is illustrated by Bring in reference to the discussions between Gustaf Aulén and Arvid Runestam.[1] Aulén is concerned to establish the historical study of religious dogma (*dogmhistoria*, history of doctrine) in methodological distinction from the psychological investigation of personal religion (*individual-psykologi*, personal psychology). For this reason he defines the theologian's object of study as "faith propositions in abstraction from their subjects." [2] Scientific systematic theology is, of course, different from the history of doctrine in purpose and procedures, but the concept of the object of study is basically the same. The direct confrontation between Runestam's *trosvetenskap* (science of faith) and Aulén's *motivhistoria* (motif history) is therefore instructive to Bring at this point.[3]

Runestam insists on distinguishing between doctrine and *åskådning* (literally outlook, or attitude). Attitudes lie much deeper in life than do teachings; perception is more basic than concepts. In seeking to understand religious propositions, therefore, one will need an eye for the attitudes of the perceiving and articulating person. In fact, religious propositions abstracted from the subject formulating them are not understandable.[4] Aulén, on his side, does not in any way negate the psychological aspects of religious experience or reject the

---

[1] Cf. *ibid.*, pp. 186 ff. Bring refers to the sharp exchange between Aulén and Runestam, *STK*, 1 and 2, 1925 and 1926, over the object of theology. Aulén defines the issue in terms of "theocentric faith" vs. "the believer".

[2] *STU*, 1933, p. 188; cf. *DhL*, 1929, p. 15, note.

[3] Lindroth, *Lutherrenässansen...*, 1941, describes Runestam's method as "subjective-psychological", while Aulén's approach is "*saklig-teologisk*" (*saklig* meaning matter-of-fact, objective). Cf. Runestam's definition of *trosvetenskapen* as "understanding psychology applied to a God-believing subject." *STK*, 2, 1926, p. 93.

[4] Cf. Runestam, "Troskunskap och vetenskap," *STK*, 2, 1926, pp. 90-98; "Dogmhistoriens object," *STK*, 4, 1928, pp. 276-386.

theoretical values of psychological research.[1] However, as he understands it, theological research is "in principle something else" than psychology of religion. There is a basic distinction between "faith as a psychological or sociological phenomenon" and "faith as the object of theology".[2] Theology approaches faith in the form of a religious type or individuality, not in the form of personal religious consciousness in individuals. Thus, while the object of psychology is the human being, the object of theology is faith.[3]

As Aulén—and Bring—sees it, the approach that Runestam suggests represents a serious methodological blunder, a twofold one. To begin with, this theology seems to assume that the way to gain recognition as a scientific discipline is to make no claims to having a particular theological method at all; theology simply applies the general psychological methods to its peculiar object of study, the religious person. Thus, systematic theology is given up; it is replaced by psychology. That is the first flaw. The second follows closely after: Since the reference to a peculiar object of study is the only basis for Runestam's argument in behalf of a separate psychology of religion, he will have to claim that the regular scientific methods—including general psychology—are unable to give insight into the meaning of religious experience, and that only those who are themselves involved in the experience which is studied will be able to

---

[1] Neither does Bring; cf. *STU*, 1933, pp. 180, 185, 189.

[2] Or as Aulén expresses it, "faith in the theological sense." *The Faith of the Christian Church*, 1960, pp. 20 f.

[3] Cf. *STU*, 1933, pp. 215 f., 220, 228 f. This formulation expresses in a nutshell the contrast between the Runestam-line and the Aulén-line in twentieth century Swedish theology. The Lundensian approach has clearly dominated the theological community. Runestam's method has been taken up, f. ex., by Harald Eklund, *Evangelisches und katholisches in Max Schelers Ethik*, UUÅ, 1932, Teologi 1, but the psychologistic emphases have appeared only as "something of an episode" in the instances where they have appeared at all. Cf. Lindroth, *op. cit.*, p. 106. Modified editions of the Runestam method are presented by Torsten Bohlin and Sigfrid von Engeström. Bohlin's dependence on experience-theology was professed, but he never considered personal faith as the epistemological presupposition for theology. His emphasis, rather, fell on the methodological importance of interpreting faith-propositions in conjunction with the experiential context within which they emerge. He applies this principle in *Gudstro och Kristustro hos Luther*, Stockholm: Diakonistyrelsen (1927), a work which is a direct antipode to Karl Holl's Luther studies, *Gesammelte Aufsätze zur Kirchengeschichte*, Bd. 1: *Luther*, Tübingen: Mohr, 1932. Von Engeström's position is somewhat closer to Lund; he attempts to defend the Lutheran concept of faith both against abstraction from human experience and against emotionist-psychologistic interpretations. Cf. his essay, "Tro och erfarenhet," *Ordet och tron*, 1931, pp. 82 ff.

understand its nature and meaning. But this means that the scientific approach to the psychology of religion is given up; it is replaced with a theological method which is clearly metaphysical and utterly unscientific.[1]

It is in order to avoid methodological traps of this nature that Bring follows Aulén's line and defines the object of study of systematic theology as "faith, objectively given", or "faith in abstraction from the believing subject." [2] What this means in practice is now clear: Systematic theology studies the objective, material manifestations of faith, *i.e.* the concrete expressions of a certain type of religion, as these become evident and available in documents of different kinds. All such documents are, of course, informed by personal attitudes and subjective commitments, and this must be taken into account as the theologian investigates, analyzes, and explicates their meaning. But this does not mean that the theologian uses the documents as sources for the study of the psychology of religious experience. His interest is in the faith, not in the believer. He investigates the various documents of faith, considering them as witnesses to different types of God-relationships or concepts of salvation, or as testimonies to the contrasting religious individualities that manifest themselves in the history of man's religion and in the experience of faithful men. For such investigations, psychological methods are entirely inadequate. Another discipline, specifically applicable to this kind of research, is necessary.

Thus Bring argues that the object of systematic theology is unique, that it is historically given, empirical in nature, and that it requires precisely the kind of investigations that scientific systematic theology proposes to undertake.

THE PURPOSE OF SYSTEMATIC THEOLOGY

There is a second element in the methodological rationale of scientific systematic theology which must be established if this discipline is to gain respectability as an independent and autonomous science: the definition of a distinctive purpose for research. The basic question,

---

[1] Cf. *supra*, pp. 134 ff. Bring finds these consequences illustrated in Lindroth, who attempts to bridge the chasm between "religious life" and "scientific investigation" by means of a certain "psychologically definable consciousness through which religion lets itself be known". This psychological consciousness can, of course, be investigated, but it does not represent more than a fraction of the real life of religion. Cf. *STU*, 1933, p. 107.

[2] *Ibid.*, pp. 186 f; *ToR*, 1937, p. 152.

of course, is whether the purposes of systematic theology are scientifically justifiable.

Once more we should note that Bring accepts the premise on which
the scrutiny of the sciences is based, namely that no discipline has
scientific justification if its purposes are in any sense metaphysical or
if they are duplicated by some other science. As we have seen, Bring
defines the theological "interest" with this in mind.[1] He explicitly
rejects the idea that the purpose of theology is to identify and define
the ultimate essence of religion.[2] It is obvious to him that if systematic
theology is to have the slightest possibility of gaining recognition
in the scientific community, it must be demonstrated in no uncertain
terms that the purposes it proposes to serve are within the capacities
of the scientific methods of research, and that no scientific discipline
already existing does the same thing or fulfills the same purposes
as systematic theology does. It is from this perspective Bring decides
that the purposes of theology must be defined in clear distinction from
both speculation and faith, and that the task of systematic theology
must be differentiated clearly from the interests of the historical-
descriptive and genetic-analytical disciplines of study.

We shall not need to repeat at this point how Bring goes about
distinguishing the purposes of systematic theology from those of
metaphysical speculation and faith. His approach to this part of the
problem is clear.[3] He has learned from Nygren the importance of
separating the theological interest from the interests of philosophy.
Nygren, of course, defined both these endeavors as scientific, but
he emphasized that scientific theology has to do with "particulars",
while philosophy is a "science of principles". As a "science of particulars", according to Bring, systematic theology must be cleansed of
all implication with metaphysical methodological presuppositions.
It is a theoretical, empirical, objective, non-evaluational and non-
normative discipline of study; and it must, for this reason, accept the
strict requirements which all responsible scientific disciplines are
obliged to fulfill. Specifically, this means that systematic theology
cannot serve the particular interests and purposes of faith. Bring is
consciously quite radical in this respect; he is, he says, a disciple of
the school of history of religion in these matters.[4] The theologian

---

[1] Cf. *supra*, pp. 107 f; 113 ff.
[2] Cf. *supra*, p. 91; 93 ff.
[3] Cf. *supra*, Ch. VI.
[4] "Teologi och religionsfilosofi," *STK*, 23, 1947, p. 62.

must, in pursuing his scientific purposes, definitively set himself apart from the faithful attitude of the believer. Faith and theology are categorically different. Theology is the science of faith, but it is not faith itself. The systematic theologian approaches his material in a detached and presuppositionless manner. His purpose is simply to investigate, to understand, and to elucidate the meaning of faith— *i.e.* the characteristic content and peculiar motif structure of the various types of faith.

The extent to which Bring separates the purposes of systematic theology from the particular interests of the religious commitment is perhaps best indicated by two specific prescriptions which he offers in support of the scientific objectivity of the discipline. The first has to do with the traditional correlation of systematic theology and certain ecclesiastical, denominational, or confessional concerns.[1] Such conceptions of the purposes of theology are much too narrow for Bring's scientific discipline. A systematic inquiry into the meaning of a certain type of faith can have no other purpose than to uncover the *motivsammanhang* that is typical of that faith itself. There are a great many secondary commitments, peculiarities and characteristics in evidence in the various sources which constitute the theological object of study; and the theologian is, of course, interested in observing these. But his primary task is to uncover the essential nature of the faith he studies. For this purpose he seeks to avoid peripheral matters, taking account of the material that has central reference to the basic motifs of the faith. But his scope must be inclusive. In the case of Christian systematic theology, specifically, the theologian cannot limit himself to a predefined selection of sources or to a few motif structures that are predetermined by reference to certain group concerns or party interests. The theologian's task is to uncover the essence and character of the Christian faith. His interest, therefore, must include all the historical-empirical material that has bearing on the question "What is the essence of Christianity?"[2]

The second of the prescriptions Bring offers in support of the scientific objectivity of systematic theology is more far-reaching yet.

---

[1] Bring refers, as an example, to John Cullberg, who defines the object of faith as "the confession". *STU*, 1933, p. 228, note 20.

[2] Cf. Aulén's emphasis on Christian symbolics, *i.e.* the "historical and statistical study" of confessional standpoints. In his view, systematic theology can never surrender "its right to evaluate any confessional documents, to determine whether and to what extent these express that which is genuinely Christian and not simply that which is peculiar to a certain section of Christendom." *Op. cit.* p. 15.

He points out that the discipline is not necessarily—or by definition—related to Christianity.[1] As a matter of fact, systematic theology is defined in very general terms as "motif-historical investigation of religious types." [2] There is nothing in the methodological framework of this discipline which limits its theoretical applicability to one faith or one religion; the scientific competence of systematic theology includes all motif-research whatever. The method is equally applicable to all other religions as to the Christian faith. Moreover, Bring makes clear that the interest in systematic theological study is not the exclusive prerogative of a specific group of scholars. The distinctive mark of this discipline is its purpose, not its performance. In Bring's words,

> "...every form of research into religion which does not stop at making historical or psychological observations but wants to understand the essential character of a concrete religious type must, in the last analysis, take the approach of systematic theology and is, in a sense, systematic theology." [3]

This goes for all branches of scholarship which focus on faith: history of religion, history of ideas, literary criticism, liturgics—all in equal measure. They all do systematic theology, whenever they approach the historical-empirical manifestations of faith in a scientific manner and for the purpose of "understanding the character of a certain religion, its type, its intentions—in other words, its essence." [4]

It may appear at this point that Bring is dangerously close to allowing systematic theology to be swallowed up by all the other disciplines that are concerned with religion. The consequences, however, could well be positive. He undertakes to broaden the basis of the discipline. This makes possible an integration of all the theological disciplines under one common purpose—the systematic interest. Systematic theology does not lose its identity by such a move; it establishes itself, instead, as the queen of the theological sciences. Each of these sciences deals with a specific facet of the historical-empirical material. Each one develops, in interaction with the general

---

[1] *ToR*, 1937, p. 174. Bring is apparently concerned to avoid the charge that systematic theology is so exclusive in its perspective that it has no place among the general disciplines of science. By arguing that the method applies to all sorts of religious material, Bring has not only strengthened the basis for the scientific recognition of motif-research; he has suggested that motif-research may serve as a tool for ecumenical dialogue and interfaith conversation as well.

[2] *STU*, 1933, pp. 116 f.

[3] *ToR*, 1937, p. 174.

[4] *Ibid.*

sciences, a method and a procedure that is appropriate to its material. Each one has a special and limited purpose, but every one contributes also to the fulfillment of an overriding purpose: the systematic theological understanding of the essential character and meaning of the faith. From this perspective, the traditional problem concerning the relationship of systematic theology and the historical, biblical, and psychological disciplines of study no longer appears insoluble. The critical approach to theological methodology has brought a solution within reach. In giving up its old life, systematic theology may, in fact, have found a new and better one.[1]

Returning to the question of the methodological autonomy of systematic theology, it is clear that Bring considers the first part of the problem solved. He has successfully demonstrated that the purpose and interest of the discipline can be defined in such a way as to be entirely appropriate for an empirical science. At this point, however, he must be able to show that the systematic purpose is distinctive, and that there is no duplication in the scientific community. The most immediate threat in this respect is, of course, historical-descriptive or historical-genetic research. Bring has given considerable emphasis to the historical givenness of the object of systematic theological study. He has stressed repeatedly that the historical manifestations of a certain faith contain the key to the understanding of its essential character and meaning, and that systematic theology for that reason must undertake an objective investigation, a critical analysis, and a theoretical illucidation of the central motifs which form the historical essence and the logical core of the religion in question. It is necessary now to demonstrate in what sense —if any—the systematic approach to

---

[1] One questions, however, whether the Lundensians have in fact been able to release this potential. Aulén is the only one among them who has attempted anything in the way of a full explication of the content and meaning of Christian faith affirmations. Cf. *The Faith of the Christian Church*, 1960. Neither Nygren nor Bring have done so. Nygren has produced a significant example of the application of the systematic-historical procedures, *Agape and Eros*, 1930-36. Bring has been engaged in more narrow endeavors of Luther-research; cf. Bibliography, below. The most important books from their pens during the second half of their academic careers have been their biblical-theological commentaries; cf. Nygren, *Commentary on Romans*, Amer. ed., 1949; Bring, *Commentary on Galatians*, Amer. ed., 1961. The reasons behind these developments must be found in the Lundensian conception of the task of systematic theology; it is difficult to ignore Wingren's comment that "a systematic theology which can consider its task fulfilled simply through the reproduction of what, for example, Luther once thought and said," cf. *supra*, p. 136, note 2, is missing an essential part of its potential significance. We shall return to this matter below; cf. Ch. IX.

the historical material differs from the description of historical facts and the analysis of historical-genetic interconnections.

Bring does so, on the most elementary level, by pointing out that systematic theology is not, strictly speaking, a historical discipline. It studies an object which is historically given, but its purpose is not simply historical. It does not merely intend to describe Christianity, to explain its historical development, or to research the genealogy of its peculiar consciousness, commitments, and concepts. Its aim, rather, is to identify, analyze, and explicate in as precise a language as possible

> "...what the various religions in the last analysis want, to what basic value judgments each individual religion goes back, and above all (in our case) what is the central intension of Christianity, what is its innermost meaning—or, as one usually says, its essence." [1]

Once more we observe how important the concept of "essence" is in Lundensian methodology. Cleansed of its metaphysical connotations, and referring to the central motifs of the various historical types of religion—their characteristic element, their organic center, their unifying idea—it serves, in a way, as the cornerstone of the methodological structure.[2] It supports the claim that a discipline can at the same time be scientific and concerned with genuine Christianity; it is the foundation also for the claim that systematic theology is not made obsolete by the historical sciences describing religious events or studying the genetic origins, the causal connections, or the logical interaction of religious types.

Systematic theology, then, is the study of the essence of historical faith; it is motif-research. Defined in this manner, the discipline obviously has two foci, both of which are important in shaping its nature: It has a historical focal point, and it has a systematic one.[3] It is precisely this interaction of historical and systematic interests which is the basis for Bring's attempt at providing a justification for the methodological autonomy of systematic theology.[4] In the past,

---

[1] *ToR*, 1937, p. 161.

[2] Cf. *STU*, 1933, pp. 174, 197, 207, 220, 229, 230.

[3] Bring acknowledges the influence of Billing in this connection; *ibid.*, pp. 110, 232 f.

[4] Billing was interested, not in the historical origin of ethical or religious types, but in their character and the inner unity of their content—what for want of a better word he called the *"logiska sammanhanget"* (logical connection). Bring prefers Nygren's term *"motivsammanhang"*, but proposes also the formulation *"det systematiska sammanhanget"* (the systematic connection). *Ibid.*

these two foci have often fallen apart in theology. Historical theology and systematic theology have, as it were, formed separate circles, the first taking the form of a descriptive summary of the various ways in which the essential meaning of Christianity has been explicated in different periods and by representative theologians, the second being a constructive presentation of a particular interpretation of Christian faith as seen from the standpoint of an individual theologian, a group, or a tradition.[1] Obviously, such a bifurcation of the historical and the systematic interests is bound to have unhealthy consequences not only for theology as a whole, but for the two separate disciplines involved as well. To guard against this, Bring has actually gone so far as to argue that a scientific approach to theology requires a close correlation of the historical and the systematic perspectives.[2] A historical study of Christian faith which has no systematic purpose whatever is meaningless from a scientific point of view; and a system of doctrine that has no reference to historical Christian faith is without value from a theological point of view.

We have come to what is in several ways the crucial point in Bring's discussions of the purposes of systematic theology. He throws light—at least by implication—on how the discipline is supposed to function; but he reveals at the same time what is, in fact, a rather limited and somewhat unimaginative conception of the nature and task of scientific systematic theology. For that reason we shall need to look a little deeper into Bring's thought at this point.

Bring indicates in one context that in Luther-research, for instance, the historical and the systematic purposes must of necessity interact and supplement one another.[3] One will not be able to understand Luther's theology simply by investigating his utterances in the context of his life story—his personal background, his historical situation, and his reformatory ambitions. Except there is also a systematic interest at work, aiming to identify the essential characteristics of his thought and the unifying motifs within his conception of Christianity, the

---

[1] Bernhard Erling, *Nature and History*, 1960, is informed by this perspective, even while describing the Lundensian methodology. He distinguishes historical and systematic theology in terms of "intent": "In historical theology the intent is to describe a theological position belonging either to the past or to the present. In systematic theology the intent is to formulate a theological position." *Ibid.*, p. 7. Erling's conception corresponds to the classical understanding of the two disciplines, but it is not Lundensian. Neither Nygren nor Bring would say, as Erling does, that "systematic theology has...a kerygmatic function." *Ibid.*, p. 272.

[2] Cf., f. ex., "Systematisk och historisk Lutherforskning," *STK*, 7, 1931, p. 32.

[3] *Ibid.*, p. 31.

many different aspects of his theology will seem utterly confusing and the scholar will, in fact, miss the genius of the Lutheran type of faith. The reverse correlation is equally true. What is needed in Luther-research, according to Bring, is a combination of the peculiar sensitivity of the systematic theologian regarding the central core of Christian theology and the conscientiousness of the historian in regard to historical accuracy.[1]

Bring argues, then, that in order to be truly historical in matters of religion and faith, one must also be systematic. The historical study of religious materials presupposes a systematic grasp of the deeper motifs of faith to which the various thoughts and expressions witness and in reference to which the material is found to have a unified and consistent meaning. It demands an extensive analysis of the conscious and concrete commitments involved, and of the unquestioned dogmatic positions, the unthought and unrecognized assumptions, as well as the many tacit personal factors which combine to give shape and character to a certain conception or faith.[2] For this reason, says Bring, the scientific investigation of the historical Christian faith,

> "...(which) aims at presenting the content of the Christian faith as it is formed in confrontation with other religious views in its time and situation,...must be systematic. The historical and the systematic perspectives are not opposites when it comes to the study of religious ideas; they presuppose one another." [3]

It is not only so that the historical perspective needs to be supplemented with the systematic approach, however. Bring turns the point

---

[1] *Ibid.*, p. 51. There are certain indications, however, that Bring's emphasis falls heavier on systematic ability than on historical exactness. F. ex., he prefers Gustaf Ljunggren's *Synd och skuld i Luther's teologi*, 1928, to Niels Nöjgaard's *Om Begrepet Synd hos Luther*, Köbenhavn: Gad, 1929, on the grounds that Ljunggren has a "shining ability" to penetrate Luther's thought and get at his central commitments; his use of the sources, compared to Nöjgaard's, is nevertheless described as "careless". In his own study of Luther, Bring can defend setting aside the basic terminological problems relating to Luther's early period, while concentrating on "purely systematic" considerations on the basis of the later sources. Cf. *DhL*, 1929, p. 28. In his discussions of the controversy between Luther and Erasmus on the freedom of the will, *Kristendomstolkningar i gammal och ny tid (KrT)*, 1950, pp. 170-282, Bring's systematic abilities have clearly dominated his research; he bases his interpretation of the controversy on Luther's response to Erasmus, *The Bondage of the Will*, and on secondary sources, not bothering to analyze Erasmus' own presentation of the issue, the *Diatribe*. On Bring's own premises, such practices cannot result in good systematic theology or good historical theology.

[2] Cf. *ToR*, 1937, pp. 206 f.

[3] *Ibid.*, p. 207.

around, arguing that when systematic theology truly becomes scientific, it is at the same time "purely historical."[1] This statement must of course be understood against the background of Bring's conception of the theological object of study and the purposes of systematic theology. The discipline is defined as the scientific investigation of the essence and character of historical faith; it is motif-research. The motifs that constitute the center and core of the various types of faith are objectively given within the many-faceted historical material in which faith manifests itself. This means that systematic theology must direct itself toward these given historical realities; its function is none other than the investigation of religious documents, the analysis of their essential character, and the identification of the different commitmental cores that give shape and meaning to individual types of faith. Strictly speaking, systematic theology is nothing else than a historical study of the shape and meaning of religious ideas. This is the reason Bring finds it difficult to explain the difference between systematic theology and idea-historical research.[2]

One should note that Bring does manage to make a delineation of the difference between the systematic approach to historical faith and the historical-genetic study of interconnecting religious ideas. The historical-genetic analysis of religious concepts consists, in the main, in determining possible causal relationships between religious ideas that emerge in different contexts, or between religious ideas and the cultural, social, and political situation. The systematic purposes are not served by such investigations. Systematic theology must ask about the essential nature and the characteristic motifs of each individual type of religion; the historical-genetic perspective does not include such questions. It concerns itself, instead, with notional roots and ideological developments, with the evolution of religious concepts and the cross fertilization of cultures and thoughtforms and traditions of faith. It analyzes certain religious materials in order to explain their ideational background and determine their subsequent influence on other, similar materials. Followed to its ultimate consequences, historical-genetic research would continue to pursue causes and effects along the lines of the historical interconnections of ideas, step by step, backwards and forwards, *ad infinitum*.[3] In Bring's view, although the resulting insights may be interesting, this approach

---

[1] *DhL*, 1929, pp. 26 f.
[2] Cf. *STU*, 1933, pp. 114 f.
[3] *Ibid.*, p. 194.

to faith is entirely inadequate as a means of understanding the authentic shape and genuine meaning of individual religious types. The Christian theologian not only needs to ask where the various elements of Christian faith came from, and how far have they influenced other religions and ideologies; he must approach Christianity as an entity by itself and ask what it is that sets it apart, what is the sterling quality of its character—the essentially and genuinely Christian.[1]

Thus, systematic theology can be clearly distinguished from historical-genetic research. The difference between scientific systematic theology and the history of ideas, on the other hand, is more elusive to Bring's mind. He has, in fact, made the correlation between the systematic and the historical purposes so close that he is forced to acknowledge that in this case there might actually be a duplication of interests. Systematic theology is primarily interested, not in showing that such and such religious ideas exist in certain select and representative faith propositions, but in analyzing their *motiv-sammanhang*: "the internal unity which because of their own content evidently exists between them and by which they appear as parts of the same basic conception."[2] But this is precisely the area in which the history of ideas also operates. Even from the idea-historical perspective, Christian ideas can only be understood fully by way of a penetrating study of the deep-running principles of organic unity that connect these ideas like a central nervous system branching out from a single point. In short, as Bring says, whether there is

> "...any principal distinction between systematic theology and the history of ideas in respect to motiv-research, we cannot say. There does not seem to be anything new in the presentation of genuine Christian faith as introduced by systematic theology."[3]

Surprising as this statement is, it is not inconsistent with the general thrust of Bring's interpretation of the purpose of scientific systematic theology. We have observed how the methodology itself is oriented on "the historical perspective".[4] Fundamental to the Lundensian method, also, is the concept of "essence", and particularly the emphasis on "the characteristic", "the typical", "the central motif", the *grundmotiv*.[5] Combine these methodological elements, and the result will be a historical discipline of study with a rather narrowly

---

[1] *Ibid.*, p. 211.
[2] *Ibid.*, p. 114, quoted from Billing.
[3] *Ibid.*
[4] Cf. *supra*, pp. 93, 114.
[5] Cf. *supra*, pp. 95 f., 107 f.

focused perspective and interest. The systematic element is, of course, important to the general make-up of the discipline, but it is no more so than the corresponding feature in the methodological make-up of a discipline such as the history of ideas. Bring has attempted to avoid the dissolution of systematic theology and the subsequent distribution of its task among the general sciences of religion, but he has not managed to chisel out a distinct and separate niche for the discipline. Its methodological autonomy is not secured. Bring, in fact, defines the discipline in such a way that its place in the scientific edifice appears to be obtained only through the good services of a close relative.

Bring had not intended it this way. What is more, the situation is not unavoidable. There are several things one can do in order to fulfill Bring's intentions and establish the methodological autonomy of systematic theology,[1] but one shall have to approach the definition of the purpose of the discipline with considerably more imagination and courage than Bring has shown. For one thing, the interest in "essential" or "characteristic" motifs must be extended to include not only the central core of faith, but the full spectrum of faith-reflective symbolism. Systematic theology cannot afford to concentrate solely on the principle of unity which connects the various faith propositions that are considered representative of a certain religious type. It must assume the task of analyzing all the facets of religious experience and faith reflection through which the fuller motif structure of a certain type of faith reveals itself and in which the entire shape of this religion becomes evident. It must take an interest, so to speak, in the full "system" of meaning by which a certain religious type is constituted. Idea-historical research does not do that. The other, more "special" theological disciplines do not either. There is need for

---

[1] Bernhard Erling's proposal, *Nature and History*, 1960, pp. 20 f., is not particularly helpful, however. In reacting to the "positivism" of recent Lundensian theology, apparent in "the uncritical acceptance of the method of the history of ideas," he suggests that motif-research offer itself as a "presupposition" for the history of ideas. Obviously, the history of ideas needs a "principle of selection" by which to choose the thought patterns to be studied. Motif-research could "supplement" the history of ideas here; its function would be to define "the relevant alternately possible ideational structures to be found in the realms of religious and ethical experience." *Ibid.*, p. 22. This approach does not provide what Lund needs; it does not guard the independent value of motif-research and the scientific systematic theology built on it. It simply suggests that motif-research function as one factor in the methodological framework of the history of ideas. Systematic theology is thereby reduced to a minor auxiliary of another antonomous scientific discipline.

a scientific discipline that will seek an integrated understanding of all the elements that combine to make up a certain type of faith. This discipline does not analyze religious types simply for the purpose of identifying, formulating, and illucidating the motif or motifs considered "typical" of each type; it considers each religion a complete personality whose individuality—appearance, thoughts, and actions—an entire motif-spectrum contributes to form and shape. Defined this way, systematic theology is not bound to the scientific routine of researching basic religious motifs; it has a much more exciting task on its hands. It utilizes the results of all of the motif-research that goes on in the different disciplines studying religion, creating a truly historical, scientific and objective portrait of the full content and meaning of each individual type of faith. This is its distinctive purpose. It is not simply motif-research; its primary task is motif-integration.

We shall need to return to this matter again.[1] In the meantime there is another facet of Bring's methodology that demands our attention. Bring has argued that systematic theology, because of its unique object of study and its distinctive purpose for research, qualifies for an autonomous place on the roster of scientific disciplines. He has managed to avoid the main methodological traps that threaten to put an end to any aspirant for scientific recognition—a metaphysical object of study, and an unjustifiable purpose for research. He is ready now to present the third link of his argument in support of the scientific status of his discipline, namely a demonstration of the claim that the procedures of systematic-theological research are purely scientific and entirely appropriate to the purposes and the object of theology. To complete the picture of Bring's theological methodology, we shall want to accompany him on this last leg of the journey, also.

---

[1] Cf. below, Ch. IX.

CHAPTER EIGHT

THEOLOGICAL PROCEDURES

Characteristically, the theological method of motif-research does not present itself before the scientific community in the form of a practical program for research or a handbook of procedural prescriptions. This methodology is more concerned with what theology is and does than with the "how" of doing it.

One reason for this lies deep within the presuppositions of the method itself. Ragnar Bring defines Christian systematic theology as "a concrete *spesialvetenskap* (special in object, scientific in approach) whose task it is to investigate an empirical material, namely the historically given Christian religion." [1] With the claim to scientific autonomy based primarily on the demonstration of a unique object of study and a distinctive purpose for research, the systematic theologian does not need to develop an entirely new and different set of procedures. As a matter of fact, theology strengthens its candidacy for scientific recognition if it takes over the general research procedures already being followed by the scientific community, simply adjusting them to the specific nature of its object and applying them to the particular purposes of its investigations.

Another reason might be hidden in the fact that systematic theology, as we have already observed, is conceived by the Lundensians as a theoretical exercise very similar to the history of ideas. [2] One may assume, therefore, that the procedures that apply in idea-historical research are also appropriate for the systematic-historical investigation of faith propositions; and if these procedures are acceptable from a scientific point of view, so will scientific motif-research be. Thus there appears to be little need for a basic consideration of scientific procedures except as one will specify their implications for systematic theology.

Bring is working throughout on the assumption that the methodology and procedures of the history of ideas are well known and generally accepted. Also, he refers to Nygren's descriptions of the modus operandi of motif research, suggesting that the basic principles on which the systematic theologian may pattern his studies are laid

---

[1] *ToR*, 1937, p. 160.
[2] Cf. *supra*, pp. 171 ff.

down there. For his own part, Bring does not give extensive attention to the procedural fundamentals.[1] However, in various contexts one may find important procedural observations, mostly practical suggestions regarding the systematic approach to religious materials, all of which give significant light to the understanding of the discipline's work. We shall focus here on five such observations and suggestions —points that seem particularly valuable in the sense that they not only contribute to our grasp of the procedures of motif-research but shed light also on the nature of scientific systematic theology itself.

THE STRUCTURAL ANALYSIS

The most elementary point in Bring's discussions of the systematic-theological approach to historical documents that witness to faith is his emphasis on the so-called "structural analysis"[2] or, as he also calls it, "the analysis of *frågeställningar*".[3] These references to "analysis" represent the third context in which Bring speaks of an analytical task. We have already observed the other two: The first, the responsibility of critical epistomology, consists of a three-fold analysis, the "analysis of experience", the "analysis of presuppositions", and "the analysis of the total framework of meaning".[4] The second, primarily the task of analytical philosophy, is defined as a "logical" or "conceptual analysis". It has reference to the need for a clear conception of the peculiar dialectic at work within the various areas of meaning, and it is the means by which to avoid the confusion of categories and the misunderstanding of language functions.[5] The third analytical task, this one assigned to the systematic theologian, takes the form of a close scrutiny of the internal structure of religious utterances. It is an attempt "to understand all concepts, thoughtforms, and...sayings in their own proper context and (according to their own) concrete intentions."[6]

---

[1] In general, the younger Lundensians have not given as much thought to the practical aspects of motif-research as Nygren has wanted. The reason might be that procedural questions are usually very complicated and only a little interesting. It might also be that motif-research, as one has come to know it, has tended to say more about the dangers of the endeavor than about the value of the method. In any case, there is a great deal of work to be done at this end of the Lundensian methodology.

[2] *STU*, 1933, p. 231.

[3] *ToR*, 1937, p. 176.

[4] Cf. *supra*, pp. 84, 88.

[5] Cf. *supra*, pp. 89 f.

[6] "Teologi och religionsfilosofi," *STK*, 23, 1947, p. 67.

Bring's terminology may appear somewhat confusing at this point, especially in view of the fact that Nygren uses "conceptual analysis" in the same sense as Bring uses "analysis of experience". [1] The picture becomes even more complex when one observes that contemporary linguistic analysts use descriptions like "logical" or "conceptual analysis" in connection with endeavors that are similar to Bring's "structural analysis". It is clear, however, that regardless of the terminological discrepancies involved there is in Bring's references to various analytical tasks—the epistemological, the philosophical, and the theological—an indication of a three-dimensional framework of understanding which is in general agreement with the modern approach to the theory of meaning. Bring has never sought an open attachment to the ongoing discussion of this problem. In this respect one may speak of a certain timidity—if not provincialism—in his work. But the possibilities for serious dialogue with the contemporary theorists of mind and meaning are there. Bring's empirical perspective should make it natural for him to pursue those possibilities.

It is clear that while Bring distinguishes between epistemological, philosophical, and theological dimensions of analysis, he sees a considerable amount of interaction between them, also. This is perhaps especially true in the relationship between the theological analysis and the philosophical analysis. Naturally, both of these are ultimately dependent upon the results of the epistemological analysis; but there is also a direct relationship between them. They are so close, in fact, that the main difference between conceptual analysis and structural analysis is simply in the degree of specificity. The philosopher concerns himself with the general delimitation of the various areas of meaning, the religious area included. He attempts to identify and define the logical presuppositions upon which the different *meningssammanhang* are based and in view of which they must be understood. The theologian is concerned with specific cases. He has before him a series of concrete documents containing a number of religious utterances. In analyzing this material, he must be informed by the insights of philosophical analysis, so that he does not approach his material on the wrong premises or apply the presuppositions of meaningfulness that are appropriate in one area of meaning to statements that belong to another; but his interests are specific and concrete.

According to Bring, there are two distinct areas in which the

---

[1] Cf. *supra*, p. 56.

structural analysis contributes to strengthening the scientific approach
to systematic theology: In the first place, in regard to the material
to be studied, it undertakes to clarify the specific intentions which
inform the utterances in question; in the second place, in regard
to the scholar himself, it seeks to identify the various factors that
influence his approach to the material. Both of these are important
to the scientific objectivity of the discipline; they form a significant
defense against the main enemies of true scholarship: superficiality
and confusion in regard to the object of study, bias and prejudice
in regard to the theologian himself.

The way in which the structural analysis undertakes these functions
is outlined by Bring only in rough sketches, but the principal aims
of the procedure are clear. Focusing on the theological object of study
for the moment, it is obvious that certain preliminary examinations
are needed prior to the detailed investigations by which the systematic
theologian seeks to uncover the essential, underlying motifs in which
he is primarily interested: First, a particular document may not be
a homogeneous unit; there may be several different intentions behind
its various statements, some of which are central, others peripheral.
Second, there may be a logical discrepancy between the form of its
language and the category of meaning to which it refers; religious
terminology is often used in theoretical contexts, and concrete
language often serve symbolic functions. Third, the propositional
utterances may clash among themselves; a superficial consideration
of religious materials often comes up with little more than paradoxes.
For these and other reasons, Bring says, it is absolutely necessary,
even at the start of the systematic investigation of a certain document
of faith, to ask what categorical question this material intends to
answer.[1]

Structural analysis is not simply concerned with identifying the
area of meaning to which the statements in question properly belong,
of course. One must examine each aspect of the propositional content
in order to unveil any multiplicity of *meningssammanhang*, any evidence
of confusion or categorical transgression, any shift in intention or
meaning of language. Within one and the same document, there
may be propositions of theoretical, aesthetic, ethical, and religious
significance. It would be disastrous for the systematic theologian
if he were to ignore these internal equivocations in the statements

---

[1] *STU*, 1933, pp. 199 ff.

that he considers on the assumption that a document which is relevant to his object of study is *eo ipso* a purely religious document. Religious meaning, particularly in ancient documents, is often hidden among propositions serving a variety of functions. The systematic theologian must, therefore, be on guard constantly, analyzing the problematics within which the document is set, the concerns to which it addresses itself, and the intentions behind each aspect of the material. Only this way will he be able to identify which of the implications that may be drawn are justified and which are illegitimate. In short, the structural analysis must be undertaken in order to make sure that a document of faith is understood within its own framework of meaning and on the basis of its own intentions.

The second task of structural analysis, that having to do with the systematic theologian himself, is equally essential to the discipline—although not so generally recognized as the first. A presupposition-less attitude to a given object of study is not a natural quality; it must be attained. There are several factors that combine to make it hard to achieve—some personal, some cultural—and these must be identified, understood, and taken into account as the systematic theologian does his work. The personal factors are, of course, closely related to the cultural ones. The particular mindset which character-izes contemporary culture tends to form the implicit presuppositions for a scholar's approach, his point of view, his way of asking questions, and his appraisal of results.[1] In the present discussion of Christianity, for instance, it is often assumed that everyone involved knows exactly what Christianity is. Central Christian concepts such as "faith", "salvation", or "eternal life" are frequently discussed as if it were a matter of accepting or rejecting a well known entity. The fact is that the parties to the discussion often approach these concepts from entirely different perspectives, and so they do not really deny or affirm the same things.[2] Structural analysis must be scrupulous in its critique of any unquestioned assumptions that tend to bias the scholar as he attempts to understand the content and meaning of the religious material.

Another aspect of the scholar's attitude which structural analysis

---

[1] One example is the general progressivistic assumption that our modern conception of things is more "advanced" than the primitive attitude informing traditional Christian concepts. Structural analysis, in Bring's view, would reveal the naiveté of such unquestioned generalizations. Cf. "Det tidsbestämda och det evigt giltiga i Bibelns ord och bud," *STK*, 35, 1959, p. 23.

[2] "Teologi och religionsfilosofi," *STK*, 23, 1947, p. 67, note 1.

must keep a close watch on has to do with the tendency to shorten
the historical investigation and move too quickly to the contemporary
reformulation of the meaning of faith. Bring is, of course, fully aware
of the double responsibility of the systematic theologian: the investigation of historical faith, and the contemporary conceptualization of
its meaning.[1] It is fully legitimate—in fact, obligatory—for the theologian to ask what is the significance and relevance of the Christian
faith in the cultural, social, political, and economic situation at the
present but this question cannot be answered until the historical-
systematic task has been undertaken in a scientifically responsible
manner and is beginning to bear fruit.[2] To rush into answering the
questions concerning the contemporary or existential meaning of
faith without the thorough preparation which the historical study
provides is to lay the faith open to all sorts of misunderstanding,
misrepresentation, and misinterpretation. One may, for example,
attempt to avoid the intellectual difficulties that are connected with
certain traditional religious concepts by taking as a starting point
some idea that seems reasonable and valuable from a modern point
of view and then proceed to read these notions back into the historical
symbols of faith. By such procedures, the historical faith is easily torn
loose from its own context of meaning and forced into conformity
with the presuppositions of modern rationality.[3] The purpose, of
course, is to make faith intellectually respectable; but the method is
not intellectually responsible. It may, in fact, be intellectually dishonest,[4] and structural analysis is there to expose it.

---

[1] See f. ex. "De kristna tankarnas sanningsvärde i olika kultursituationer,"
STK, 16, 1940, pp. 39 ff; "Det tidbestämda och det eviga...," *STK*, 35, 1959.
Bring refers to Schleiermacher, showing that he did not conceive of the theological
task merely in terms of recording what Christianity is; he also faced the question
how Christianity could be formulated so as to become a cultural force in the
contemporary setting.

[2] Bring urges theology, in fact, to abstain from the immediate concerns over
relevancy in order to give its full attention to the objective, scientific analysis of
the essential intentions of historical Christianity. His reasons for stressing the
systematic-historical task are simple: There is still much work to be done, and
theology has only begun to get at the meaning and intentions of the Christian
message. Some questions are, perhaps, answered; and where the answers seem
adequate the move to contemporary conceptualization and application is legitimate. But in other cases (for example, the virgin birth), theologians are not yet certain of the original intentions behind the biblical or doctrinal symbolism, and here
the modern reformulation of the meaning of the symbols must wait. "De kristna
tankarnas sanningsvärde...." *STK*, 16, 1940, p. 41.

[3] "Teologi och religionsfilosofi," *STK*, 23, 1947, pp. 62 f.

[4] "De kristna tankarnas sanningsvärde...," *STK*, 16, 1940, pp. 43 ff. There is,

Focus on the Central

A second procedural observation that keeps recurring in Bring's descriptions of the historical-systematic study of faith is closely related to the emphasis—so central to the Lundensian methodological framework—on the significance of seeking the essential and characteristic motifs of faith. In practice, the systematic theologian is urged to focus on the central, and this rule is given explixit application to both the selection of sources and the actual investigation of them.

We have noted that Bring defines the purpose of systematic theology as the discovery of the essential or intentional core of the several types of historical faith.[1] The essence of faith is historically given; it lies deep within the historical-empirical material in which the various types of religion become manifest in the world. Systematic theology, as a scientific discipline of study, approaches this material by way of historical-analytical and historical-critical methods in order to identify and understand and elucidate the basic motifs which form the organic center of the various types of faith.

In approaching the historical-empirical material, however, the systematic theologian is faced with a practical problem: the massive multiplicity of the documents that witness to faith. It is obvious that the scientific investigation cannot encompass everything—not even all the material that gives expression to one specific type of faith. The many experiences, events, interpretations, confessions, and explications—the countless statements, propositions, and concepts—will have to be sorted out and reduced to a manageable object of study; and for this purpose the theologian must have a principle of selection. Moreover, when his field of study is properly delimited and he has chosen the sources which are representative of the object of his interest, the systematic theologian is in need of a definite aim to guide his approach to the material. In other words, the systematic theologian must have both a clearly defined scope and a clearly formulated focus: The first has to do with selecting his documents and delimiting a

---

says Bring, an inevitable tension between what seems reasonable in the present cultural setting and what, for example, the Bible considers meaningful. For this reason, it is of prime importance to understand what lies behind the biblical concepts before attempting to relate their content to present ways of thinking. Any other procedure would be intellectually dishonest; what is commonly called "intellectual honesty" is often just an uncritical acceptance of the metaphysical commitments of a contemporary cultural orientation.

[1] Cf. *supra*, pp. 169 ff.

field of study which he can reasonably hope to cover; the second has
to do with the formulation of a tangible target for the investigations
that are undertaken. In both contexts, Bring's advice is to focus on
the central.

There is nothing extraordinarily hazardous, from a scientific
point of view, in making a selection among the many historical
faith propositions and bringing together some that are considered
representative. Most scientific research follows similar procedures;
it is a question of making a discriminating choice of relevant evidence.
A good scientist proves himself by a wise choice of material; a bad
scholar is one whose scope is locked on the peripheral or the circumstantial. But a choice has to be made. In Bring's view, the good systematic theologian will select primarily material that contains a consistent explication of the content of the faith.[1] The more strongly a
document is dominated by motifs that are central to the faith, the more
it lends itself as an object for systematic theological investigations.
The best sources available are those that contain a full and clear
exposition of the basic ideas or formative concepts within the faith;
and in as much as the various types of faith receive a particularly full
and clear expression in the works of certain men, and at various
junctions in history, these men's works and documents from these
specific periods are of particular significance to the theologian.

One should note, at this point, that the criteria by which the
various faith propositions are judged to be central and representative,
or peripheral and irrelevant, are considered given within the historical material itself. The theologian does not first define the central
motifs and then go to the historical material to look for the clearest
expositions of them. Such procedures would be completely unscientific.
The theologian would be developing a system of true doctrines in a
metaphysical manner, arbitrarily forcing the historical material into
conformity with it. Bring will have none of this. In his view, the norm
—if one must use such a term—by which one determines whether
or not the historical propositions of faith are essentially Christian is
only a provisional and tentative hypothesis, dependent upon subsequent verification in reference to the historical material. It is the
given motif-connections which are typical of historical Christianity
that are decisive to the Christian theologian.[2] These are the normative

---

[1] *STU*, 1933, p. 19.
[2] "Individual faith-concepts are tested by being analyzed in reference to the
center of the Christian faith. That which is connected with this center is accepted

principles. Only in so far as the theologian's hypotheses correspond to this norm are they valid. In practice, this means that their relativity —the relativity of all scientific hypotheses—must be explicitly acknowledged.

Bring's delimitation of the scope and perspective of systematic theological investigations is closely related to his definition of the focus of research. In fact, Bring's emphasis on the central—whether in perspective or purpose—comes down to one single point: the *grundmotiv*, serving as the organic core around which a certain type of faith is structured. Here is the key to theological understanding. The various conceptions of religion are not understandable apart from the nature and meaning of their *grundmotiv*. Only by reference to the *grundmotiv* which unites them can the many different concepts and propositions that express the meaning of a certain religion be held together and interpreted consistently, *i.e.* in terms of a single center of meaning. The *grundmotiv*, in a sense, is the very core of the meaning of a religious type. It lies deep within the many individual parts that together constitute the shape of a religion. It is because their *grundmotiv* is the same that all these different concepts and propositions can be seen to form an organic and meaningful unity. The core motif is also, of course, a concept. It is, in Bring's terms, "the organizing concept within a religious type, that which so to speak takes the others in its service, or which the others intend to explicate." [1] With the importance of the *grundmotiv* stated this way, it is clear that the systematic theologian must direct his research to

---

as Christian. The 'normative' character of dogmatics, if one will use such a term, does not mean that it defines what must be believed or what is a true and right conception of the God-relationship, but that it presents systematically what is typically Christian...." *Ibid.*, pp. 229 f. Bring's formulation is rather interesting in a subsidiary way; he does not often talk of "dogmatics", and he does not usually describe the "presentation" of what is typically Christian as "systematic". We have here a reference—albeit very minor—to a task of systematic theological construction and integration which is otherwise largely absent from Bring's methodology. Cf. *supra*, pp. 166 f., 169 ff., 172-174.

[1] *STU*, 1933, p. 229. A terminological problem arises in connection with the Swedish word *åskådning*. Its primary English correlatives are "view," "way of thinking", "conception"; it refers to a total conception or a type of orientation, such as a religious *åskådning*. Individual concepts, or ideas that combine to make up an *åskådning*, are referred to as *föreställningar*. In the English context, "concept(s)" is probably the better rendition of both Swedish words, but where the context needs clarification, I find it useful to talk of *åskådning* as a "conception of religion" or "conception of ethics", etc., and of *föreställning(ar)* as "religious" or "ethical concept(s)". "Conception of religion" is also, here and there, rendered as a "type" or a "view" of religion.

the discovery and explication of such basic motifs. Says Bring,"...
when faith is considered as an organic unity, the direction of theology
toward its center is also given." [1]

If one should desire to know more specifically what kind of concept
is capable of serving as the organizing principle within a religious
type, one will find that Bring's answer is vague by design. He says:
"That which is decisive for the unity of the *åskådning* (religious
type) and makes it what it is, that which indicates the basic structure
within the whole, that is the *grundmotiv*." [2] It is, in a sense, the principal
religious commitment, that fundamental factor which determines
the type of God-relationship or religious consciousness which is
involved. It is the most elementary of all the concepts that enter
into the make-up of a religious type, that which serves as "the
answer to the categorical question of religion." [3]

Bring cannot be more specific than this, for several reasons:
In the first place, he is committed to the historical givenness of the
essence and center of religious meaning. The closer definition of its
content can only be sought by way of historical-systematic research,
motif-research. Any other approach would be metaphysical and
illegitimate. In the second place, Bring has consistently emphasized
that the categorical question is a pure and empty form; the formulation of it can only be given in a hypothetical, tentative, or preliminary
way. The *form* of religion is given *a priori*, but not its *content*. If it were,
theology would be able to deduce the answers from the categorical
question, and such a procedure would be clearly metaphysical—and
therefore illegitimate. Instead, according to Bring, theology locates
the answer in the historical material, and the question is left open
so that various formulations—all of them hypothetical—may be
tested.

In the practice of motif-research, then, the theologian is free to
decide for himself what is to be the particular angle from which to
approach the historical material and seek to identify the central
motifs within it. The formal categorical question to which the material
gives the answers can be formulated in a variety of ways, and as a
consequence the basic motifs which characterize the different types of
faith will vary in their formulation, also. In this sense—and only
in this sense—the form of the answer depends on the form of the

---

[1] *Ibid.*, p. 77.
[2] *Ibid.*, p. 229.
[3] *Ibid.*

question: The formulation of the religious question is at the option of the theologian, and the material will yield its answer in a corresponding frame of reference.

One way to approach the material and seek its central motif structure is to ask the categorical question in terms of the God-concept.[1] Another, closely related way is to investigate the historical material by asking for the basic nature of the God-relationship.[2] A third approach, one particularly useful in the attempt to understand the peculiar nature of Christian thought, is to ask the question of essence by reference to the character of the concept of faith.[3] Fourthly, one may investigate the material in search of the basic elements in the understanding of salvation.[4] Or again, one may simply ask what the material witnesses to as being the central concept in the confession of faith.[5] Any one of these options may be followed as a

---

[1] "Since the inner unity (within a conception of religion) is of an organic nature and the *åskådning* thus has a definite center, one can find within the God-concept that which is typical of a faith; the God-concept indicates the characteristics of a faith-*åskådning*." *Ibid.*, p. 221. Examples of motif-research from the perspective of the God-concept are Aulén's *Den kristna gudsbilden genom seklerna och i nutiden*, 1927; Nygren's *Agape and Eros*, 1930-36; and Bring's *DhL*, 1929.

[2] Cf. Nygren, *Filosofi och motivforskning*, 1940, pp. 80-81: "All real religion seeks to be God-relationship. This means that we cannot remain with a number of Christian motifs, but must press on to the basic motif. If Christianity were only a religious teaching, it would be possible to point to a number of its characteristic views and thought-motifs. It would then seem somewhat arbitrary if one of these views were distinguished from others and given the rank of a basic motif. The situation becomes altogether different when one thinks of Christianity as God-relationship. Then one must ask, 'Of what kind is the relationship which Christianity establishes between God and man?' The answer to this question will be the basic Christian motif."

[3] *STU*, 1933, p. 19. Cf. Aulén, *The Faith of the Christian Church*, 1960, p. 4: "The function of systematic theology is, therefore, to elucidate the content and meaning of the Christian faith by use of all available resources. The purpose of the study must continually be directed toward this one central point. The task is to unveil and reveal everything that is essential, to brush aside all non-essential and foreign elements, to remove all unnecessary accretions, and to bring out clearly the very heart of the matter.... By a critical analysis it must penetrate through the shifting forms to the unterlying and fundamental religious motifs and at the same time be continually mindful of that which is uniquely and essentially Christian." It is significant that Aulén's focus on faith, though directed toward the essential, includes "everything that is essential", *i.e.* the entire "system" of essential Christian faith.

[4] Bring seems to prefer this perspective; cf. *ToR*, 1937, pp. 199 f. It gives particular sharpness to the comparison of religious types; cf. below pp. 192 ff. Examples of motif-research under this symbol are his *FTG*, 1934, which focuses on Melanchton and post-Reformation Orthodoxy, and *KrT*, 1950, particulary two chapters dealing with the controversy between Luther and Erasmus.

[5] This is Aulén's approach in *Reformation och katolicitet*, 1959; here he sets con-

way of getting at the unique character of the fundamental motifs of the different historical types of religion. All these formulations focus on an elementary and determining factor in the religious experience of men. One need not argue for one specific approach and against the others. Instead, the theologian does well to change his approach from time to time, at one point confronting the material to analyze the essential nature of the God-concept, at another point asking for the basic shape of soteriology. Behind all the different formulations, however, the intention must always be the same: to uncover the central motifs of faith.

The Hypothetical 'Grundmotiv'

We must return, for a moment, to Bring's emphasis on the hypothetical nature of the theologian's work—of his presuppositions as well as his results. This constitutes an important aspect of his procedural observations, one designed to counter any suspicions as to the scientific objectivity of motif-research.

It is interesting, in this context, to observe that the term motif, or *grundmotiv*, is employed by Bring in two different ways: It stands, on the one hand, for the objectively given ideational core which constitutes the unifying principle within a certain type of religion; [1] and it serves, on the other hand, to describe the working hypothesis of the systematic theologian or the result of his research, so far as it is clear.[2] There is no inconsistency involved in these two uses of the term. The one is the presupposition of the other: The formulation of a hypothetical *grundmotiv* includes an implicit assumption of the appropriateness of doing so; but it signifies also that the objectively given basic motifs are not considered known *a priori*. Together these two considerations serve to guarantee that the theologian approaches the work of motif-research scientifically.

The systematic theologian setting out to investigate the essence of a certain conception of religion has no way of knowing in advance what this essence is. He may assume that he knows, and approach the material with a definite, preconceived idea, but this procedure is open to critique both on scientific and theological grounds. He may

---

fession and dogmas in contrast to one another and defines the *bestående* (the lasting, unchangeable) elements of Christianity as the kerygmatic confession of Christ, while the formulation of dogmas is a constantly changing, ever progressing endeavor. Cf. Bring's review, *STK*, 35, 1959, pp. 111 ff.

[1] *STU*, 1933, pp. 228 f.

[2] *ToR*, 1937, p. 127.

assume nothing, and confront the material simply as a reporter, but this is unacceptable from the point of view of the systematic-theological purposes. A scientific procedure in motif-research demands that a hypothesis be formulated by which one is guided in selecting the material and confronting its content. But the hypothesis is no more than that—at least not to begin with. As the investigation proceeds, the hypothesis is either strengthened or discredited by reference to the material. If the hypothesis is verified, it gains the status of a scientific theory; it has empirical proofs to back up its claims to validity. But proofs of validity are never final; the material is always stronger than the theory. The systematic theologian is not interested in defending his hypotheses or proving his theories; he remains open at all times to new insight, new truth, and the necessity for new hypotheses.[1]

Bring is eager to emphasize this point, especially in connection with the investigation of the essence of Christianity. The comparative study of religion has long followed such scientific practices regarding hypotheses and results. Christian systematic theology, however, has not been used to thinking of itself as an empirical science. But that is precisely what it is, says Bring:

> "...The affirmation of an idea as essential to Christianity can only mean that one approaches the matter empirically; one has, as always in such matters, to set up a working hypothesis.... This working hypothesis must subsequently be corrected or verified by the historically given material, *i.e.* by the history of Christian ideas; and the criterion of rightness must be whether it makes the meaning of the Christian witness to faith and the Christian history of ideas understandable." [2]

Nothing subjective or metaphysical can be allowed in the affirmation of essential Christian faith. Christianity is a historical entity and must be understood the way everything else historical becomes understandable; theology must approach its task like any other empirical science.[3]

The scientific nature of Christian systematic theology is thereby carried through to the details of theological procedure. But there is another important implication to this point. The fact that the theologian approaches the understanding of Christianity in an empirical manner, *i.e.* on the basis of a scientific hypothesis concerning its *grundmotiv*, an hypothesis which is to be tested in confrontation with

---

[1] *Ibid.*, p. 208.
[2] *Ibid.*, pp. 174 f; cf. *STU*, 1933, pp. 77, 114; *DhL*, 1929, pp. 27 f.
[3] *ToR*, 1937, p. 125.

the historical manifestations of Christian faith, means that essential
Christianity will be allowed to rise out of the historical material and
declare itself in its own characteristic voice.[1] The systematic theologian
has freed himself of the subjective predispositions which tended to
make him the ruler of the material. Metaphysics is gone. Historical
Christianity is now the center of attention, and the theologian humbly
formulates his hypotheses in order to allow the historical faith to
express its essence and character on its own terms. Bring argues,
in effect, that the scientific approach to Christian theology is the best
guarantee for the authenticity of the understanding of the faith.

This point is well worth attention. Theologians have struggled
for some time to iron out the relationship between authentic Christian
truth and modern scientific methods of research, and often the result
has been an inverse correlation of the two. In the Lundensian way
of looking at it, the relationship is direct, positive, and definite.
Bring declares not only that authentic Christian faith content and
strictly scientific research procedures represent genuinely compatible
entities; he considers the two mutually dependent on one another. A
theology which aspires to be truly scientific will be concerned to
allow the historical Christian faith to express itself in all its peculiarity
and depth. Similarly, a faith that is concerned to be truly Christian
will desire to have the essential character of historical Christianity
analyzed and explicated by way of scientific objectivity, not by reference
to subjective preconceptions or uncritical dogmatism. Strict scientific
objectivity—to be guided in the confrontation with the historical
manifestations of Christian faith by a series of tentative hypotheses
which are subsequently corrected or verified in reference to the given
material—is in fact the best possible orientation for the systematic
theologian as he seeks to understand the authentic nature and the
essential core of Christianity.

Here, then, is the answer to the question which the Lundensians
raised: how and in what sense systematic theology can be both
positively Christian and strictly scientific. It is precisely by being
strictly scientific in the way it conceives its nature and task, its purpose
and procedures, that systematic theology has the possibility for gaining
a true understanding of the faith and giving a right exposition of its
Christian character.

One further point should be noted here. When Bring says that

---

[1] *Ibid.*, p. 127.

"the criterion of rightness" on which the hypothesis of the systematic theologian is constantly to be tested "must be whether it makes the meaning of the Christian witness to faith and the Christian history of ideas understandable,"[1] he means this in a plain and common sense. His criterion is a rational and theoretical one; it has nothing whatever to do with any "spiritual" principle of understanding or a "special" logic of faith. Bring rejects, as we have seen,[2] both the notion of a special religious way of knowledge and the flight from rationality into paradoxality. What is historical, empirical, given in reality—as the Christian faith is—must be understandable in terms of rational and theoretical criteria of understanding. Reason will study Christian faith propositions—even those that are formulated by way of paradox—in order to understand their meaning and intention; and it will do so honestly, with a view to their religious *meningssammanhang*, and in the light of common logic.

This is the way the theologian approaches both the Bible and the Christian history of ideas:[3] he applies the tools of reason and logic in order to understand the faith and identify the internal and external factors that determine its content, its character, and its relationships to other faiths.[4] He considers the paradoxes of the faith the same way. In Bring's judgment, the paradoxality of faith statements is fully understandable on logical terms.[5] Paradoxes can be made to make sense, therefore; their nature and function can be fully analyzed, and their meaning can be explained from a rational point of view. The theologian confronts the historical-empirical manifestations of Christianity precisely for the purpose of analyzing and explaining the "sense" of the material. He does so in terms of a hypothetical "essence" or *grundmotiv*, but his hypothesis is always tested against the question whether the material makes sense in light of it. The aim of theology is to provide a clear and cogent understanding of the basic motifs which form the center of meaning or the principle of unity within the larger motif structures of Christianity; and the understanding which is in question here is purely theoretical, available to all, but attainable only by way of a rational and scientific approach.

---

[1] Cf. *supra*, p. 187.
[2] Cf. *supra*, pp. 96 ff., 101 f.
[3] *ToR*, 1937, p. 125.
[4] *STU*, 1933, p. 231.
[5] Cf. "Paradoxtanken i teologien," *STK*, 10, 1934, pp. 3 ff.

THE TYPOLOGICAL CONTRAST

A fourth practical observation which receives special emphasis in Bring's methodology has to do with the ideational contrast between various types of faith. On this Bring builds a practical, explicitly dualistic theological procedure. He is a typical Lundensian in this respect—a disciple of Eklund, Aulén, and Nygren. But he is also—and perhaps more—influenced by the dramatic-dualistic perspectives of Söderblom and Billing. There is a very fine line to be drawn here: On the one side, the procedure is quite consistent with the critical philosophical commitments; on the other side, there are clear tendencies to making Christian dualism determinative for theological method. Which of these sides receives the main emphasis in Bring's various considerations of this point is difficult to say.

The existence of typological contrasts is, of course, presupposed by Bring already in his delineation of the religious category as an empty, transcendental form and the various historical religions as so many different religious types.[1] He understands religious experience generally as representing a series of independent "individualities", each containing a central idea or *grundmotiv* which functions as the unifying principle within all the empirical manifestations of a certain type of faith. With the religious category functioning as "an open question" concerning the nature of religion (a question which in its various formulations may focus on different aspects of religious existence, the God-concept, soteriology, etc.), the different religions are seen as a number of basically dissimilar "answers", *i.e.* alternative concepts of God, or the world, or salvation. Thus there are, built into the very nature of the historical religious material, a series of sharp typological contrasts.

The scientific systematic theologian will be especially aware of this; it is his task to investigate the various types of faith and identify the particular *grundmotiv* which is characteristic of each one. For the purposes of systematic theology it is, in fact, of great value to set the various conceptions of religion in direct contrast to each other, and to compare their motif structures point by point.[2] Such comparisons

---

[1] Cf. *supra*, pp. 93 f.

[2] *STU*, 1933, p. 116. In spite of strong tendencies, characteristic of Bring and of his predecessors in Lund, to think of the various religions as pure and unique types, each representing a nonduplicated individuality, Bring does not usually consider the historical religions typified by one single motif in pure form; cf. *ToR*, 1937, p. 175 f. A faith is, rather, made up of several *grundämnen* (basic elements,

shall have to be kept strictly within the requirements of scientific objectivity, of course; the same scientific methods apply to the comparison of several different religions as to the investigation of a single one.[1] It is all a part of motif-research,[2] and it is undertaken simply for the purposes of analysis and explication, not in the interest of absolutization or evaluation. Comparative motif-research serves to put the essential character of the different types of *grundmotiv* into particularly sharp focus; Bring is even inclined to go so far as to say that their typological uniqueness only becomes clear by typological comparison.

Against this background it is obvious that Christian systematic theology, that brand of motif-research which concerns itself with the essential character of historical Christian faith, must also be a comparitive discipline, concerned with the relationship between basic Christian motifs and the corresponding motifs in other types of religion. Bring at one point makes this explicit, assigning to Christian systematic theology the twofold task of "investigating and understanding the Christian faith in terms of its inner organic unity and positing its typological character or *Gestalt* in contrast to other kinds of religious *grundmotiv*." [3] The double task of systematic theology, the analytic and the comparative, unites two elements which must, according to Bring, supplement one another: In the investigation of historical Christian faith, the theologian will only come to understand the peculiar properties of the Christian *grundmotiv* as he sets it in contrast to the *motivsammanhang* that characterize other major types of faith.[4] Conversely, the theologian needs the deep systematic analysis of the basic motifs of each individual type of religion in order to compare them responsibly.

So far, Bring's observations on the study of typological contrasts seem consistent with his methodological presuppositions; they can easily be incorporated into the framework of scientific theology. But at this point another factor appears: The perspective seems to narrow

materials), different motifs brought together and synthesized into a distinct religious „personality".

[1] *STU*, 1933, p. 116.

[2] *Ibid.*, pp. 224 f; *ToR*, 1937, pp. 199 f.

[3] *STU*, 1933, p. 75.

[4] "It is undoubtedly very useful for the precise definition of the outstanding features of Christianity to set the Christian conception of religion over against another conception of religion which has an entirely different structure, but with which Christianity has contact and is engaged in ideological encounter." *Ibid.*, p. 115.

and harden into a dualistic theory of religion; a particular theological hypothesis is promoted as a general methodological principle.

Surveying the religious scene in terms of his favorite symbolism, namely soteriology, Bring finds that "the different conceptions of salvation are really quite few." [1] In fact, as Bring sees it, they come down to two basic types: on the one hand, the conception dominated by egocentricity, legalism, and *eros*; and on the other the conception informed by theocentricity, grace, and *agape*. [2] These two ways of understanding salvation are, clearly, part of two diamentrically opposite conceptions of religion; they go back to religious commitments that are "direct opposites" in intention and direction, [3] and a struggle between them is therefore "inevitable". All historical religion can be analyzed in terms of "diametrically contrasting answers to the categorical question of religion." [4]

One cannot but wonder where in the development of Bring's thought the scientific intentions of motif-research—the objective study of the *grundmotiv* of different types of religion, and the non-evaluational comparison of typological contrasts—first came to be compromised and replaced by the unyielding application of the theory of soteriological polarities. The answer is not hard to find. The first of Bring's theological works, his academic dissertation on *Dualismen hos Luther*, revealed to him the usefulness of the dualistic hypothesis. By the time he produced his third book, *Förhållandet mellan tro och gärningar inom Luthersk teologi*, which came five years later, the pattern was deeply ingrained in his thought. Here Pehr Eklund's "cliches", Billing's *längdsnitt* and *tvärrsnitt*, and Aulén's "typological ruler" were all brought together and reduced after the pattern of Nygren's egocentricity/theocentricity dialectic, and in Bring's perspective the result is a theoretical principle of crystalline simplicity: the dramatic-dualistic theory of religion.

In his dissertation, Bring defines the dualistic perspective the following way: "It does not refer to a contrast between God and the natural world, but to the view of faith which divides existence into con-

---

[1] *ToR*, 1937, p. 153.

[2] Bring has obviously taken over Nygren's fundamental typological distinction. See Nygren, "Egoism och religion," *STK*, 3, 1927, pp. 129-150, for the early form of the egocentricity/theocentricity pattern. Bring used this in his academic dissertation; cf. *DhL*, 1929, p. 22. Cf. also "Lag och evangelium," *STK*, 12, 1936, pp. 207-227.

[3] *ToR*, 1937, p. 176.

[4] *Ibid.*, p. 172.

flicting opposites and considers it the battlefield of good and evil forces." [1] The definition is significant; it shows clearly that Bring is not working with a metaphysical concept of reality, intending to argue a theistic-dualistic ontology in opposition to naturalistic or humanistic world-views. Bring's dualism is explicitly a "view of faith", *i.e.* an hypothesis designed to help the theologian in his endeavors to understand the nature of the religious material before him. Nevertheless, one is bound to ask whether Bring's hypothesis is adequate, and whether in his use of it Bring himself is sufficiently aware of its hypothetical character. [2]

We shall not stop to consider the practical aspects of this question at this point. [3] Here, only a general comment is relevant; it is necessary to remind ourselves of the scientific nature of systematic theological investigations. According to Bring, systematic theology is categorically different from faith-reflection. [4] The one is theoretical, the other religious; the one represents knowledge, the other does not. The theological interest in essential Christianity is an empirical-historical interest, and must be pursued by way of scientific-analytical procedures. This includes the formulation of a research hypothesis which is entirely tentative, open to correction, always softer in substance than the material with which it is confronted.

It is on this point that Bring's soteriological polarity needs testing. Applied to the theology of Luther, as in *Dualismen hos Luther*, the hypothesis is evidently very useful; Luther's theology shows a singular concentration on the theocentric motif in opposition to all soteriological implications of the human ego. Likewise, in the study of faith and works within Lutheran theology, the dualistic perspective appears to be sound. The Lutheran concept of faith does represent in nearly pure form the theocentric motif—God being the subject of faith, who establishes the God-relationship and determines its nature, and who overwhelms man by his Word and takes him into his fellowship by grace. Bring tends to identify Luther-research and the systematic-theological analysis of essential Christianity, however;

---

[1] *DhL*, 1929, p. iii.

[2] Helge Nyman, in a review of Bring's *KrT*, *STK*, 27, 1951, pp. 201 ff, says that "a common criticism against Bring's theology" is that it is "much too schematic", and that it "utilizes the material onesidedly", simplifying the problems, and overstressing certain preset viewpoints.

[3] A fuller discussion is included in the Conclusion of my dissertation, *A Study of Lundensian Theological Methodology*, 1962, pp. 289 ff.

[4] Cf. *supra*, pp. 117 ff.

and the hypothesis which has proven appropriate to the study of Luther and Lutheran theology is thereby considered indispensable for systematic theology as a whole.

To Bring, the Lutheran understanding of Christianity serves as the key to the essential motifs of the faith.[1] The New Testament, together with—and interpreted on the basis of—Luther's religious *åskådning*, are "the deepest sources for (the study of) Christian faith available anywhere." [2] This is, of course, a respectable personal commitment; but it is not a scientific observation, and it must not be allowed to influence the theoretical methodological perspective. In the context of Christian systematic theology in general, the particular hypothesis which is applicable to the Lutheran understanding of the faith must be tested again. The soteriological polarity between theocentricity and egocentricity—*agape* and *eros*—may not, in fact, be the best hypothesis for uncovering the characteristic nature of historical Christian faith. At any rate, one must be sure to observe that the working hypothesis is simply a prism through which the light of the historical material is reflected and by which it is broken into an ordered and meaningful spectrum, and not a filter that is put on top of the material and through which only one acceptable light wave is allowed to shine. It is clear that Bring's strict application of the theory of soteriological polarities, when applied to Christianity as a whole, functions much in the way of a filter.

In connection with the comparative aspect of scientific systematic theology, Bring makes two subsidiary observations of significance for the understanding of his methodology. The first has to do with illegitimate comparisons. The Christian faith is, of course, part of the religious area of experience. It does not function as a theoretical world explanation or a system of metaphysical truths; its intentions are categorically different from these. In practice, however, Christianity finds itself in conflict with a series of metaphysical world-views which in addition to their theoretical aspirations also intend to function as religious types. Some of them claim to represent the ultimate truth about reality. The temptation is that the Christian theologian, in comparing Christian faith with such metaphysical systems, allows the

---

[1] His procedure, then, is in many ways quite similar to that which he uncovered in Billing; cf. *supra*, pp. 126 ff. He has formulated an hypothesis in terms of a particular theological tradition, and he allows the hypothesis to play a role in the foundations of the scientific methodology as well.

[2] *STK*, 7, 1931, p. 375.

explication of Christian *grundmotiv* to be drawn into dialectic involvements with the problematics to which metaphysical concepts answer. Christianity, in Bring's way of putting it, is the "direct opposite" of naturalistic or idealistic metaphysics, yet the contrast is not one that should be argued by way of philosophical antitheses. If the context of the contrast is philosophical, so will the theologian's understanding of the Christian faith be.[1] The systematic theologian must be sure to approach the comparison of *grundmotiv* within the context to which such an undertaking properly belongs. The typological contrast between Christianity and the metaphysical-religious world-views is in reality a twofold one; it has to do with the difference between religion and metaphysics, and it takes the form of a conflict between different conceptions of religion. The first calls for a critical analysis of the relationship between the various categories of human experience, and this is a matter for the philosophers to iron out; the second calls for an objective analysis of the various forms of human religiosity, and this is the task of scientific systematic theology.

Secondly, Bring speaks of a certain intra-theological relevance of the study of typological contrasts. Comparative systematic theology is not only concerned with the relationship between the *grundmotiv* of a number of different conceptions of religion. The history of Christian faith reveals how several kinds of *grundmotiv* do in fact struggle to put their imprint on a single religion, at times challenging one another in open controversy, at other times coexisting by way of uneasy compromises or tacit interconditioning. The systematic theologian must therefore apply the procedures of typological comparison to the history of Christian ideas itself, and by doing so seek to identify the purest expressions of essential Christian faith against all unchristian or subchristian notions. This is both a necessary and a fruitful

---

[1] In opposing a naturalistic world-view, for instance, the Christian faith must be kept clear of the naturalistic metaphysical problematics. When it is lured by its opponents into making absolute claims, it becomes itself metaphysics and loses the character of a religious faith Cf. *STU*, 1933, pp. 156, note 52; p. 170, note 26. From this perspective, one is bound to ask whether Bring himself succeeds in keeping the Christian faith from being pulled into dialectic dependence upon the views he opposes. Bring's soteriological contrast is formulated so that the opposition to egoism dominates his interpretation of Christianity completely. This contrast is intended as a tool for analyzing religious motifs, but in Bring's theological work it hardens into a principle of logical opposites; Christian faith is the counterpoint to egocentric idealism. As a result, Bring's systematic-historical analysis of the essence of Christianity reveals a religion characterized by theodynamism and predestinarianism, antinomianism and fideism.

endeavor, according to Bring. Especially instructive are those periods in the history of the faith which are marked by theological strife and disagreement. It is "in theological controversy it appears most clearly when something that is essential or fundamental to Christian faith is at stake." [1] Where there is no controversy, or where doctrines are not the object of theological discussion, there the faith is often overpowered by the mind of the times, and foreign elements tend to suppress the essential Christian motifs. The systematic theologian, in seeking the authentic Christian faith, must utilize the insights gained from the investigation of theological controversy and delineate what is what in the various interpretations of Christianity that have appeared through the centuries. Scientific systematic theology must be a critical discipline, for it is committed to the task of identifying the essential, the *bestående*, the characteristic *grundmotiv* of historical faith.

NORM AND EVALUATION IN THEOLOGY

A fifth and final procedural observation which receives recurring emphasis in Bring's thought is the explicit rejection of an evaluational, demonstrative, or normative role for systematic thology. This marks the capstone in Bring's methodological structure, and it serves as an additional guarantee for the scientific objectivity of systematic theology. It does not mean, however, that the systematic theologian is simply an analyst of recorded religious phenomena.

The theological interest, as Bring describes it, focuses on the characteristic features and essential motifs of religious types. A particularly profitable procedure in this connection is the typological contrasting of different *grundmotiv*. Bring makes it quite clear that the confrontation and comparison of religious motifs must be undertaken with scientific objectivity, purely for the purposes of analysis and explication, and not for the sake of evaluation and absolutization. The systematic theologian has no other function than to undertake the analysis, search for an understanding, and attempt the explication of the essential nature of each historical conception of religion.[2] The fact that one historical faith interests him more than any other type of religion does not mean that the theologian has lost his objectivity; nor does the fact that he sets over against one another the typological characteristics of the different religions necessarily involve a

---

[1] *ToR*, 1937, p. 152.
[2] *STU*, 1933, p. 176.

compromise of the scientific status of his discipline. He must only be on guard against using his science to prove one faith as "right" or establish one motif as "norm". Such endeavors have no place in an objective science.

Bring does not mean, of course, that science contains no form of evaluation. The positive sciences are not without standards of correctness and value. On the contrary, they have developed certain principles that are considered normative for a scientific undertaking, such as the correct reproduction of facts, the proper handling of evidence, and the logical consistency of conclusions.[1] On the basis of a common acceptance of such standards, a certain scientific work can be evaluated and pronounced better—of higher scientific quality—than another.[2] Even the quality of a philosophical system can be evaluated in the same manner, provided a certain rule of logic is explicitly accepted as the basis of discussion.[3] In all these cases, the evaluation is made by reference to some commonly recognized— and therefore, in a sense, objective—criterion. It is not, for that reason, a subjective value judgment; it has the character of a statement of fact. The evaluation takes the form of an objective comparison between a given entity and a stated principle of value.

Such a "factual evaluation" is integral to the procedures of scientific systematic theology, also.[4] The general standards of scholarly research apply, of course, to this discipline as they do to other historical sciences. Furthermore, the theologian is involved in evaluating his sources—the many propositional formulations of faith—against the standard of a responsibly formulated scientific hypothesis. This evaluation is always hypothetical and tentative, always open to review and correction, as the theologian's hypothesis itself is. Still, it has validity. It is not an arbitrary value judgment on the part of an individual theologian; it is, in a sense, an objective evaluation, for it is undertaken in reference to a hypothesis which is also, in a sense, objective.[5]

Bring is very anxious to underscore that the evaluation which is an essential part of scientific procedure must not be confused with a subjective commitment concerning the absolute truth of one type

---

[1] *Ibid.*, p. 124.
[2] *Ibid.*, p. 97.
[3] Cf. *ibid.*, pp. 122 f.
[4] *Ibid.*, p. 125.
[5] *Ibid.*, p. 173.

of faith or one conception of religion.[1] There is no way to prove absolute truth or ultimate value scientifically. The truth of Christianity cannot be demonstrated by way of scientific systematic theology. It is one thing to analyze and determine what can rightly be said to belong to essential Christian faith; it is another thing entirely to claim that the Christian faith is "right", and to attempt to demonstrate this judgment as "true". The first is a legitimate scientific task; the second is not at all scientific.[2] If the systematic theologian moves beyond the first and engages himself in the second, he has immediately fallen from grace in any scientific context; he has submitted to metaphysical confusion.[3] In Bring's terminology, to attempt to prove the truth of an ideal is "absurd". An ideal exists only for him who stands in a relation of personal commitment to it, and who "hallows" it; value presupposes a personal standpoint. A "provable ideal" is, therefore, a meaningless configuration of terms.[4]

The reason Bring must emphasize the non-evaluational, non-normative character of systematic theology is clear. In the first place, religious value judgments and theoretical investigation of religious types belong to two categorically different areas of experience.[5] In the second place, there is no absolute, objective standard by which to arbitrate between the claims of various religious types.[6] Both of these considerations are consistent with Bring's methodological presuppositions. The first is a consequence of his philosophical analysis of the categories of experience and the subsequent emphasis on the autonomy of the different areas of meaning; the second is a direct corollary to his critical understanding of the religious category and the consistent rejection of a metaphysical definition of the essence of religion. Obviously, on Bring's presuppositions the scientific systematic theologian can have no part in the value judgments that are legitimate only in the religious area of meaning; neither can he be engaged in a search for an absolute value standard by which to evaluate value judgments. As a scientific theologian, he approaches

---

[1] *Ibid.*, p. 72.

[2] *Ibid.*, p. 180.

[3] *Ibid.*, p. 76.

[4] *Ibid.*, p. 70.

[5] *Ibid.*, p. 122; cf. also *ToR*, 1937, p. 159: "...no science whatever can evaluate, *i.e.* make value judgments; it can only state facts."

[6] "Within the positive sciences, certain principles are developed by which these sciences gain grounds for judgment. When it is a question of two religious types, however, there exists no common measuring stick... by which one type can be said to be superior to another." *Ibid.*, p. 124.

religion empirically and theoretically, working by way of generally accepted procedures for historical-critical research, and aiming toward the discovery, the understanding, and the explication of the essential meaning and basic motifs of each individual type of faith.

We have come to a turn in the road that we set before us in the introduction. The primary purpose of this study was to investigate the theoretical framework of theology that was conceived and constructed by Ragnar Bring; to focus particularly on the way he holds together the two aspects of the contemporary theological renewal, the emphasis on intellectual respectability in method and theological responsibility in content; and to do so by way of a detailed analysis of his methodology, from the critical-philosophical foundations of his epistemology to his practical observations concerning the procedures of motif-research. Our main program was simply to uncover and represent, in a systematic fashion, the basic elements of Bring's own thought on the subject. That in itself seemed an important endeavor, in so far as the world-wide theological community has not yet had the benefit of a thorough systematic presentation of the full spectrum of Lundensian theological methodology.

But it was more than an academic interest that formed the motivation for the undertaking. Clearly, to this author's mind the Lundensian approach to theology represents a most viable option for the theological community in the twentieth century. Lund has developed an invaluable means by which contemporary theologians may orient themselves in the modern age and find a way to do theology understandably and respectably in the present. Lundensian methodology gives contemporary theology a basis that is intellectually honest, and a sense of direction which is genuinely Christian, thus helping it avoid the traps on both sides of the modern theological dilemma. Moreover, the method provides the presuppositions for a new integration of the theological disciplines. It opens the possibility for interfaith conversation and lays the groundwork for an ecumenical understanding of Christian faith. Theology, as Bring delineates it, has a future, and the future is meaningful. It holds promises of a significant role for theology among the sciences of men, and it gives visions of a meaningful interaction between theological scholarship and the community of faith whose traditions it investigates and whose development it contributes to shape. All these things are important for modern theology—there can be no two opinions about this.

That the Lundensian approach to the work of theology contributes in significant ways to making these things attainable, is also undeniably clear. This author, at least, finds it so.

But at this point, another facet of our work comes into view. We indicated at the beginning that a second part of our task would be to reveal the problems involved in Bring's methodology, to ask questions, and perhaps even suggest answers. We have kept this in mind along the way. Here and there we have submitted critical observations, pointed to weaknesses, indicated possibilities, and offered corrections; but so far these points have been argued in rather disjunctive and perfunctory ways. It remains now to bring these considerations together in a responsible manner and to determine explicitly where the limits of Bring's methodology are.

It will be recognized that our critique of Bring's methodology does not include a rejection of the presuppositions upon which the system is built. We do not take up an alternative methodological position from which we then proceed to make comparisons and pronounce value judgments. Others have done this, and their discussions have been little helpful. One may even ask whether such procedures represent a fair treatment of a man's thought. Instead, we shall develop our criticism from within the presuppositions of the Lundensian system, *i.e.* in full identification with the critical philosophical perspective. The difficulties we have uncovered in Bring's methodology are not of such a nature that they discredit the fundamental principles upon which the structure is built, and the revisions we are proposing are not so as to establish an entirely new concept of the contemporary methodological task. Yet, we are deeply conscious of the limitations and the incompleteness of Bring's methodology.

We affirm, then, that the Lundensians have begun well the task of constructing a modern framework for faith. They have advanced the work of their predecessors in the enterprise in several significant ways. But they have also left a number of loose ends about; there are a series of gaping holes in their methodological structure. Bring is himself conscious of some of them; others he has not seen. Moreover, there are examples of internal inconsistencies in the architecture—elements of confusion which, if left alone, will tend to discredit the value of the whole undertaking. All these things combine to limit the usefulness of the Lundensian perspective; only by facing them honestly can the future of the method be secured.

If our critique of Bring's thought is to have any positive value, however, we must go beyond the mere discussion of the weaknesses apparent in the present form of Lundensian methodology. There must be a constructive quality to our conclusions. We must at least be prepared to suggest ways to solve the difficulties, go beyond the limitations, and complete the methodological structure. And if these proposals are to be at all relevant, they must be made in explicit reference to the methodological presuppositions on which the Lundensian system is itself built.

This is the task before us in the final part of this book.

PART THREE

BRING'S LIMITS

CHAPTER NINE

THE UNFINISHED STRUCTURE

Lundensian theological methodology has many disciples but few leaders. The leaders of the school are actually only two, Anders Nygren and Ragnar Bring. No other scholars have given such thorough-going and consistent attention to the foundations of Lundensian motif-research as these men, and no one at the University of Lund or in its immediate sphere of influence has risen from the ranks of the followers to shoulder the task of developing the method further, now that the two originators have moved on to retirement. The prospects for the future of the method —at least in Lund— seem rather dim.

LUNDENSIAN METHODOLOGY AT THE PRESENT

The first and most obvious reason for the lack of new leadership in the Nygren-Bring tradition lies in the nature of these men's own work in recent decades. Having laid the philosophical foundations of the method many years ago, and having then also developed the basic principles of scientific motif-research, the leaders of the school moved on in their scholarly careers to other, more directly theological concerns: Nygren to motif-historical and biblical-theological writings (besides the ecclesiastical responsibilities of a resident bishop), Bring to Luther-research, and later to biblical-theological and exegetical interests. The indications were, perhaps, that they considered the methodological task finished. Nygren and Bring have themselves given no support to such conclusions. They are both aware of the underdeveloped areas in their thought, and they have repeatedly underscored that more work is needed to complete the methodological structure. But they have not been able to inspire younger Lundensian scholars to join them in a critical-philosophical braintrust or to assume leadership in methodological matters. Bring, on his side, has tended to look to Nygren for the further development of the philosophical perspective, and Nygren has only in recent years had the leisure to return to his first love. His long projected work, billed to be his magnum opus in the field of philosophy of religion, has been slow in coming, and in the meantime others have been kept in a state of intellectual suspension, waiting for the word from the man who is without comparison the foremost in Sweden in this field.

A second reason for the dirth of new leadership in Lundensian methodology has to do with the developments in the theological community in general during the last thirty or forty years. The traditional tension between philosophy and theology, which was beginning to lessen under the influence of various nineteenth and early twentieth century attempts at developing a rational understanding of the theological endeavor, later returned in full force under the theological hegemony of the neo-orthodox giants. From their dialectic standpoint, theological methodology was defined as an internal theological concern, not a subject that should be approached from a "heteronomous" philosophical point of view. Defining philosophy in terms of specific philosophical content, neo-orthodoxy set out to free theology from its Babylonian captivity to "foreign" thoughtforms. Instead of grounding theology in the perspectives of reason and speculation, it was said, theologians concerned with the recovery of Christian thought should find their starting point in "theonomous" doctrinal symbols such as "revelation", "kerygma", "divine-human encounter", or "the Word of God". Thus, as a consequence of the great impact of dialectic theology, methodology was once more—as in pre-critical times—considered as part of an exclusively doctrinal orientation, and the theology that emerged shows clear signs of intellectual isolation. It was, in Lutheran terminology, *incurvatur in se*.

This attitude to methodological matters has invaded Scandinavia also. It is, in a sense, more immediately acceptable to the traditionally conservative mindset of Scandinavian Christians than the critical and scientific orientation of the Lundensians. As we shall see, the continental theological standpoint has invaded the center of Lundensian methodology itself, finding its most prominent spokesman in Nygren's own successor in the chair of systematic theology, Gustaf Wingren. The influence of the Nygren-Bring tradition at the University of Lund was thus deliberately broken.

The few younger Scandinavian scholars who have continued to be interested in the problems of contemporary theology have apparently not found much inspiration from new developments in philosophy or new structures of methodology. The theological community is only slowly finding its way to a modern methodological orientation, though some significant attempts at bridging the gap between theology and philosophy have occurred during the last twenty years. They are identified primarily with the form-critical school and its prime mover, Rudolf Bultmann, who sought openly to attach his thought to the philosophical framework of existentialism, especially Martin Heidegger, and with the radical theologians in England and America, who are more or less directly indebted to the ontology of logical positivism and the semantics of linguistic analysis. Unfortunately, the discussion of Bultmann's work has come to focus primarily on his program of demythologization and its consequences for biblical hermeneutics and historical interpretation, not on his methodological foundations in Heideggerian epistemology and Kierkegaardian philosophy of religion. At present, the response to Bultmann—particularly in Germany—seems to crystallize itself in the development of several more conservative methodological positions, characterized by a metaphysical interpretation of history (as in Wolfhart Pannenberg) or a metaphysical theory of language (as in the so-called "new hermeneutic" of Gerhard Ebeling and Ernst Fuchs). On its side, radical theology has not managed to develop its methodology to any significant degree. Whereas several popular presentations of the intellectual difficulties of modern theology have originated in this circle (f. ex. by John A. T. Robinson, Thomas Altizer, and Gabriel Vahanian), radical theologians have so far given only sporadic attention to the deeper epistemological and philosophical problems of contemporary religious existence. The rethinking of theological categories has been given some attention, and the study of the nature of religious language has made some progress. Radical reformulations of theological concepts have been presented, in terms of sociology (as in Harvey Cox), linguistics (as in Paul van Buren), ethics (as in Herbert Braun and William Hamilton), and personalistic existentialism (as in Manfred Mezger and Schubert Ogden). Other, less radical attempts at bringing together philosophical and theological considerations have been undertaken by John Macquarrie, who uses the insights of religious existentialism in his approach to ecumenical Christian thought; Heinrich Ott, who seeks to relate Barthian dogmatics and Heideggerian ontology; and Jürgen Moltmann, who works on a correlation of secular eschatology and the Christian concept of hope. Of all these methodological attempts it appears true to say, however, that the principal questions regarding the epistemological presuppositions for religious knowledge, the nature of religious experience, and the relationship between religion and other dimensions of human existence remain largely unanswered. There appears to be a widespread unwillingness to consider such elementary questions; few theologians seem prepared to go back to the fundamental philosophical problems lying at the very heart of the methodological undertaking.

A third reason for the lack of new methodological leadership in the Lundensian tradition must undoubtedly be found in the present orientation of the faculty of theology at the University of Lund itself. Recent developments in the school show clear tendencies toward a renewed disintegration of philosophical and theological concerns. This is the result of the influence of two men in particular: Gustaf Wingren, the systematic theologian, and Hampus Lyttkens, the philosopher of religion. In different ways these leaders of the present faculty have expressed open dissatisfaction with Nygren's and Bring's work. In what amounts to a demonstration of intellectual independence, they have both explicitly disassociated themselves —though on different grounds— from the presuppositions of their predecessors' methodological framework; and Nygren's and Bring's influence is thereby virtually ended in Lund.

Gustaf Wingren, who is in some ways the most influential of the Scandinavian theologians at the present, found himself early attracted to the systematic foundations of continental neo-orthodoxy and the conservative biblical orientation of German Protestantism. Already in the 1930's, as a student, he experienced a certain disenchantment with the directions in which the Lundensian theological methodology was developing. Later, receiving scholarships for study abroad, he went to Berlin and Basel to find his bearings. Convinced that the philosophical presuppositions of Nygren's method actually hindered the true exposition of essential Christianity, he returned to Sweden a confirmed theologian of the Word. After he was established as Nygren's successor in theology, Wingren decided to challenge his predecessor openly, by a frontal attack on his methodology, first through a series of discussions in *Svensk teologisk kvartalsskrift*, 1956, and then through a critical study of Nygren's method together with those of Bultmann and Barth, *Theology in Conflict*, 1958.

Wingren's own methodological concerns focus on a "correct" interpretation of Scripture and a "right" presentation of its meaning in the present. His theology has a dual aim: the true understanding of the biblical message, and the kerygmatic proclamation of its truth in direct confrontation with the human situation in the world.[1]

---

[1] This is especially evident in his book *The Living Word*, 1960.

The historical question concerning the content of the Word of God is closely combined with the hermeneutical question concerning the meaning of the Word now. Wingren is critical of Nygren in both these contexts. He claims that Nygren's philosophical orientation in reality "hinders" the proper understanding of Christianity; [1] and he argues that questions concerning the relevance of Christian faith for present existence are "foreign" to Nygren's system. [2]

We shall not enter into the controversy between the two men at this point. It is clear, even on the surface, that the discussions between them are pervaded with unhappy elements. Wingren's interpretation of Nygren's philosophy is manifestly weak, [3] and Nygren's answers are not free from personal irritation and a little condescension. The fact of the matter is that the two men's thinking is not on the same wavelength. [4] The debate, therefore, is not particularly instructive— except perhaps as an example of philosophical-theological confusion. In our context it is relevant only in so far as it helps us understand why Wingren finds it necessary not only to criticize certain features in Nygren's methodology, but to undertake "a purposive demolition of the religious-philosophical foundation (of his theology)." [5]

Wingren's own methodological presuppositions are simple: He considers the question of methodology a subject for theology, not

---

[1] *Theology in Conflict*, 1958, p. 17.

[2] *Ibid.*, p. 88.

[3] This is particularly the case with his strange argumentation against the "formalism" of Nygren's categorical question of religion. Wingren claims that it is too "definite", on the one hand, yet he complains that it does not focus the attention on the question that the material— *i.e.* the Bible— asks: the "pregnant" question of guilt. Says Wingren, "The formal character of Nygren's philosophy is in a deeper sense a lack of radical formality, *i.e.* the absence of postulation in the original question". *Ibid.*, p. 98. Nygren's formal question "interferes" with the material; he does not allow the biblical question of guilt to be asked. *Ibid.* p. 102. Behind Wingren's odd reasoning, there is a legitimate concern. The purity of Nygren's *agape* motif has bothered many who are aware of the strong biblical emphases on law, responsibility and judgment. But Nygren's error is simply in the narrow scope of his research hypothesis—possibly the result of a hardening of an evangelical Lutheran motif of faith—; it is not, as Wingren says, a hindrance to the proper understanding of Christianity which "cannot be removed within the presuppositions of Nygren's theology." *Ibid.*, p. 17. By such reasoning, Wingren simply proves that he does not recognize the presuppositions of the critical philosophical perspective.

[4] Jarl Hemberg rightly criticizes Wingren for arguing by way of logical "type errors": ". . . Wingren mixes together philosophy of religion and Christian faith, scientific construction of theory and a commitment to a worldview." *Op. cit.*, p. 276.

[5] *Theology in Conflict*, 1958, p. 90.

for philosophy.[1] The methodological presuppositions of theology must be tested by way of a "purely theological question", *i.e.* whether or not they are "valid on the basis of the Bible and specifically the New Testament?"[2] It is the biblical perspective that determines whether a philosophical position or a methodological "blueprint" is valid. According to Wingren, if such a test were made of contemporary theology, the results would be devastating: "If the correction demanded on the basis of the Bible were to be taken seriously, everything that had been achieved so far (in methodology) would have to be destroyed and the work begun anew," for "the conflict is fundamental."[3] Against this background, one could have expected, perhaps, that Wingren would proceed to develop his own theological perspective, revealing the presuppositions of his biblical interpretation and specifying the Scriptural foundations for the understanding of theology; but he does not. He seems to think that the Bible is clear on its own basis and that he, Wingren, is presuppositionless in his openness to the biblical thoughtworld. His clearest commitment in regard to theological methodology, it seems, is that "Nygren's attempt to define the task and method of theology is not tenable."[4] Concerning the shape of the new methodology he envisions, he has little to say.

Wingren has thereby infused into the Lundensian context an explicitly intra-theological and anti-philosophical attitude. This is in itself a strange move, especially since his own understanding of the Christian faith seems influenced by the broad historical perspectives of the Old Testament and its doctrines of creation and redemption rather than the narrower Lutheran emphases on the Pauline concepts of salvation and justification.[5] There should be room within Wingren's point of view for an opening toward the problems of man's cultural and intellectual situation. Dietrich Bonhoeffer experienced such an opening on the basis of a similar theological orientation. Wingren does have this opening, though only in a dialectic sense. His conception of the task of theology goes beyond Nygren's and Bring's more one-sided emphasis on historical-systematic motif-research. He is eager to unite what he calls "anthropology" and "hermeneutics",

---

[1] *Ibid.*, p. xi.

[2] *Ibid.*

[3] *Ibid.*, p. xv.

[4] *Ibid.*, pp. 21 f.

[5] Cf. his *Creation and Law*, 1961; also *Man and the Incarnation*, Edinburgh and London: Oliver and Boyd, 1959.

i.e. the concern for the contemporary meaning of faith and the historical-theological investigation of its content.[1] This is positive. But when one analyzes Wingren's attitude to the anthropological situation, the picture becomes another. His openness turns to rejection. He considers the modern intellectual orientation the direct opposite of Christian faith, and makes theology responsible for confronting it with truth. He charges Bultmann, Barth, and Nygren with "harmonizing" (!) the biblical message and the anthropological situation, and declares that it is a "sign of living theology" that there is a dynamic "tension" between the two.[2] Clearly, the dialectic commitments dominate Wingren's thought. Whatever else one might say about his position, he will not inspire younger scholars to take up the methodological task left by his predecessor and his former colleague in Lund.

Hampus Lyttkens, Wingren's counterweight, has probably had more influence in this respect, though not even he appears to have any desire to identify himself with the Nygren-Bring tradition. Educated at Uppsala, he is thoroughly familiar with Hägerström's epistemological and axiological analyses; and his own philosophical perspective shows definite effects of the confrontation with logical positivism. Lyttkens' scholarly writings have so far focused on Thomas Aquinas and neo-Thomism,[3] but recently his primary interests have moved in the direction of analytical philosophy, specifically the linguistic analysis of religious propositions. In a way he is continuing the methodological task.

Perhaps the most relevant picture of the philosophical orientation of the Lundensian faculty at the present time is one provided by Hampus Lyttkens in a presentation of the work of the school's department of philosophy of religion.[4] He describes its orientation as "analytical", and defines the task of analytical philosophy of religion as follows:

> "The analytical philosophy of religion considers as its task the analysis—by utilization and development of methods and models

---

[1] *Theology in Conflict*, 1958, p. 106.

[2] *Ibid.*, p. xxi.

[3] Cf. *The Analogy between God and the World. An Investigation of its Background and Interpretation of its Use by Thomas of Aquino*, Uppsala: UUÅ, 5, 1953; *Nythomismen. En Religiös filosofi*, Stockholm: Diakonistyrelsen, 1962.

[4] Signed mimeographed sheet, "Religionsfilosofi", summarized in Lunds Universitet Teologiska Fakulteten, *Förslag angående utbyggnad och omstrukturering av de teologiska fakulteterna*, Mimeographed, Lund (March 1968), pp. 27 f.

of analysis from analytical philosophy—of central religious concepts, religious propositions, religious language, and religious argumentation."

Lyttkens delineates four specific problem complexes that are of primary interest to the analytical philosophy of religion: a) *The internal logical analysis of religious texts* (which consists in clarifying the basic concepts, assumptions, and ways of reasoning present in religious texts; explicating vagueness and equivocations; analyzing the determining elements in central religious concepts; reconstructing the internal argument of various texts; testing the logical status of propositions with regard to clarity and consistency; seeking verification and falsification criteria; and investigating the symbolic character of religious language, especially language about God). b) *The scientific theory of the sciences of religion* (which is a widening of the internal logical analysis to include the concepts and theories of religion; the relationship between religion, theology and the general sciences of religion; and especially the scientific theory of systematic theology). c) *Empirical semantics applied to certain religious texts* (which focuses on the problems of understanding and interpretation; religious debate; the relationship between sender and receiver in communication; functional analysis and the analysis of the structure of arguments, thus serving to give the logical analysis relevance for the empirical use of language). d) *The epistemological question of truth* (which concerns the critical-epistemological testing of the assertions of truth that occur in various religions; questions involved in the criticism of religion; the confrontation between religious propositions and the propositions of philosophy, natural science, etc.; it may be approached analytically, *i.e.* by determining the limits and conditions, necessary or adequate, for the objective truth of religious content, or it can be approached in an apologetic manner, from the standpoint of a positive commitment to a certain religious content).

It is evident from this syllabus that certain aspects of Nygren's and Bring's methodology have in fact been taken up and continued in the work of the department of philosophy of religion at Lund. Parts of Lyttkens' delineations of the analytical task can be seen as a significant superstructure on the more rudimentary references in the framework of motif-research. However, some items indicate also that there is a basic discontinuity between what has been and what is now the direction of Lundensian methodology.

Point "b)" in Lyttkens' presentation corresponds rather closely to the fundamental concerns of Nygren's and Bring's methodology, particularly the close correlation of the analytical philosophical perspective and the scientific conception of the nature and task of systematic theology. A certain continuity could be established at this point. Also, points "a)" and "c)", which are mutually interdependent, can be considered explicit extensions of Bring's references to "logical" or "conceptual analysis", on the one hand, and his descriptions of the so-called "structural analysis" on the other. Lyttkens' detailed delimitations of the subject areas of these two forms of analysis do not, of course, have clear parallels in Bring's rather general definitions of the analytical task; but this does not constitute a major obstacle to synthesizing the two systems, if their methodological orientation be otherwise the same. Lyttkens' more informed and up-to-date conception of the analytical task can indeed serve to supplement several of the underdeveloped areas in Nygren's and Bring's framework.

However, point "d)" in Lyttkens' syllabus contains items which reveal the discontinuity between the present faculty's philosophy of religion and that of the formative Lundensian methodologians. Lyttkens refers to the involvement of analytical philosophy of religion in the "epistemological question of truth". This is clearly inconsistent with the critical intentions of his predecessors in Lund. Moreover, his interest in the "limits and conditions (necessary, adequate) for the objective truth of religious content" marks a definite break in relation to the critical tradition of Nygren and Bring. As we have observed, these men consider the epistemological question concerning the presuppositions of validity (the criteria of truth or falsity) logically preliminary to the task of philosophy of religion; it is of strictly theoretical and purely logical nature, and must be answered by an epistemology that functions as a "science of principles", *i.e.* by way of transcendental-analytical investigations of the formal presuppositions at work in the various autonomous areas of experience. Lyttkens, presumably, has no principal objection to this way of looking at it, except that he locates the epistemological task under point "a)" in the syllabus of philosophy of religion. He accepts the assumption that the criteria of truth and falsity involved in the natural sciences are different from those that apply in religious reflection. But Nygren and Bring go further. In their view, the epistemological analysis of experience results in a fundamental differentiation between the theoretical and the a-theoretical (and especially the religious) areas of meaning. Lyttkens' question concerning "the objective

truth of religious content" represents, therefore, an altogether illegitimate consideration, first because religion does not function in
the way of objective truth, and second because the procedure tends
to confuse the theoretical, non-religious criteria of truth and falsity
with the a-theoretical, religious category of meaning, thus impinging
on the categorical autonomy of both theoretical epistemology and
religious convictions.

Lyttkens, on his side, does not work within the framework of the
Kant-Schleiermacher-Nygren-Bring problematics. His epistemological
background is closer to Hägerström and to the Uppsala-tradition of
positivistic empiricism. He recognizes, of course, a certain distinction
between theoretical and a-theoretical experiences; but he is not, as
Nygren and Bring, eager to separate between several autonomous
areas of experience. The deduction of the formal category of religion
is not a subject of interest to him. He sees no need for such an analytical tool; the religious phenomenon (or rather, the religious
statement) is all he needs in order to function as a philosopher of
religion. As he sees it, the relationship of theoretical and religious
experience must not be constructed so as to involve two different
concepts of truth. There may be certain differences between the
criteria of truth and falsity that are applicable to the two classes of
propositions, but they are still criteria of objective truth. Religious
propositions must be tested by reference to their objective truth
value; only thus can they be validated and considered significant.
Without such testing, the religious material will contain a great
deal of subjective delusion or corporate illusion. With it—that is
with the determination of the limits and conditions of the objective
truth of religious content—the scheme of "true" religious propositions
may become extremely small; but this would only lead us closer to
true religion, and that is precisely the aim of analysis. The analyst is
not at all threatened by such a reduction of the doctrinal spectrum;
on the contrary, he welcomes it. Even if religion proves to be nothing
more than a configuration of known experiential factors—psychological, sociological, cultural, logical, or semantic—the modern
philosopher of religion does not panic. The religious phenomenon
is still there, and the religiously functioning texts can still be analyzed
and tested as to their objective truth.

Between Lyttkens and Wingren there is little logical contact —except
that Wingren's sort of statements may become the objects of Lyttkens'
kind of analysis.

In general, philosophy and theology appear to have fallen apart in Lund. Moreover, the Lundensian tradition is broken. Between Wingren and Lyttkens, on the one hand, and Nygren and Bring, on the other, there is little sense of continuity. In their own way the new leaders of the faculty have put the spotlight on certain areas of unfinished business in the methodological system of Nygren and Bring, and this methodology can undoubtedly learn much from these men. But Wingren and Lyttkens have made it clear that they consider the type of methodology that was formulated by their predecessors either theologically invalidated or philosophically outdated, and they strike out in other directions, leaving Nygren and Bring aside. The results, so far, are not convincing. Wingren's attempt to recapture theological methodology within an unquestioning reliance upon biblical categories of thought represents an unfortunate return to the philosophical naivité of the pre-critical age. Lyttkens' approach to the analysis of religious propositions, for all its modernity and sophistication, is fraught with epistemological problems, and with it the philosophy of religion is tied into a process of steadily diminishing returns.

In contrast to the present trend at Lund, we do not consider Nygren's and Bring's contributions passé. The original aim of their methodological work has not been fulfilled; there are still problems to be solved before theology is able to show itself at one and the same time intellectually respectable and theologically responsible; but a beginning has been made, a good foundation for further construction has been laid, and the aim is valid. The question now is how this unfinished methodology can be brought to completion and made to function according to its original intentions.

THE EPISTEMOLOGICAL REORIENTATION

In our analysis of the theological methodology of Ragnar Bring, we have identified a series of difficulties that may be seen to converge into three major problem areas. Each of these complexes of problems has its basis in certain methodological assumptions that are problematic or that have not been consistently followed through, and these are therefore the principal points on which the critique must focus and with which the reconstruction of the method must take its beginning. These problematic methodological assumptions we shall now need to identify, dissect, and adjust. They are located at different levels in the system, but their consequences are in evidence throughout.

We shall have to follow these cause and effect relationships as they criss-cross the entire methodological structure.

The first problem area has to do with the radical epistemological reorientation proposed by Nygren and Bring: the rejection of the subject/object perspective and the affirmation of the validity of human experience. The most immediate consequences of this move are positive. The new perspective has the effect of dissolving the traditional epistemological dilemma and releasing the human intellect from its long-standing captivity to the paradoxality of existence and the dubiety of knowledge. In this sense, the Lundensian methodology has cut through the Gordian knot of traditional philosophical epistemology and set the mind on the road to significant progress in selfunderstanding and world awareness. For all its simplicity, the epistemological reorientation is undoubtedly the most radical feature in the philosophical foundations of Lundensian methodology—though this is not always clearly recognized by the interpreters.

Nygren and Bring came to it almost unexpectedly. They were faced with a problematic fact: the modern mind's dissatisfaction with metaphysical speculation. On the surface, the general rejection of metaphysics appeared as a commonsensical desire to avoid the claims and counterclaims of the many systems of transcendent truth and to affirm the validity of more tangible and manageable realities, but on further analysis it became apparent that the metaphysical problem was deeper than that. The commonsensical solution, the rejection of metaphysical realities and the subsequent redefinition of reality in terms of physical or intuitive experience, obviously could not solve the underlying problem, the uncertainty of knowledge itself. As Bring sought his way back to the presuppositions of the metaphysical problem, he found on every level of consideration the assumption of a fundamental chasm between the knower and the known, forming an unavoidable hindrance to indubitable knowledge. At the core of the problem of metaphysics was another problem, an epistemological one: the problem of valid knowledge; and behind it, the ontological dilemma itself, the subject/object dichotomy. Forced this far back into the logical origins of human thought, Bring had no way to turn but to ask the basic question whether such problems are inevitable. Is the presupposition of the subject/object dichotomy necessary to the philosophical perspective, or is there perhaps another way to think? Bring's answer—the same as Nygren had also come to— was direct: there is. By dissolving the subject/object problematics, by refusing to be involved in the traditional ontological dilemma, by declaring that valid knowledge starts where man's experience reaches awareness, and by claiming that philosophy, far from having to prove the validity of knowledge simply functions to analyze the formal presuppositions upon which knowledge in fact rests, Bring —with Nygren—broke free from a centuries' old tradition of epistemological misconception. This is the most dramatic thing about them.

We should note that the Lundensians are not the only twentieth century philosophers who have made this move. The most illustrious example, perhaps, is Martin Heidegger. His radical *Kehrung* from the "ontic-existential" perspective of speculative metaphysics to the "ontological-existential" perspective of transcendental phenomenology corresponds, in several respects, to Bring's epistemological reorientation. It is a move from closed logical systems to radical openness toward existence, from epistemological uncertainty to an attitude of acceptance in relation to life. It was this *Kehrung* that lay at the base of Heidegger's thought as he issued his dramatic challenge to theologians, at the meeting of "the old Marburgers" in 1959, that they consider two elementary questions: "What do we mean by thinking?" and "What sort of thinking does faith represent?" By that time, Heidegger had already gone through deep dimensions of intellectual quest in order to free himself from the post-Socratic subject/object scheme. He had sought his way back to more "original" ways of thinking, characterized by immediacy of understanding, openness to the forms of language, and response to the meaning of existence. One may describe his new epistemology as built on two factors: a primal awareness of life (cf. Bring's validity of experience), and a transcendental phenomenology (cf. Bring's analysis of categorical presuppositions). Characteristically, Heidegger insists on keeping the phenomenological analysis entirely "transcendental", *i.e.* formal, or in more typical Heideggerian terminology, "ontological", as distinct from the "ontic" (or content-defined) ways of thought. On closer examination, it becomes quite apparent that Heidegger's epistemology and Ragnar Bring's critical perspective match at several crucial points.[1]

The old Marburgers, on their side, did not do much to answer Heidegger's challenge. Heinrich Ott was requested to present a

---

[1] Cf. Heidegger's reflections on his philosophical foundations; *Holzwege*, Frankfurt am Main: Klostermann, 1950.

paper in response to Heidegger the following year, which he did, under the title "Was ist systematische Theologie." [1] In it, he first paid tribute to Heidegger's "inestimable service in teaching us to see in a more primal way the nature of thinking, of language, and thus of understanding"; and then he proceeded to fill the formal-ontological categories of Heidegger's thought with the material-ontic concepts of Christian doctrine—thus revealing that theology is still involved in ontic-objectivistic metaphysical speculation and is seeking to rendezvous with the philosopher's analyses only to prove the intellectual "respectability" of Christian dogmatics. [2] Heidegger himself has issued explicit warnings against the temptation to making direct correlations between the transcendental-ontological analysis and the theological commitments of Christian faith. [3] His emphasis corresponds, in fact, rather closely to Nygren's and Bring's views on the illegitimacy of defining the religious category in such a way as to identify it with certain positive Christian concepts.

Heidegger's challenge to theology was, in a sense, already answered in Lund—though not, of course, in every detail. A new epistemological perspective had been developed, the presuppositions of valid knowledge being located in the validity of experience itself. The task of analysis had been taken up, the analysis of experience and the analysis of presuppositions both being considered basic to the concept of philosophy. And the first consequences had been drawn, namely the identification of a number of "areas" or "contexts" of experience, and the preliminary deduction of certain categorical *a priori* that are considered basic to the form and meaning of experience. But the epistemological reorientation was so radical, and its consequences so far-reaching, that the Lundensians were not able to survey the full significance of it all at once. There are still, in fact, a number of points in Bring's methodology that give evidence of the continuing influence of the old philosophical perspective. We shall mention three in particular: a) the fear of subjectivity, b) the definition of the

---

[1] *Zeitschrift für Theologie und Kirche*, Beiheft, 2, 1961, 19-46; English translation in *The Later Heidegger and Theology*, James M. Robinson and John B. Cobb, Jr., editors, New York: Harper & Row, 1963.

[2] For a fuller explication of Ott's view, cf. his *Denken und Sein. Der Weg Martin Heideggers und der Weg der Theologie*, Zürich: Zollikon, 1959.

[3] Cf. *Sein und Zeit*, Tübingen: Klostermann, 1949, pp. 179 f, 306 (footnote); *Holzwege*, 1950, p. 343; *Was heisst Denken?*, Tübingen: Max Niemeyer Verlag, 1954, p. 110; *Einführung in die Metaphysik*, Tübingen: Max Niemeyer Verlag, 1953, p. 6.

theological object of study, and c) the defense against positivism.

Bring's references to "subjectivity" and "subjectivism" appear for the most part in his discussions of the nature of religious experience and in his endeavors to secure the scientific objectivity of systematic theology. In the first context the importance of personal decisions or value judgments is freely acknowledged, and what we might call the epistemological subjectivity of religion is accepted in principle. In the second context the influence of subjective factors is considered methodologically embarrassing and therefore illegitimate; here subjectivism must be avoided at all cost. Thus Bring's commitments are clear: Religion is necessarily involved in epistemological subjectivity, but theology is to be guided by scientific objectivity.

One wonders, perhaps, why Bring, who has left the subject/object dichotomy behind, should continue to speak in such outdated terminology. This, however, is not a major problem. Bring's language may be excused as an allowance to the "old" philosophical perspective. His problem occurs when he allows his embarrassment on behalf of methodological subjectivism to dominate his thought to the extent that all subjectivity—even the epistemological subjectivity of religious experience itself—becomes a liability to him. Such tendencies are evident at several places in Bring's thought. Most notable, perhaps, is his careful differentiation between the presuppositions of faith and the presuppositions of scientific theology. From a scientific standpoint, this differentiation is, of course, very important. Moreover, the critical philosophical perspective demands that the religious and the theoretical categories be kept entirely separate and distinct. But in Bring's case there is more to it. He defines theology itself so that the methodological requirements of scientific systematic theology are met, *i.e.* apart from subjective involvements, apart from the presuppositions of faith. The role of faith-reflection and religious experience all but disappear from view. The task of developing a methodological framework for theology is actually abandoned at the point where the subjectivity of faith appears.

We shall consider Bring's definition of theology in a moment. Closely related to his fear of subjectivity, and further evidence of Bring's inability to draw the full consequences of his epistemological reorientation, is his delimitations of the theological object of study. Bring follows Aulén in this matter, declaring that theology is the study of the historical Christian faith, in abstraction from both its object, God, and its subject, the believer. As an explicit attempt to disengage theology from rationalistic metaphysics and personalistic psychology, and from the old philosophical point of view, this move is perhaps understandable. But on Bring's own epistemological presuppositions, and especially on the basis of his understanding of the nature of religious experience, the point is not only overdone; it is unnecessary, even illegitimate.

For one thing, if the epistemological subjectivity of religion is consistently acknowledged, faith need not be explicitly abstracted from its "object"; it already is, by the very nature of the case. From the critical point of view, all references to a metaphysical object of faith are excluded on principle. Religion is an area of human experience, valid and meaningful as such. Theoretical questions concerning the object of faith represent an illegitimate desire to extend the epistemological grasp of human reason. They are signs, also, of a metaphysical confusion of *meningssammanhang*. Such questions are therefore irrelevant to the study of faith, and an explicit argument to secure a non-metaphysical understanding of faith is unnecessary. Bring has not seen this. He has not managed to hold on to his epistemological assumptions in this context. He has not been ready to allow the full meaning of his epistemological reorientation to take effect.

A more surprising example of this is Bring's attempt to extrapolate faith from its subject, the person or the community of people who believe. Against the background of his critical philosophical orientation and the principal commitment to the epistemological subjectivity of faith, it is a riddle how Bring can even think in such terms. Religion, as he understands it, is a part of human experience, and faith expresses its nature. Between the experience of religious meaning and the expression of this meaning in propositions of faith, no separation is possible. A statement of faith is what it is primarily in terms of the intentions of the person or persons who formulate it. Thus, strictly speaking, faith does not exist except in reference to a subject; it has no meaning except in view of the experience of a subject who believes. To consider faith in abstraction from its subject, as an object or a thing in itself, is in obvious contradiction to Bring's methodological presuppositions. Moreover, the study of such an abstraction must inevitably lead to misunderstanding and misinterpretations of faith. Yet Bring insists on defining the theological object of study this way. Why does he, virtually inviting methodological inconsistency and theological distortion?

The reason lies, not in his principal commitments, not in the presuppositions of his system per se, but in the address and structure of his arguments, *i.e.* in his polemic involvements. Bring has apparently been drawn into dialectic opposition to the so-called theology of experience. He is anxious to avoid the methodological subjectivism which characterizes this school's orientation; and over-reacting to the dangers of methodological subjectivism, he allows his own concept of faith to lose its subjective reference and slip into pure historical objectivism. His basic commitment concerning the epistemological subjectivity of religion is thus compromised.[1] Bring's methodology does not, in fact, reveal itself as the product of a radical epistemological reorientation.

A third manifestation of Bring's tendency to fall back into the old philosophical perspective comes to light at those points where he is pressed by the impact of positivism and conservative theology into assuming an apologetic stance, feeling obliged to answer questions concerning the "truth" or "reality" of religious concepts. Principally Bring would argue on the basis of the categorical differentiation between the theoretical and the religious areas of meaning, explaining that religious statements do not function as descriptions of reality and that they are not, for that reason, to be considered true or false in the same sense that theoretical statements are. The truth of faith, if one must use such terminology, is of a religious kind. This reference to a principal distinction between the two kinds of statements, based on their respective intentions, is clearly in line with Bring's epistemological presuppositions. It represents a helpful approach to the trivial problems involved in the observation of a certain "conflict" between the truth claims of science and those of faith. In Bring's view, the

---

[1] The correctness of this analysis is supported by Bring's own view of Schleiermacher's concept of the object of faith. Bring argues that Schleiermacher is interested in the "broader historical-empirical" concept of faith, not in the "narrow psychological" perspective of his later followers. Cf. *supra*, pp. 160 f. Bring's reading of Schleiermacher's mind is ludicrously oversimplified at this point. It is true that Schleiermacher did not onesidedly focus on the psychology of the religious consciousness, but it is manifestly incorrect to imply that his "historical-empirical" approach to Christianity in any way abstracted faith from its subject. On the contrary, it was precisely Schleiermacher's strength that he interpreted the Christian faith from the perspective of the religious consciousness of the Christian community. He was, after all, raised in the tradition of the Brethren of the Common Life. A fuller explication of Schleiermacher's approach to theology would show that his emphasis on historical-empirical or scientific theology is closely integrated with another—perhaps more basic—concept which can best be described as faith-reflection. Cf. *Die christliche Glaube*, §§ 3, 4, 11, 15.

two kinds of utterances are categorically different from one another, and they cannot therefore be in conflict with each other.

Yet Bring is not satisfied to let the matter rest there. Positivists, on the one side, confront theology with the charge that since religious statements do not refer to real or true conditions and cannot therefore be verified, they are actually nothing but illusions; they are meaningless or nonsensical. Conservative believers, on the other side, confront the theologian with the challenge that unless he considers the dogmas of faith as referring to real and true things, he has, in fact, undermined the faith and is no longer a believer. The pressure of this double attack is enough to push Bring back from the clear-cut affirmation of the autonomous validity of religious experience to more traditional defense lines. He counter-attacks the positivists and pacifies the conservatives in one polemic-apologetic move, namely by explaining that the statements of faith refer to "realities" that lie "beyond" the narrow definitions with which the positive sciences operate, and that they are therefore "true" and "valid" in their own way.

By strict logic, the possibility of this kind of turn should be principally excluded for Bring. He has rejected the philosophical orientation on questions of reality, basing his epistemology instead on the validity of experience. He acknowledges the epistemological subjectivity of faith and considers the meaning of faith statements categorically different from the theoretical predication of objective truth. And he has stated positively that the truth value of faith lies in the realm of personal value judgment and commitment, not in the realm of objective verification. A consistent *Durchführung* of the critical philosophical understanding of religion would involve accepting the positivistic charge of subjectivity (but not the old-fashioned implication that this at the same time invalidates faith and makes religion into illusion), and living with a faith that is precariously agnostic (without submitting to the traditional fear that this robs religion of all meaning and assurance). The critical concept of faith is problematic only from the perspective of the old understanding of knowledge and reality. In the new way of thinking, faith is a valid aspect of experience, and its content plays a significant role in life.

Bring has laid the basis, in his critical philosophy, for leaving both the positivistic critique of religion and the traditional, objectivistic conception of Christian dogmas aside, yet he has not managed to free himself from the shackles of the old thoughtworld. There are other philosophers and theologians in our time who have done just that, however, and Bring's methodology could well be brought closer to completion by relating to such contemporary developments. They are two in particular: the new understanding of the function of religious language which has emerged within the camp of linguistic analysis, and the new understanding of the meaning of Christian dogmas that is developing in radical Protestant theology.

One need not subscribe to every facet of these movements in order to reap the benefit of the new thrust. Bring could learn two important things here: First, he could learn that logical positivism is philosophically passé, and that the philosopher of religion need no longer argue the case for a meaningful faith by reference to a "wider", pseudo-metaphysical concept of reality. Linguistic analysis has broken through the positivistic restrictions, simply by observing certain experiential variations in the functions of language. The verification principle of logical positivism has been limited to the particular language game to which such rules are relevant. Religious language games are now considered valid and meaningful in their own way, even though they do not answer to the rules of ordinary language. Secondly, Bring could learn that a de-objectified interpretation of Christian dogmas does not undermine the faith, but serves, instead, to redeem religious symbols from a centuries long process of secularization and metaphysicalization. It is the means to make faith come alive to contemporary men in a more meaningful and truly religious way. The old dogmatic perspective tends to absolutize and idolize human ideas. Its reference to the "reality" of dogmas signifies a loss of faith, not a concern for it. In the new perspective, faith is once more faith.

Clearly, then, two of the foremost movements of thought at the present constitute the logical continuation of the Lundensian methodological tradition. With these, the Lundensians do have an opening for the further development of their thought.

THE RELIGIOUS CATEGORY

The second major problem area in Bring's methodology has to do with the transcendental deduction—or, as one should rather put it, the lack of a deduction—of the religious category. We have already indicated several likely reasons for the Lundensian reticence in this respect.[1] There may be other explanations.

---

[1] Cf. *supra*, pp. 91 ff.

One possible explanation may be that the Lundensians simply did not need a clearer grasp of the nature of religious experience. The impression is unavoidable that the principal motivation behind Nygren's and Bring's development of a theological methodology was their desire to establish the autonomy of the religious area of experience and their interest in securing the scientific respectability of the discipline of systematic theology. Certainly, these are their primary emphases throughout, and on the surface they appear to demand a broad and inclusive methodological program. If one examines the Lundensian framework of thought a little closer, however, one will be struck by its limitations. One discovers that the program actually demands very little of its philosophical substructure. All that needs to be established in order to secure the autonomous validity of religious experience is the claim that this experience is *different* from, for example, theoretical or ethical experience. Again, all that is required in order to support the systematic-theological claim to scientific objectivity is a definite commitment to the *formality* of the concept of religion and an explicit reference to the historical *givenness* of the material that is to be investigated.

Thus, in view of the limited methodological task which Nygren and Bring defined for themselves, they have not, strictly speaking, had a need for completing the transcendental deduction of the religious category. They have expressed a certain interest in seeing it done, of course. Bring has also stressed the need for an analysis of the interrelationships and interdependencies of the various areas of experience, and the development of an integrated view of the formal categorical presuppositions. But he has managed to get along without these, most likely for the simple reason that his methodological purposes were after all so limited as not to require such philosophical refinements. Bring is not concerned to secure a contemporary understanding of the theological activity of faith-reflection. He is only secondarily interested in the problems involved in the reformulation of traditional motifs of faith in the current situation of the church. And he does not have much to say on the problems connected with the communication of Christian faith in the context of a modern secularistic society.

We shall return to the problems converging around Bring's rather narrow definition of theology in a moment. At this point we shall only observe that his two main methodological interests—the philosophical apologetic on behalf of the autonomy of religion, and the theoretical rationale for the scientific status of systematic theology—both focus on the theoretical status of religion and theology respectively, and are not directed toward the larger problems concerning the utilization of philosophical and theological media in the attempt to make sense of religious experience and Christian faith in the contemporary intellectual setting.

This observation is in itself a cause for disappointment, particularly in view of the fact that Bring at the outset did intend to hold together a double interest in intellectual respectability and authentic Christianity. But, somewhere along the line of its development Bring's methodology was reduced in scope; intellectual respectability became almost exclusively a question of scientific status, and scientific status was considered possible only for historical-systematic research. Whether in the last analysis the reduction in the scope of Bring's methodology is a result of his failure to complete the transcendental deduction of the religious category, or the absence of the transcendental deduction is instead a consequence of his limitation of the methodological purposes, we shall not venture to determine. But that the vacuum which exists in Lundensian philosophy at this point is closely related to the particular conception of theology with which these methodologians work seems reasonably clear.

Another possible reason that Nygren and Bring have not completed the transcendental deduction of the religious category may be that they simply did not know how to proceed. Their progress in this matter may have been blocked by the way they defined what they were looking for, namely "the religious category" or "the religious a priori". Their difficulties may, in fact, have started already at the point where they began to talk of religion as an "area" or a "context of experience". They did not, of course, intend to identify themselves with the idealistic approach to the categorical a priori. Neither did they desire to be involved in the pietistic compartmentalization of human experience or the classification of human affairs and historical events in terms of a sharp differentiation between secular and sacred things. But how can one talk about the autonomy of religious experience without being identified with these traditions? That was the problem.

The Lundensians quickly realized that the idea of a religious "area" of experience is easily misunderstood. So they began to speak of *meningssammanhang* (connections of meaning) or *meningsområden* (areas of meaning), instead. However, the change of terminology did not solve all their problems. It did not make it any easier to conceptualize what sort of formal category would be functioning as the transcendent presuppositon for the religious "connection" or "area" of meaning. Nygren proposed that the concept "eternity" might serve; but he had difficulties explaining its precise meaning and relating it to the other transcendent categories. Bring suggested that perhaps "salvation" might be better. They both realized, however, that these proposals simply substituted for a clear concept of the formal religious category, which could only be reached by way of the transcendental deduction. They also acknowledged that their own concepts were probably too close to the Christian understanding of religion to be fully acceptable. So, in a determined move toward categorical formality, but capitulating to the analytical problem, Nygren and Bring began to describe the religious category simply in terms of "the religious question". This opened the door for a variety of possible formulations to be tried out, but again the vagueness of the categorical form created difficulties. There was nothing in this approach to indicate, for example, what distinguishes the religious question from other categorical questions.

Nygren and Bring have never found a solution to their dilemma over the religious category. They have simply continued to emphasize that it must be kept entirely formal, and that as far as they are concerned there are perhaps several different formulations that will do.

The consequences of this embarrassing inability to provide an acceptable definition of the formal category of religion are evident at various crucial points in Bring's methodology. We shall discuss three: a) the understanding of religious experience, b) the conception of the nature of religious language, and c) the lack of an integrated view of experience.

We have noted that Bring in several places argues on the presupposition of an essential unity of the emotive and the reflective aspects of religious experience. He rejects the traditional differentiation between *fides qua creditur* and *fides quae creditur*. Religious life and religious understanding are inseparable; there is no way to distinguish between primary (religious) and secondary (theoretical) elements of faith. The methodological functions of this feature in Bring's thought are clear. He desires to avoid the liabilities of an extreme subjectivistic concept of faith; the scientific status of theology depends on it. Furthermore, he is afraid that theology might be subsumed by and made dependent on psychology. In order to undergird the scientific respectability of systematic theology, he must be able to show that its object of study is historically given, and that it is such as to require precisely the kind of study which this discipline proposes to undertake.

From a methodological standpoint, and in view of Bring's own purposes, his interpretation of religious experience is well taken. One can even demonstrate that Bring's approach to the interpretation of religious experience corresponds to the more advanced theories of psychologists who look at man not as a conglomeration of several different faculties, some of which function in one context while others predominate in other contexts, but as a whole being. In some ways, his conception of religion may be seen to predate the modern psychological discovery of the involvement of the total man in all facets of experience. Bring seems once more to have backed into an important contemporary intellectual reorientation, namely the death of the old psychologies of instincts and faculties, and the rise of the "wholistic" view of man. Other theologians of the modern era have embraced this revision in the psychological scheme openly. Some point with gratification at the fact that the Hebrew conception of man was always characterized by the idea of a body-soul unity, and that the Greek-inspired systems of psychological dualism or categorization of faculties have no place in the Hebrew-Christian perspective. Bring comes to the same conviction, but via his own route, and he is not able to orient himself fully on it.

In one sense one might say that Bring's interpretation of religious experience represents a daring innovation in his time and a sign of his openness to the current advancements in the understanding of man. But, unfortunately, the vagueness of Bring's concept of religion reduces the impact of his psychological reorientation; he is simply not clear on what sort of experience faith is. He has frequently described it as having its essence in "God-relationship", but since the principal analysis of the religious category is lacking, every symbol that he might propose to describe its form loses its logical justification. No concept can symbolize a transcendent category when its nature is formal and its form is not determined.

Bring is, in fact, caught in a vicious circle, and he finds no way out. The nature of religious experience is not defined; Bring can only refer to "the religious area of experience". Attempting to get a grip on the nature of religious experience by describing its content, faith, Bring finds himself without the means to break through to a principal understanding of the nature of faith. His only recourse is to identify faith with "the religious material", and to investigate its historical content as expressed in the documents at hand. This move is fully legitimate, if the purpose is to show that scientific theology is directed toward the historically given Christian faith. But if it signifies a capitulation to the philosophical problem of the nature of faith, and a flight into the scientific activities of motif-research, then the move is a declaration of failure.

In close conjunction with Bring's problems in understanding the nature of religious experience is the problem of developing a clear understanding of the nature of religious language. We have indicated in various contexts in preceding chapters a distinct need for further developments in the Lundensian perspective on this subject. Nygren has shown some preliminary interest in these matters, and Bring has provided some rudimentary references to the basic elements of a modern understanding of language—such as the analysis of language functions, appropriate categorical contexts, inner intentions, etc. There is a possibility for establishing a significant relationship between Lund and, for example, the Cambridge circle here. We must keep in mind, however, that the Lundensian methodology will not be able to support any cogent thought on the nature and function of religious language until it develops a principal concept of the nature of religious experience itself. And as we have seen, the Lundensians cannot reach a clear understanding of the nature of religious experience until they undertake the crucial task of analyzing the empirical manifestations of religion in the specific interest of completing the transcendental deduction of the religious category. In short, Lund must go deeper before it can go on.

Examples of the weaknesses in the Lundensian understanding of the nature of religious language come to light at several points in Bring's methodology. One cannot exclude the possibility of its playing a role even at the level of definitions and commitments. For instance, in reference to Bring's disinterest toward the methodological problems of faith-reflection or the contemporary reconceptualization and communication of Christian doctrine, it may be relevant to ask whether he leaves these aside simply because he does not have the tools with which to handle them. Both these areas of theology are, of course, intimately related to the understanding of religious experience and religious language. Bring knows this. He gives emphasis to the point that in order to understand the meaning of religious symbolism one must consider the statements of faith in their own proper context and according to their own characteristic intentions.

But what are the characteristic intentions of religious symbolism? All that Bring is able to say is negative: they are not theoretical, not metaphysical. What religious language positively intends, Bring does not explain. He cannot explain it, for he has not gone far enough in the analysis of religious experience and religious language to be able to do so. There is a roadblock in the way of Bring's progress in the faith-reflective field. In this situation, he is forced to look for another way to do theology, and he finds it: Instead of struggling to complete the critical-analytical theory of religious experience and religious language and presenting a thorough reinterpretation of the meaning of Christian faith in a contemporary linguistic framework, Bring turns to the history of the faith, to the study of the doctrinal intentions of the best theologians of the past. Besides being a scientifically respectable endeavor, this historical-systematic motif-research gives the theologian a certain understanding of the essential motifs of Christian faith. A personal and contemporary and constructive understanding of the meaning of the faith it is not, of course; but it gives significant theological insights, even if it does lack the satisfaction of the deeper dimensions of theology.

Other, more obvious consequences of the failure to analyze the nature of religious language are evident in Bring's occasional attempts at theological reformulation. Observe, for instance, his specifications regarding the Christian God-concept: It is not an hypothesis on the level of the natural sciences; it is not an attempt to understand God or claim him accessible to human conceptualization; it is an expression of the fact that man is being encountered and overwhelmed by the ultimate power of his being, and that he subjects himself to this power.[1]

Observe also this Christological passage:

> "The idea of Christ's divinity does not mean a curious metaphysical theory concerning a man being something between God and man; it indicates, rather, that in Christ's work, in his incarnation from birth to death, and in his suffering on the cross, God's own salvation came down to us and was given to us, so that here, and only here, do we find God as the self-giving God of love." [2]

---

[1] "Kristen tro och vetenskaplig forskning," *STK*, 25, 1949, p. 202.
[2] *ToR*, 1937, pp. 27 f.

At first glance, such reformulations may seem significant. But on closer examination it is evident that the main strength in Bring's approach lies not in what he affirms, but in the rejection of the theoretical or speculative understanding of Christian dogmas. In this respect, Bring's reformulations are characteristic of the way the Lundensian philosophy of religion sets the intentions of religious statements in sharp relief against the theoretical perspective on things, and they are helpful, negatively. But when it comes to the positive explication of the intentions and meaning of Christian concepts, Bring must rely on the traditional technique of substituting symbols, bringing in a different set of Christian concepts to explain the ones in question. There is no other way for Bring. He lacks the most essential tool for breaking open the symbols and getting at their intentions, namely a clear understanding of the essential nature of religious language. His present approach to theological explication—the substitution of symbols—cannot be a very meaningful one. Religious symbols constitute closed systems until one has opened them up, and Bring cannot do so until he has a clear understanding of the nature of religious experience and a sure grasp of the presuppositional form of the religious category.

A third major problem related to Bring's failure to undertake the analytical deduction of the religious category has to do with his interest in developing an integrated view of human experience and making an understandable delineation of the logical relationships between the various categories of experience. Bring has repeatedly emphasized the necessity of analyzing these matters. He considers it the next step in the development of the Lundensian philosophical-analytical program. Yet his own work does not focus on the mutual relationships or logical interaction between the different categories of experience. His emphasis, rather, falls on their mutual separation and autonomous validity. In a sense, this is inevitable in Bring's case. His methodology demands it. Moreover, he cannot himself hope to contribute to the development of an integrated view of the experiential categories—he has not even contributed to the clear grasp of the category closest to his own concern. Since the underpinnings of the categorical structure are not provided, the structure itself must wait.

We must ask at this point whether the fact that Bring considers the analysis of the overall categorical scheme the final, crowning stage of the Lundensian philosophical system does not in itself constitute a fundamental logical error. Does it not, in fact, run counter to the presuppositions of the system itself? As we have observed, two of the fundamental assumptions of Bring's epistemology are a) that human experience is valid, and b) that man is a psychological unity in all of his experience. The first of these assumptions clearly implies an integrated view of human experience; experience is, after all, the experience of man. The second assumption explicitly predicates a wholistic conception of the man who experiences, and whose experience is valid. With his methodological groundwork resting on these presuppositions, Bring ought not only to be able to understand the distinctive nature of the various facets of human experience; he has, in fact, a perspective from which to understand human experience as a united whole. It would seem logical, therefore, that he should start the philosophical analysis with the totality. The unity of human experience is given; it does not need to be constructed. The inclusive perspective on life is logically prior to the categorical distinctions within experience.

In their methodology, the Lundensians have reversed this logical order. That may well be the basic cause of their philosophical blockage. Impatient to get on with the task of presenting a philosophical apologetic on behalf of an independent category of religious experience, they rushed past the first stage in the presuppositional analytic—the deduction of a formal model for the understanding of the total spectrum of man's experience—and to the second stage, where they gave attention, primarily, to establishing the categorical autonomy of the several areas of experience. They did intend to undertake the transcendental deduction of the individual categorical presuppositions, of course, but they did not come far in this regard. The fundamental unity of human experience was lost to their view, and as a consequence the multiplicity of experience became problematical, also. The individual categories did not seem to fit into an integrated whole. The attainment of an inclusive perspective seemed difficult. Thus the Lundensians forgot what is actually the basic epistemological presupposition of the critical methodological system; and in its place they entertained only a remote philosophical *desideratum*.

In order to overcome the problem and accomplish the integration of experience, the Lundensians need to go back to the very beginnings of their philosophy and start again where things began to fall apart. Perhaps, after all, the solutions are at the roots of the problems; maybe the correction of the Lundensian errors must begin with the analysis of experience itself. It is our contention that it must. We shall indicate here, though only sketchily, the direction in which a critical analysis of experience could be developed. Much work is required to clear the Lundensian methodology of inconsistency and free it from subsidiary interests and foreign notions.

As we have seen, Nygren and Bring rushed to the analysis of the individual categories of experience under the impact of a predominant apologetic concern. They were not clear about the methodological consequences of their philosophical reorientation. In contrast, the starting point for our reconstruction of the method is to take the critical philosophical commitments seriously. These commitments center on the fundamental assumption of the validity of human experience, including religious experience. Clearly, if this assumption is taken seriously, the philosopher of religion need not feel under any immediate obligation to seek to establish the autonomous validity of religious experience; it is valid, and it forms a significant aspect of human life. The primary philosophical task, instead, is to analyze the nature and structure of human experience as a whole. The philosopher of religion is first an analyst of experience. In this primary analysis of experience, the philosopher is interested in developing a theoretical model for the conceptualization of the unified multiplicity of experience. That human experience is organized in several categorically different "areas" or *sammanhang* is obvious. Still, it is all the experience of man, and its unity is therefore given. Man functions in different ways in different contexts of life, but the wholistic concept of man makes it possible to see the unity of experience throughout. The basic analytical task, then, is to show how one can think of human experience at one and the same time in terms of unity and multiplicity.

The approach which we call for—and which, we suggest, is consistent with the fundamental assumptions of the Lundensian philosophical presuppositions—represents a reversal of the logical priorities in Bring's analysis of experience. It also requires a change of perspective. Nygren's and Bring's references to "areas" or "contexts" of experience tend—unintentionally—toward the disintegration of experience. The expressions "areas of meaning" or *meningssammanhang* are somewhat less prone to cause distortion, but they are still carriers of a non-unified concept of life. They point, in a sense, outward, to things or events in themselves, to the world or history per se; and they seem to indicate that certain ontological or axiological distinctions are present out there—objectively given, so to speak.

It is necessary to correct the Lundensian approach to experience. The fear of the so-called theology of experience has had a certain effect, also, on the Lundensians' philosophical perspective. In the same manner as they abstract the theological object of study, faith, from its subject, the believer, they tend also to abstract the categories of experience from their subject, the experiencer. All such inconsistencies—non-critical philosophical commitments—must be cleansed away. Clearly, on the basis of the critical epistemological orientation the experiential references are not only *not* problematic; they are essential to the cogency of the system as a whole. We propose, therefore, to seek a perspective and develop a terminology which will correspond to the fact that the categorically distinct areas of experience or contexts of meaning belong within the framework of every man's experience of life. They are, so to speak, nothing more than "dimensions" of human awareness.

If, from this perspective, we should suggest a model for the conceptualization and analysis of the totality of human experience, we would choose to speak of it as a multidimensional dynamic field made up of several concentric spheres that symbolize the distinctions between the various dimensions of life. (Cf. sketch).

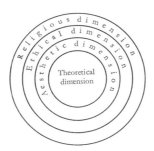

The most narrow and concentrated dimension of our awareness of life is the *theoretical* one. It is the dimension of science; it is ruled by the categories of human knowledge; it concerns itself with the investigation of facts; and its purpose is the progressive discovery of truth.

A second, more inclusive dimension of experience is the *aesthetic* one. It is the dimension of sensitivity; it functions by way of complex processes of appreciation; it is interested in the responsive acknowledgement of form and sense; and its goal is the expanding awareness of beauty.

The third dimension, more inclusive yet, is the *ethical* dimension of man's consciousness. It is the dimension of obligation; its dynamic is a commitment to a standpoint, an imperative, a principle of evaluation; it is directed toward the responsible recognition of value; and its aim is the growing obedience to the good.

Finally, there is the most inclusive of all the dimensions of life and awareness, the *religious* dimension. It is the dimension of faith; its principle of operation is the interpretation of existence from the perspective of a certain framework of meaning, a "story", a "Word", or a "message"; it is concerned to uncover the meaning of life; and its fulfillment lies in the complete openness to the ultimate.

One will note that in this model the fundamental presuppositions of the Lundensian form of philosophical criticism are in full view. The autonomy of the various dimensions of experience is guarded, yet they belong together within an integrated whole. The various dimensions are described in a formal way—they do not in any sense exclude any experiential varieties that might occur among men— yet they have a distinct and recognizable character. The model is not based on a categorization of experiential events into different "areas" or "contexts" which are the exclusive functions of separate and autonomous categorical presuppositions. It is in the awareness of experience that the categorization takes place. The presuppositional *a priori* are at work in the perspective of the experiencer, directing his approach to the things of life. The dimensions of awareness are not, however, described in such a way as to require a divisioning of the psychological faculties of man, or the assignment of different dimensions to different psychological functions. All of man—body and soul, reason and will—is involved in each and every dimension of experience.

If this model represents the essential philosophical intentions of the Nygren-Bring tradition of thought, it could well point the way to overcoming the difficulties that have continued to haunt the Lundensian leaders. Regarding the understanding of the religious dimension of life, for example, the model assures the autonomy of the religious category, its full integration with other dimensions of experience, and its complete formality. Religious experience is characterized by an autonomous principle of operation, a unique function, and a distinct intention. It is related to each of the other dimensions of life in a meaningful and significant way, and it is incorporated into a unified concept of existence. Thus, by means of this model, we may begin to make progress where the Lundensians so far have been hindered—in the understanding of religious experience, in the development of a critical theory of religious language, and in the logical explanation of the relationships between the religious dimension of life and other aspects of experience. It may even open the possibility for developing an intellectually acceptable methodological framework for the theology of faith-reflection.

THE DEFINITION OF THEOLOGY

We shall consider, finally, the third of the major problem areas which we have identified in Bring's methodology, that having to do with his definition of theology itself. Though closely related to the principal epistemological and philosophical problems which we have already discussed, Bring's difficulties here are at the same time more subtle and more obvious than the ones we have considered so far.

We have seen how Bring's failure to follow through on the presuppositions of his epistemological reorientation has had serious consequences for his definition of the theological object of study. Again, we have observed how his failure to complete the deduction of the religious category has influenced his understanding of religious experience, religious language, and the relationships between religious experience and the other categories of meaning. The question we are concerned with here is whether these factors, together with his fundamental methodological concerns, have had a bearing on Bring's definition of theology itself, thus causing a failure not only in the foundations of the methodological system, but in the very conception of the framework of theology as a whole. It is our contention that this is the case.

When Bring defines Christian theology as a scientific discipline engaged in the historical-critical study of the Christian faith, and aiming at the discovery, the identification, and the explication of its essential and characteristic motifs, he is doing so in a conscious attempt to avoid the traditional involvement of theology in speculative metaphysics, and to dissolve the close association of theology and authoritarian traditionalism, ecclesiastical dogmatism, and sectarian confessionalism. Bring has learned that no theology that is involved in metaphysics is intellectually acceptable in the post-critical philosophical situation. He is convinced that a theology which is less than open to the radical demands of scientific objectivity will have no possibility for claiming recognition in the future; it will be doomed to exist in an intellectual ghetto, and it will have no assurance of being true to the authentic character of Christian faith. The only basis on which Bring could see himself acceptable and responsible as a theologian in the present was to denounce metaphysical and authoritarian starting points for theology, to renounce all subjectivistic and arbitrary methodological commitments, and to define the task of theology as the objective, scientific investigation of essential religious motifs.

We shall not raise an argument against Bring's reading of the contemporary situation of theology. His understanding of the postcritical mind's reaction to metaphysics is corroborated by innumerable sources in the contemporary context. Likewise, his sensitivity to the methodological liabilities of subjectivism or dogmatism is clearly realistic. What is surprising—and disappointing—from our perspective is that Bring has not seen that the options for theology are not quite as limited as he has assumed; the option he has chosen represents, in fact, only a fraction of what a modern theology can be.

Theology, traditionally, has been given two opposite definitions. Corresponding roughly to the two main traditions of Western philosophy, idealism and realism, they may be referred to by way of the Greek terms *theologia* and *theologikè*. The first is a "strong" concept of theology, identified with the idealistic approach to reality; and it defines the task of theology as the presentation and explication of God's own logic or *logia*, the Wisdom or the Word of God. The second is a "soft" concept of theology, typical of the realistic philosophical orientation; and it shows the theologian satisfied to engage his own intellect in the interest of expressing and interpreting man's logic concerning the ultimate. *Theologia* claims that theology represents the truth of God, and that it has—in so far as that is the case—a degree of absoluteness; *theologikè* only claims to represent man's best thought concerning God, and it recognizes its own relativity.[1]

This division of theology into two main traditions is further complicated by the fact that Western philosophy is also divided along epistemological lines—the subject/object scheme of thought breaking into the conceptions of ontology and dividing both idealists and realists into several different camps. There are idealists of objectivistic and subjectivistic persuasions, and there are realists of existentialist

---

[1] For a fuller, though more popular discussion of this distinction, cf. my little book *A Theology of Christian Devotion*, Nashville: The Upper Room, 1969, Part II.

and positivistic points of view. And there are theologians in all these groups. Thus, schematically, one may describe four major types of theology as follows:

I. *Theologia*:   1. Subjectivistic
        —Metaphysical speculation concerning God's being and truth
                      2. Objectivistic
        —Transcendent truth from God and concerning God
II. *Theologikè*: 1. Subjectivistic
        —Religious reflection on the basis of faith
                      2. Objectivistic
        —Historical-critical study of the characteristics of man's faith.

When we consider Bring's definition of theology against this background, two things are becoming apparent. First, Bring's basic concept of theology is definitely of the *theologikè* variety, "soft" in regard to metaphysical references. It could not be otherwise. Bring lays a critical philosophical groundwork for his theology. He has undergone a fundamental epistemological reorientation that thas altered radically his entire approach to thought. Not only are questions regarding ultimate reality and truth beyond the capacity of man's perception and language; Bring considers the epistemological orientation which separates between man's experience and reality logically passé. It can only lead to a single choice: metaphysical speculation or absolute scepticism—neither alternative being a meaningful way to approach the ontological or epistemological questions. Bring rejects, therefore, the dichotomy of essence and existence, assuming instead that all significant thought must start from the presupposition of the validity of the human awareness of experience.

Philosophical idealism is thus an impossible position for Ragnar Bring, and the concept of theology as *theologia* is, for that reason, principally excluded from his perspective. He does, as we have seen, still allow for a certain "metaphysical interest" on behalf of theology;[1] and he does occasionally slip into the "old" separation between a limited, "positivistic" concept of reality and a reality which is "wider", which lies "beyond" these limitations, and to which the symbols of faith refer.[2] But these items are clearly inconsistent with the basic presuppositions of his thought. They must be ascribed to

---

[1] Cf. *supra*, pp. 145 f.
[2] Cf. *supra*, pp. 221 ff.

the fact that Bring has not in every respect managed to build a consistent structure on his critical groundwork.

Secondly, in terms of our theological spectrum, it is clear that
Bring's methodological emphasis falls on the objectivistic type of
theologikè, and that the subjective or existential form of *theologikè*
—faith-reflection—is forced into the background. This is nearly
inevitable in Bring's case. We have observed that his predominant
methodological interests evolve around two foci: He wants to establish the autonomy of the religious category of experience, and he
wants to secure the intellectual respectability of authentic Christian
theology. The first is accomplished by means of the critical analysis
of experience, and by the identification of the religious area of experience as an independently valid category or context of meaning.
The second, as Bring sees it, is primarily a matter of avoiding metaphysical thoughtforms and proving the scientific objectivity of theology. Metaphysical thoughtforms consist partly in an attempt to
define ultimate reality or truth in terms of certain arbitrarily chosen
concepts or ideas, partly in a confusion of *meningssammanhang* and
the subsequent tendencies toward logical transgression and loss of
categorical autonomy.

Theology as Bring defines it is largely free of the first form of
metaphysics; the critical point of view makes metaphysical identity-
speculation logically illegitimate. To avoid the second kind of metaphysics, Bring finds it necessary to draw a sharp dividing line between
theology defined as an objective science and theology understood
as religious faith-reflection. Faith-reflection contains features which
immediately disqualify it as a science: It is a religious exercise, not
theoretical; it is involved in the subjectivity of all religious commitments, ergo incapable of the objectivity and detachment that are
required of a scientific discipline. If theology is to be recognized
from a scientific point of view, it must be free of all traces of faith-
reflective presuppositions, being defined as a theoretical discipline
engaged in the historical-critical study of religious motifs. In short,
Bring's concept of theology, *theologikè*, assumes an explicitly objec-
tistic—even positivistic—character; he defines it as a scientific discipline
with a very limited scope and with only the most contingent relationship to the constructive, creative, faith-reflective brand of theology.

It is clear that Bring's problems in establishing an inclusive and
integrated concept of theology have their roots deep in the epistemological and philosophical complexes we have already analyzed. For

one thing, Bring's failure to complete the epistemological transition —the move from the assumption of the subject/object dichotomy to the unified but multi-dimensional concept of experience—plays a definite role here. The radical separation between the subjectivistic and the objectivistic kinds of *theologikè* is part and parcel of a pre-critical epistemological orientation, and Bring would have refused it on principle if he were consistent. A dichotomy between faith-reflection and scientific systematic theology is not in line with the basic assumptions of a critical methodology. According to the critical point of view, both faith and science belong together within the total experience-spectrum of man. Separate them, and man's experience disintegrates. Construct a separate theology on the two, and theology itself disintegrates. With two such separate and unrelated kinds of theology one can never claim to have overcome the subject/object dichotomy. There is, of course, a possibility for differentiating, even within the critical concept of theology, between different dimensions of theology: There is a *theologikè* which is integral to the religious dimension of experience, and there is a *theologikè* which is part of the theoretical category. But these are both aspects of one and the same endeavor. They represent two different *dimensions of theology*, not two separate and autonomous *theologies*.

The second of Bring's problem complexes, his confusion of epistemological and methodological subjectivism and his subsequent disavowal of the experiential focal point in theology—the abstraction of faith from its subject—has a definite influence on his concept of *theologikè*, also. Within a critical framework of thought, one would expect that a methodological preoccupation with the scientific or theoretical kind of *theologikè* and a corresponding de-emphasis of the faith-reflective, religious dimension of theology would immediately appear to represent a reversal in the proper order of priorities. Theology has to do with religious experience. According to the critical analysis of experience, the religious dimension constitutes a distinct category of meaning, valid and significant per se. Any aspect of religious experience, be it non-verbal and immediate or rational and articulate, is meaningful only as it participates in or is explicated by reference to the peculiar presuppositions and intentions of the religious context of meaning. Clearly faith-reflection, representing a rational superstructure on the confessional-commitmental substructure of religious experience, is in a position of logical priority as compared to the theoretical investigation of the historical manifestations of faith. Bring has not been willing to say this, however. He has made his methodological commitments in direct opposition to the "theology of experience", disassociating himself from the existentialism and subjectivity of faith-reflection, and the proper priorities of the critical theological methodology have thus been reversed.

A third aspect of Bring's philosophical problems that has also influenced the definition of theology is his failure to analyze the nature of the religious dimension of experience and its relationship to the other—and specifically the theoretical—dimensions of life. Bring has managed to establish the autonomy of the various categories, and he has made significant contributions to the understanding of the nature of scientific theology. These were his primary methodological purposes. But Bring could have done more. His methodological framework is much too limited to be representative of the critical methodological orientation. A critical methodologian is by virtue of his perspective interested in delineating the nature and function of faith-reflective theology, in explaining the relationship between faith-reflection and scientific motif-research, in engaging in a constructive theological endeavor to understand the meaning of faith in the thoughtforms and language of contemporary culture, and in solving the problems of communicating the faith to men who are living in a secular context. In so far as these interests demand a solid underpinning in the philosophical analysis of the nature of religious experience, religious language, and the place of religion within the total experience of man, Bring has not been in a position to take them up; and in so far as they represent real methodological needs on the part of the contemporary theological community, Bring's methodology must be said to have left the major part of the task undone. To the extent that Bring's philosophical perspective provides the clue to the fulfillment of these methodological tasks, one can say that he has been successful as a methodologian; but to the extent that he has not managed to complete the framework for faith, his methodology must be termed a failure.

Bring's peculiar definition of theology has given rise to three methodological weaknesses which we have identified already, but which we shall now, in closing, need to correct. They are: a) the demise of faith-reflective theology, b) the historicism and essentism of systematic theology, and c) the disintegration of the various dimensions of theology. The question we must consider here is whether the revisions we have proposed as means of solving the problems in Bring's methodology—the radical acceptance of the epistemological reorientation and the reversal of Bring's approach to the analysis of experience—can be seen to have positive effects even in regard to these more practical issues.

What will a consistent *Durchführung* of the critical perspective mean for the concept of faith-reflective theology? Stated simply, it will put the faith-reflective *theologikè* back in the center of the methodological structure. Once theology has abstracted itself from the philosophical perspective in which the subjective and the objective are considered opposites, it need not be abstracted from religious experience and defined solely in terms of scientific objectivity in order to reach intellectual respectability. Religious experience is valid. It is a major dimension within the total spectrum of man's awareness of existence, and it is autonomous and meaningful on its own presuppositions. The experiential anchoring of theology is not a methodological liability. The epistemological subjectivity of religious experience is not at all an embarrassment to the critical philosopher of religion or to the theological methodologian; on the contrary, it is precisely the basis on which the intellectual respectability—and not only the scientific status—of theology can be established. It means that theology itself is accepted as a meaningful part of life. The validity of religious experience carries with it the validity of all aspects of religious experience, theology included. The meaningfulness of religion includes the meaningfulness of theology. Faith-reflection, freed of all speculative, theoretical, and metaphysical intentions, and functioning on the basis of existential, religious, and interpretive motivations, is in fact the only form of theology that can undertake the basic task of holding together the authentic meaning of historical Christian faith and an honest involvement in the thoughtforms and rationality of contemporary culture.

In order to accomplish this task—the fundamental purpose of a responsible and respectable theology—faith-reflection must, of course, relate itself to the historical-critical disciplines which are studying the historical manifestations of Christian faith. This is where scientific theology comes into the picture. Christian theology will go wrong if it is not informed by the spirit and content of historical Christian faith. The epistemological subjectivity of religion will lead to individualistic arbitrariness and religious isolation if it is not counterbalanced by way of responsible cross references to a tradition of faith or a community of believers. Faith-reflection must therefore be assumed into a more inclusive systematic theology, a discipline which includes a significant participation in historical-critical research, an honest involvement in contemporary thoughtforms and language, and a conscious commitment to seeking and disseminating a constructive concept of the meaning of Christian faith in the present.

Besides incorporating faith-reflection in a larger context, this view sets the task of motif-research within its proper framework, also. All the different disciplines engaged in the theoretical investigation of Christian faith, Christian origins, Christian doctrine, and Christian history are inrolled as participants in and contributors to a single, overriding purpose. Moreover, the scope of systematic theology is widened considerably. A onesided emphasis on scientific theology tends to restrict the theologian within a theoretical, detached, and purely descriptive historicistic perspective. Also, a definition of the task of systematic theology as the scientific investigation of essential and characteristic Christian *grundmotiv* tends to reduce the theologian's scope and cause him to take a simplistic or atomistic attitude to the faith. With systematic theology defined as the unity of faith-reflective and scientific *theologikè*, and with scientific theology explicitly assigned to inform the theologian of the given historical character of Christian faith, the dangers of historical positivism and atomistic essentism are minimal. The theoretical study of the faith is then meaningfully related to the existential involvement in constructive faith-reflection. The purpose of motif-research is then no longer limited to the identification of the central or essential core of the faith; the historical-critical disciplines of theology are responsible for investigating the full meaning of the traditions and developing an inclusive understanding of the whole spectrum of Christian symbolism.

Theology, in a sum, is one. It has two dimensions, one theoretical, one religious; one scientific, one faith-reflective. But the two dimensions are intregrated within a unified concept of theology, existing side by side in mutual interaction and cooperation—not falling apart, to the deterioration of the whole, or being confused, to the detriment of each. With a consistent application of the critical view of experience, and with a clear concept of the relationship between the various dimensions of meaning, such an integration is possible. For in the critical perspective, the theoretical and the religious brands of theology are not considered two separate and mutually exclusive entities; they represent two different dimensions within the total theological awareness of man, each manifesting a distinct character, but both contributing to the larger whole.

We have come to the end of our present task, but the road goes on.[1] The methodological work is still unfinished. The Lundensians have made important strides, but they have only gone part of the way. Their course, however, is sound, and the road ahead is open. The contemporary theological community would be well served by what the Lundensians have done if their example could now inspire a new round of works on *frågan om den systematiska teologiens uppgift.*

---

[1] Cf. our Appendix, pp. 244 ff., for a series of theses toward a critical methodology for theology.

APPENDIX

A FRAMEWORK FOR FAITH

59 Theses Toward a Critical Methodology for Theology

On the Nature of Theology

1. Theology is man's thinking about God. It is a human language, an expression of faith, and it is significant not so much for what it says about the object of faith as for what it says about the man who theologizes.

2. The appropriate context for theology is within a community of men who share a certain faith and who desire to live in the light of this faith in the present.

3. The presuppositions for theology are present when a certain body of materials, constituting a historical tradition of faith, is acknowledged as constitutive of a certain community of believers and this community is committed to the continuing recapitulation and reappropriation of the meaning of the tradition here and now.

4. Theology functions partly as a historical science, describing objectively the given content of the tradition, and partly as contemporary faith-reflection, interpreting the meaning of the faith and drawing its implications for life in the present.

On Christian Theology

5. In regard to the Christian tradition of faith, theology undertakes to uncover the sources, investigate their content, and explicate their meaning. This is a scientific task, and it calls for the utilization of historical-critical methods of research.

6. Christian faith-reflection, springing from the corporate life of the Christian community or from the personal experience of individual believers, must be in continuing dialogue with the historical-critical disciplines of theology, both so as to be informed of the historical characteristics of the faith and so as to be aware of the relativity of all interpretation and language.

On the Sources of Christian Theology

7. The Bible is the primary source of Christian theology. It is the constitutive element in the Christian tradition, in so far as it

represents the crucial witness to the historical origins of the faith.

8.   The creeds of the church are significant for theology in that they represent an attempt to define, delimit, and explicate the central tenets of the Christian faith in the language and thoughtforms of their period.

9.   The history of the Christian community, in all its multiplicity, is an important source for theology in that it witnesses to the many and varied ways in which Christians have sought to express their faith, in life and work as well as in doctrine and order, in various periods.

10.   The corporate life of the community of believers is a valid source for Christian theology in so far as it is informed by the historical Christian faith. In the ongoing recapitulation and reappropriation of the faith, the community both celebrates its tradition and nurtures its commitment. As a member of the church, the theologian participates in both.

11.   Personal and individual religious experience is an acceptable source for Christian theology to the extent that the religious commitment is in harmony with the character of Christian faith, such as it has established itself in history.

On Systematic Theology

12.   It is the task of systematic theology to bring together the historical-critical and the faith-reflective aspects of theology, and to develop an understanding of faith which is both true to the intentions of the tradition and meaningful to men in the present.

13.   A crisis occurs in theology whenever the concern for the authenticity of the tradition takes precedence over the concern for the contemporary understanding of faith (the crisis of irrelevance). Similarly, a crisis occurs also whenever theology allows the contemporary mindset to set the limits for what is an acceptable and meaningful faith (the crisis of heresy).

Methodological Prerequisites

14.   Systematic theology must at all times recognize its involvement in the epistemological, philosophical, and methodological traditions that are influencing the intellectual life of man. The Christian faith is not itself a philosophical system, nor does it have a vested interest in any particular intellectual orientation. The theologian

is both free to function as part of his culture and responsible for participating in the advancement of thought.

15. Christian theology must demonstrate its intellectual honesty by establishing its selfconsciousness in direct reference to the presuppositions of thought that prevail in the present cultural context. This is the general purpose of theological methodology.

16. In the context of the contemporary intellectual situation, it is imperative that theology develop an awareness of its peculiar nature and establish itself as a meaningful intellectual exercise, autonomous within the spectrum of human thought, yet clearly related to other activities of the mind.

17. Theology must be able to define its categorical profile in such a way that it is not confused with metaphysical speculation or scientific explanation, *i.e.* with theoretical knowledge. Such confusion leads to intolerable intellectual conflicts and causes theology to lose its autonomous validity.

Methodological Goals

18. The theology which is needed to overcome the theological crises in our time must be true to the tradition, yet intellectually honest; genuinely faithful, yet capable of communication in the twentieth century; clearly ecumenical, yet having a distinct character.

19. Theology must strive toward a methodological orientation in which the various theological systems are considered objectively, not in terms of an absolute standard, not by way of eclecticism or reductionism, but by reference to the task of systematic theology itself: the explication of the historical Christian faith.

20. The relative value of a theological system must be considered on the basis of a double criterion: its capacity for uncovering the essential character of the historical faith, and its ability to make faith meaningful to contemporary man.

21. Theological systems must be studied with clear reference to the presuppositional commitments on which they are structured; a theologian's view of faith must be interpreted and evaluated on the basis of his own methodological presuppositions, not on principles foreign to his thought.

Epistemological Foundations

22. While theological methodology must be developed within the epistemological and philosophical perspectives that are character-

istic of the cultural context, it must also join in the continuing critique of the presuppositional foundations of culture. This is the point at which theological methodology intersects with the history of ideas and with critical epistemology.

23. Recent analyses of the presuppositional foundations of Western thought have revealed that most of the problems involved in developing consistent theories of knowledge and reality are due to the general acceptance of the post-Socratic philosophical perspective, which sets the knowing subject and the known object in polarity to each other. Where knowledge of reality becomes problematical, the only options for thought are scepticism and metaphysics.

24. Metaphysics represents an unsatisfactory epistemological option and an illegitimate way of thinking. It poses insoluble onto-logical problems, proposes unverifiable speculative solutions, and makes claims to ultimate truth on behalf of arbitrary intellectual com-mitments.

25. In the interest of avoiding the epistemological dilemma and its consequences—identity-philosophical speculation and philosophi-cal scepticism—critical philosophy rejects the subject/object frame of reference and proposes instead the following four presuppositions for thought: a) human experience is significant, b) human awareness represents valid knowledge, c) human experience is multidimensional, d) each dimension of experience presupposes an autonomous *a priori* category that functions as its formal context for meaning.

On the Analytical Task

26. The first step toward understanding the various dimensions of experience is the analysis of human awareness; this is the general task of analytic philosophy. Its aims are: a) to develop a model for the understanding of the total spectrum of man's experience, b) to sort out the various autonomous contexts or levels or dimensions of human experience, and c) to explain the relationships between the different dimensions so as to alleviate confusion and safeguard the integration of experience.

27. The second step toward understanding the dimensions of experience is the analysis of logical presuppositions; this is the specific purpose of analytic philosophy. Its functions are: a) to identify and delimit the essential nature of each of the dimensions of experience, b) to undertake the logical deduction of the formal *a priori* governing

the various categorical contexts, and c) to observe how the formal categories appear in the understanding of specific individuals or groups.

On the a priori *Categories*

28. An *a priori* category is a formal principle which functions as the presupposition for meaning within a certain dimension of experience to which autonomous validity must be ascribed.

29. A separate categorical *a priori* must be defined for each dimension of experience whose meaning cannot be understood by reference to other categories.

30. The formal *a priori* serving as categorical presuppositions for the various dimensions of experience are identified not for the purpose of establishing the validity of human experience, but simply as means of understanding it.

31. The *a priori* categories governing the various dimensions of human experience are not to be defined as to content, so as to serve as criteria by which to evaluate experience, but only as open or formal principles under which all experiential content is subsumed.

On Philosophy of Religion

32. It is the specific task of philosophy of religion to analyze, on the basis of the various forms of historical religion, the essential nature of religious experience, to undertake the logical deduction of the formal category of religion, and to explain the relationships between the religious dimension and other dimensions of human experience.

33. The quest for the essence of religion must be undertaken by way of a responsible investigation of the historical religions of man. The essence of religion is partly a formal concept, partly a material concept; the formal concept points to the religious *a priori*, the material concept to the specific content of each religion. These must be kept separate.

34. The analytical philosophy of religion must guard against any tendencies toward defining the essence of religion in terms of specific religious commitments or proving that a certain historical religion is the ultimate form of faith. Such tendencies are the results of a confusion of philosophy and theology; they signify a loss of integrity in both disciplines.

35. The judgment that Christianity is the ultimate manifestation of religion is a theological utterance, representing the peculiar commitment of Christian believers. The analytical philosophy of religion cannot lend support to any claims to metaphysical absoluteness.

On the Religious Category

36. The formal category of religion must be defined in such a way that man's religious experience is understood not as a function of a certain psychological faculty, not as a series of special or sacred events, but as engaging all of man and encompassing all of life, *i.e.* as an inclusive dimension of his awareness.

37. In its most formal delimitation, religion can be described as man's commitment to a certain interpretation of the ultimate meaning of existence.

On the Religious Types

38. A number of different commitments as to the interpretation of the ultimate meaning of existence appear in the history of religion, each representing a distinct religious type. Each individual religious type is characterized by a distinctive commitmental center, a basic motif of faith which forms the unifying core in all the historical manifestations of this religion.

39. The Christian faith is a distinct historical religion which was originated in the selfinterpretation of Jesus of Nazareth as the Christ, and in which the ultimate meaning of existence is interpreted in the light of the New Testament kerygma concerning the acts of God the Father, God the Son, and God the Holy Spirit.

40. A religious commitment represents the confluence, within the consciousness of an individual or a group, of the formal religious category and a particular religious tradition.

41. It is of fundamental importance for the religious development of an individual that he enter into a meaningful relationship with a particular religious community or tradition, thus avoiding the hazards of individualism, arbitrariness, and isolation.

42. In any religious community, there is both a tradition of confession and a tradition of doctrine. The first is a deep substratum of kerygma, cult, and symbolism; the second a distinct superstructure of didache, reflection, and interpretation. The tradition of confession

contains the constitutive elements of the faith and is binding on
each believer; the tradition of doctrine represents a series of contingent
interpretations of the faith and is informative for believers, but
relative.

On the Nature of Faith

43. The concept 'faith' is used in different ways in different
contexts: a) as a description of the religious category of meaning
(faith as differentiated from knowledge), b) as a description of a
certain religious type (Christian faith as differentiated from Jewish
faith), c) as a description of a particular theological tradition within
a certain religious type (the faith of a Calvinist as differentiated from
that of an Arminian), and d) as a description of a conscious commitment on the part of an individual to a certain religious tradition
(personal faith).

44. Having defined the nature of religious experience in terms
of man's commitment to a certain interpretation of the ultimate
meaning of existence, we have at the same time laid the basis for
establishing the autonomy of the religious dimension and relating
faith without conflicts and confusion to other dimensions of experience.
"Meaning" is distinct from "fact", and the interpretation of the
ultimate meaning of facts is different from the theoretical investigation,
the aesthetic appreciation, and the ethical evaluation of facts.

45. The religious interpretation of the ultimate meaning of
existence does not in any sense represent theoretical insight into
the scientific truth or the metaphysical essence of reality; its function
is not to uncover natural or supernatural facts, but to express man's
awareness of meaning, whether immanent or transcendent.

46. The distinction of faith and science must be expressed not
in terms of two different "objects", not in terms of two different
kinds of knowledge, but in terms of the different intentions evident in
their approach to existence. Science intends to investigate, faith to
interpret; science explains, faith elucidates; science asks for the "what"
and the "why" and the "how" of facts, faith confesses the "what"
and the "why" and the "how" of religious commitments.

47. The distinction of faith and metaphysics must be expressed
not by reference to competing epistemologies or contrasting
ontologies, not by reference to divine revelation versus human reason,
but by reference to the different intentions informing their approach

to reality. Metaphysics intends to define reality, faith to confess an interpretation of it; metaphysics will describe transcendent objects, faith expresses its own point of view; metaphysics seeks to answer the "what" and the "why" and the "how" of essential reality, faith expresses the "what" and the "why" and the "how" of religious awareness.

48. Within the critical orientation, "reason" describes the dynamics of thought from the perspective of the theoretical dimension of experience, while "revelation" symbolizes the believer's interpretation of the dynamics of thought from the perspective of the religious dimension. Reason and revelation represent two different perspectives on life; both find room within a man's awareness of experience, and there is no conflict or confusion between them.

On Religious Language

49. Language functions to express man's awareness of experience. Parallel to the differentiation of various dimensions of experience is the differentiation between several dimensions of language, each of which constitutes a distinct context of meaning. Statements are meaningful only as they are understood within their own context of meaning and in reference to their own intended purpose. Religious language is meaningful only in the sense that it signifies in symbolic ways the interpretation of the ultimate meaning of existence.

50. Parallel to the distinction of a confessional-cultic substratum and a rational-doctrinal superstructure within religious traditions is the distinction in religious language between liturgical language (language functioning within the intentional framework of worship) and doctrinal language (language functioning within the intentional framework of theological explication). Both serve a significant purpose within the religious dimension of experience and both are valid in the light of their intentions.

51. The symbolism of liturgical language is less direct and exact than that of doctrinal language; however, doctrinal language lacks the spontaneity and vitality of liturgical language. The believer must be acquainted with both language functions and must understand each aspect of religious language on its own presuppositions.

On the Nature of Doctrine

52. The nature of doctrine is best defined by reference to its double orientation: the religious tradition and the contemporary

thoughtforms. It is faith-reflection. Christian doctrine is grounded in the kerygmatic essence of historical Christian faith and developed by way of logical reflection and modern concepts. Doctrine participates, therefore, both in the dynamics of faith and in the intellectual life of its time.

53.   The formulations of Christian doctrine represent, in symbolic language, an explication of the meaning of existence as interpreted by an individual believer or a group of Christians who reflect on the content and consequences of the Christian faith from the standpoint of a definite commitment to this faith and by means of the conceptual and linguistic tools available to them.

54.   In the development of Christian doctrine, it is imperative that all reformulations of the meaning of the Christian kerygma be checked against the traditions of confession and doctrine. In confronting new doctrinal formulations with the traditions, however, one must guard against the tendency to absolutize one part of the tradition and declare it "orthodox".

55.   There is no absolute norm by which doctrinal reformulations can be judged "true" or "false". Such a norm would itself represent an explication of the meaning of the faith from the point of view of an individual Christian or a community of believers, and it would therefore participate in the relativity which it were designed to test. The criterion by which doctrinal reformulations are to be evaluated lies deep within the kerygmatic symbols that are constitutive for Christian faith, functioning as their unifying core: the Christian *grundmotiv*.

56.   In seeking the criterion of authentic Christian doctrine—the essence of the Christian faith—it is necessary to investigate all the historical manifestations of this faith, and primarily the documents from its constitutive period, *i.e.* the Bible, especially the New Testament, and the Fathers. This is the general task of scientific theology (biblical exegesis, historical theology).

57.   In order to get at the motif-structures that characterize the Christian faith, the scientific theologian must penetrate all contingent historical factors of thought and language and seek to describe the formative elements of the Christian kerygma. Scientific theology endeavors to understand the authentic Christian message.

58.   Scientific theology undertakes the investigation of the historical manifestations of Christian faith—the tradition of confession

and the tradition of reflection, the language of liturgy and the language of doctrine—by means of historical-critical methods of research. It is a theoretical exercise, tentative and non-normative. It aims to identify, within the vast variety of Christian symbols, that which is the underlying intention, the essence of meaning, the *grundmotiv*; this is the specific purpose of scientific theology (motif-research). The definition of the essence of Christianity will always be hypothetical, however, always open to modification by way of new research.

On Christian Communication

59. Christian theology will of necessity involve a concern for the contemporary communication of the faith. The basic means of Christian communication are: a) Christian liturgy, b) Christian preaching, c) Christian teaching, and d) Christian action. Christian communication is primarily evocative, not indicative or imperative; it aims not to impart factual knowledge or metaphysical ideas, not to inculcate ethical ideals, but to witness to the Christian faith by way of celebration, proclamation, explication, and application, and to awaken in persons an awareness of its meaning and a commitment to live in its light.

BIBLIOGRAPHY OF WORKS CITED

AALEN, Leiv, "Principal Systematic Problems of Present-Day Scandinavian Theology," *Lutheran World*, 3 (1956), 44-58.

ANDRAE, Tor, *Nathan Söderblom*. Uppsala: Lindblad, 1931.

AUBREY, Edwin Ewart, *Present Theological Tendencies*. New York and London: Harper, 1936.

AULÉN, Gustaf, "Adertonhundratalets kristologiska brytningar och nutiden," *STK*, 6 (1930), 32-46.

——, *Christus Victor*. London: S.P.C.K., 1931.

——, "Diskussionsinlägg. Ennu ett svar till professor Runestam," *STK*, 2 (1926), 98-104.

——, *Die Dogmengeschichte im Lichte der Lutherforschung*. ("Studien der Luther-Akademie," nr. I.) Gütersloh: Bertelsmann, 1932.

——, *Dogmhistoria*. ("Handböcker i teologi," nr. 5.) Stockholm: Nordstedt, 1917.

——, *Dramat och symbolerna*. 2d ed. Stockholm: Diakonistyrelsen, 1965.

——, "Den evangeliska teologiens tvänne huvudskeden och vår tid," *STK*, 2 (1926), 232-52.

——, *Evangeliskt kyrklighet*. ("Sveriges kristliga studentrörelse. Skriftserie," nr. 50.) Uppsala: Sveriges kristliga studentrörelse, 1916.

——, *Evangeliskt och romerskt*. ("Sveriges kristliga studentrörelse. Skriftserie," nr. 139.) Stockholm: Sveriges kristliga studentrörelse, 1922.

——, *The Faith of the Christian Church*. Philadelphia: Muhlenberg Press [1960].

——, "Från den teologiska samtiden. (Adolf von Harnack)," *STK*, 6 (1930), 211-16.

——, *Gammalkyrkligt och reformatoriskt*. ("LUÅ," n.f., avd. I, bd. 26, 3.) Lund: Gleerup, 1930.

——, *I vilken riktning går nutidens teologiska tänkande?* ("Sveriges kristliga studentrörelse. Skriftserie," nr. 133.) Stockholm: Sveriges kristliga studentrörelse, 1921.

——, "Inför Einar Billings sextioårsdag," *STK*, 7 (1931), 236-40.

——, *Kristendomens själ*. ("Sveriges kristliga studentrörelse. Skriftserie," nr. 148.) Stockholm: Sveriges kristliga studentrörelse, 1922.

——, *Den kristna försoningstanken*. Stockholm: Diakonistyrelsen, 1930.

——, *Den kristna gudsbilden genom seklerna och i nutiden*. Stockholm: Diakonistyrelsen, 1927.

——, *Den kristna tankens tolkning av Jesu person*. Uppsala: Norblad, 1910.

——, *Liturgiska förnyelsesträvanden och evangelisk kristendom*. Lund: Gleerup, 1928.

——, "Lundensisk teologisk tradition," *STK*, 30 (1954), 229-45.

——, *Martin Eric Ahlman och Ebbe Gustaf Bring*. ("LUÅ," n.f., avd. I, bd. 14, 5.) Lund: Gleerup, 1918.

——, "Nathan Söderblom och nutida svensk teologi," *STK*, 2 (1926), 3-19.

——, *Reformation och katolicitet*. Stockholm: Diakonistyrelsen, 1959.

——, "Sekelskiftets teologi. En återblick," *STK*, 1 (1925), 61-80.

——, "Teologisk litteratur. Ny svensk litteratur på systematikens och den kristna idéhistoriens område," *STK*, 6 (1930), 357-81.

——, "Det teologiska nutidsläget," *STK*, 5 (1929), 119-46.

——, *Till belynsning af den lutherska kyrkoiden*. ("Uppsala. Vilhelm Ekmans fond. Arbeten," 11.) Uppsala: Almqvist & Wiksell, 1912.

——, "Teologisk litteratur. Troskunskap och vetenskap," *STK*, 1 (1925), 360-71.

AULÉN, Gustaf, *Uppenbarelse och historia i den nutida teologien*. Uppsala: Almqvist & Wiksell, 1912.

BARTH, Karl, *Church Dogmatics*. Vol. I, 1. New York: Scribner, 1955.

———, *The Epistle to the Romans*. Translated from the 6th German edition. London [etc.]: Oxford University Press, [1957, c. 1933].

———, *Protestant Thought: from Rousseau to Ritschl*. New York: Harper [1959].

BENKTSON, Benkt-Erik, *Christus und die Religion*. ("Arbeiten zur Theologie," II. Reihe, Bd. 9.) Stuttgart: Calwer Verlag [c. 1967].

———, "Eros och agape hos Karl Barth," *STK*, 36 (1960), 214-42.

———, *Den naturliga teologiens problem hos Karl Barth*. Lund: Gleerup, 1948.

BILLING, Einar, *De etiska tankarna i urkristendomen*. ("Ur kristendomens historia och tankevärld," 3.) Uppsala: Schultz, 1907.

———, *Försoningen*. Uppsala: Almqvist & Wiksell i distr., 1908.

———, *Folkkyrkan och förkunnelsen*. ("Sveriges kristliga studentrörelse. Skriftserie," nr. 16.) Stockholm: Sveriges kristliga studentrörelse, 1912.

———, *Herdabref till prästeskapet i Västerås stift*. Stockholm: Sveriges kristliga studentrörelse, 1920.

———, *Luthers lära om staten*. Uppsala: Almqvist & Wiksell, 1900.

———, *Luthers storhet*. (Sveriges kristliga studentrörelse, Skriftserie," nr. 73.) Stockholm: Sveriges kristliga studentrörelse, 1917.

———, *Den svenska folkkyrkan*. ("Religionsvetenskapliga skrifter," 15.) Stockholm: Sveriges kristliga studentrörelse, 1930.

———, *Universitet och kyrka*. Stockholm: Sveriges kristliga studentrörelse, 1923.

BOHLIN, Torsten, *Gudsto och Kristustro hos Luther*. Stockholm: Diakonistyrelsen [1927].

———, "Den historiska uppenbarelsen och den dialektiska teologin," *STK*, 1 (1925), 219-32.

———, *Kierkegaards dogmatiska åskådning*. Stockholm: Diakonistyrelsen, 1925.

———, *Tro och uppenbarelse*. Stockholm: Diakonistyrelsen, 1926.

———, "Trosbegreppet i den dialektiska teologin," *STK*, 1 (1925), 156-76.

———, "Vetenskap—troslära—förkunnelse," *Gåva och krav. Skrifter tillägnade Manfred Björkquist*. Stockholm: Sveriges kristliga studentrörelse, 1934.

En bok om bibeln. Lund: Gleerup, 1947.

En bok om kyrkan. Stockholm: Diakonistyrelsen, 1943.

BRILIOTH, Yngve, *Kampen om kyrkan*. ("Skrifter i teologiska och kyrkliga ämnen," 6.) Lund: Gleerup, 1937.

———, *Kyrkokristendom*. Stockholm: Diakonistyrelsen, 1943.

———, "Nyanglikansk renässans," *Kyrkohistoriska föreningen, Uppsala. Skrifter, I, Kyrkohistorisk årsskrift* (1921-23).

———, *Svensk kyrkokunskap*. Stockholm: Diakonistyrelsen, 1933.

BRING, Gustaf, *Immanuel Kants förhållande till den filosofiska teologien*. Lund: Gleerup, 1876.

BRING, Ragnar, "Anders Nygren. Teologen och kyrkomannen," *STK*, 26 (1950), 161-66.

———, "Anders Nygrens teologiska gärning," *STK*, 16 (1940), 315-21.

———, *Att lyda bibeln. Luthers förhållande till bibelns bud*. Stockholm: Diakonistyrelsen, 1961.

———, "Bibeln och uppenbarelsen," *STK*, 22 (1946), 319-41.

———, *Bibelns auktoritet och bibelns bruk*. Lund: Gleerup [1958].

———, *Der Brief des Paulus an die Galater*. Berlin: Lutherisches Verlagshaus, 1967.

———, "Christologie und Gottes Monarchie," *Die Leibhaftigkeit des Wortes*. Hamburg: Furche-Verlag [1958].

———, *Christus und das Gesetz*. Leiden: Brill, 1969.

BRING, Ragnar, *Commentary on Galatians.* Philadelphia: Muhlenberg Press [1961].
——, *Dualismen hos Luther.* Stockholm: Diakonistyrelsen, 1929.
——, "Einige Blätter aus der schwedische Lutherforschung," *ZST*, 8 (1931), 615-70.
——, "Die Erfüllung des Gesetzes durch Christus," *Kerygma und Dogma*, 5, 1959.
——, "Die Erfüllung des Gesetzes. Vergleich zwischen Paulus und Luther," *Vierhundertfünfzig Jahre lutherische Reformation. 1517-1967. Festschrift für Franz Lau*, Berlin: Evangelische Verlags Anst., 1967.
——, "Förhållandet mellan teologi och religion i historisk belysning," *STK*, 10 (1934), 260-74.
——, *Förhållandet mellan tro och gärningar inom luthersk teologi.* ("Acta Akademiae Aboensis," Humaniora, IX.) Helsingfors: Åbo Akademi, 1934.
——, "Från den teologiska samtiden," *STK*, 15 (1939), 161-63.
——, "Der Glaube an die Zukunft und die Hoffnung auf das ewige Leben," *Lutherische Rundschau*, 4 (1954), 225-37.
——, "Glaube und Werke," *ZST*, 12 (1934-35), 498-551.
——, *Das göttliche Wort. Grundfragen unseres Glaubens.* Gütersloh: Gerd Mohn, 1964.
——, *How God Speaks to Us: The Dymanics of the Living Word.* Philadelphia: Fortress Press, 1962.
——, "Kristen tro och vetenskaplig forskning," *STK*, 25 (1949), 201-43.
——, *Kristendomstolkningar i gammal och ny tid.* Stockholm: Diakonistyrelsen, 1950.
——, "De kristna tankarnas sanningsvärde i olika kultursituationer," *STK*, 16 (1940), 39-49.
——, "Lag och evangelium," *STK*, 12 (1936), 207-27.
——, *Lutherische Theologie angesichts der ökumenischen Arbeit.* ("Luthertum," Hft. 1, pt. 2.) Berlin: Lutherisches Verlagshaus, 1951.
——, *Luthers Anschauung von der Bibel.* ("Luthertum," Hft. 3.) Berlin: Lutherisches Verlagshaus, 1951.
——, "Luthers Lehre von Gesetz und Evangelium als Beitrag der Lutherischen Theologie für die Oekumene," *Luther-Jahrbuch*, 26 (1957).
——, "Luthersk bibelsyn," *En bok on bibeln.* Lund: Gleerup [1948, c. 1947].
——, "Der Mittler und das Gesetz," *Kerygma und Dogma*, 12, 1966.
——, "Die neuere schwedische Theologie," *Ekklesia*, Bd. II, 5: *Die Kirche in Schweden.* Gotha: Klotz, 1935.
——, "On the Lutheran Concept of the Sacrament," *World Lutheranism of Today. A Tribute to Anders Nygren.* Stockholm: Diakonistyrelsen, 1950.
——, "Ordet, samvetet och den inre människan," *Ordet och tron. Till Einar Billing på hans sexioårsdag.* Stockholm: Diakonistyrelsen, 1931.
——, "Paradoxtanken i teologien, " *STK*, 10 (1934), 3-17.
——, *Pauli brev till galaterna, Tolkning.* ("Tolkning av Nya testamentet," 8.) Stockholm: Diakonistyrelsen, 1958.
——, *Die paulinische Begründung der Lutherischen Theologie.* ("Luthertum," Hft. 17.) Berlin: Lutherisches Verlagshaus, 1955.
——, "The Subjective and the Objective in the Concept of the Church," *This is the Church.* Philadelphia: Muhlenberg Press [1952].
——, "Swensk kyrkotidnings teologi," *STK*, 35 (1959), 153-74.
——, *Teologi och religion.* Lund: Gleerup [1937].
——, "Teologi och religionsfilosofi," *STK*, 23 (1947), 37-70.
——, "Teologisk litteratur. Anders Nygren: Dogmatikens vetenskapliga grundläggning," *STK*, 12 (1936), 287-90.
——, "Teologisk litteratur. Gåva och krav. Till Manfred Björkquist," *STK*, 10 (1934), 383-87.

BRING, Ragnar, "Teologisk litteratur. Gustaf Aulén: Reformation och katolicitet," *STK*, 35 (1959), 111-20.

——, "Teologisk litteratur. Några randanteckningar till andra upplagan av Nygren: Filosofisk och kristen etik," *STK*, 9 (1933), 50-66.

——, "Teologisk litteratur. Några randanmärkningar till vissa den svenska systematiska teologiens senaste landvinningar," *STK*, 7 (1931), 385-75.

——, "Teologisk litteratur. Systematisk och historisk Lutherforskning," *STK*, 7 (1931), 32-51.

——, "Det tidsbestämda och det evigt giltiga i Bibelns ord och bud," *STK*, 35 (1959), 21-42.

——, *Till frågan om den systematiska teologiens uppgift*. ("LUÅ," n.f., avd. I, bd. 29, 1). Lund: Gleerup, 1933.

——, *Das Verhältnis von Glauben und Werken in der lutherischen Theologie*. ("Forschungen zur Geschichte und Lehre des Protestantismus," Zehnte Reihe, Bd. VII.) München: Kaiser Verlag, 1955.

——, "Ein Versuch dogmengeschichtlicher Neuorientierung," *Theologisches Literaturblatt*, 53 (1932), 257-61.

——, *Wie ist nicht-metaphysische Philosophie möglich?* ("Kungliga humanistiska vetenskapssamfundet i Lund. Årsberättelse," 1939-40.) Lund: Gleerup, 1940.

BRUNNER, Heinrich Emil, *Revelation and Reason*. Philadelphia: Westminster Press [1964].

CARLFELT, Carl Gustaf, "Recent Swedish Theologians and Their Theology," *American Lutheran Conference. Journal*, VII (1942), 481-510.

CARLSON, Edgar Magnus, *The Reinterpretation of Luther*. Philadelphia: Westminster Press [1948].

CULLBERG, John, *Das Problem der Etik in der Dialektischen Theologie. I. Karl Barth*. ("UUÅ," 4.) Uppsala: Lundequistska bokhandeln, 1938.

——, *Religion och vetenskap*. Stockholm: Diakonistyrelsen, 1930.

EHNMARK, Erland, *Religionsproblemet hos Nathan Söderblom*. Lund: Gleerup, 1949.

EKLUND, Harald, *Evangelisches und katholisches in Max Schelers Ethik*. ("UUÅ," Teologi, I.) Uppsala: Lundequistska bokhandeln, 1932.

ENGESTRÖM, Sigfrid von, "Arvet från Albrecht Ritschl i den svenska teologien," *Nordisk teologi. Ideer och män*. Lund: Gleerup [1955].

——, *Luthers trosbegrepp. Med särskild hänsyn till församthållandets betydelse*. ("UUÅ," Teologi, 3.) Uppsala: Lundequistska bokhandeln, 1933.

——, "Tro och erfarenhet," *Ordet och tron. Till Einar Billing på hans sextioårsdag*. Stockholm: Diakonistyrelsen, 1931.

ERASMUS, Desiderius, *Vom freien Willen*. Verdeutscht von Otto Schumacher. 2. Aufl. Göttingen: Vandenhoeck & Ruprecht, 1956.

ERLING, Bernhard, *Nature and History*. ("Studia theologica Lundensia," 19.) Lund: Gleerup, 1960.

——, "Swedish Theology from Nygren to Wingren," *Religion in Life*, Spring (1961), 196-208.

FERRÉ, Nels, *Swedish Contributions to Modern Theology*. New York, London: Harper [1939].

FRIES, Martin, *Metafysiken i modern svensk teologi*. Stockholm: Natur och kultur, 1948.

GÖRANSSON, Nils Johan, *Luthers reformation. Historisk psychologisk trosskildring*. Stockholm: Norstedt, 1920.

GORDH, George R., *Criticism of Reason in Contemporary Theological Methodology*. Unpublished Ph. D. dissertation, University of Chicago, 1941.

HÄGERSTRÖM, Axel, *Axel Hägerström*. (*Selbstdarstellung*). ("Die Philosophie der Gegenwart in Selbstdarstellungen," Vol. 7.) Leipzig: F. Melner [1929].

——, Hägerström, Axel, "Kritiska punkter i värdepsykologien," *Festskrift tillägnad E. O. Burman*. Uppsala: Akademisk Bokhandel, 1910.

——, "Om moraliska föreställningars sanning," *Socialfilosofiska uppsatser*. Stockholm: Bonnier, 1939.

Hall, Thor, "Nygren's Ethics," *The Philosophy and Theology of Anders Nygren*. ("Library of Living Theology.") Carbondale, Ill.: Southern Illinois University Press (forthcoming).

——, *A Study of Lundensian Theological Methodology as Represented in the Thought of Ragnar Bring*. Unpublished Ph. D. dissertation, Duke University, 1962.

——, *A Theology of Christian Devotion*. Nashville: The Upper Room, 1969.

Harnack, Adolf von, *What is Christianity*. New York: Harper, 1957.

Hedenius, Ingemar, *Tro och livsåskådning*. Stockholm: Bonnier, 1958.

——, *Tro och vetande*. Stockholm: Bonnier, 1949.

Heidegger, Martin, *Einführung in die Metaphysik*. Tübingen: Max Niemeyer Verlag, 1953.

——, *Holzwege*. Frankfurt am Main: Klostermann, 1950.

——, *Sein und Zeit*. 5th ed. rev. Frankfurt am Main: Klostermann, 1949.

——, *Was heisst Denken?* Tübingen: Max Niemeyer Verlag, 1954.

Hemberg, Jarl, *Religion och metafysik. Axel Hägerströms och Anders Nygrens religionsteorier och dess inflytande i svensk religionsdebatt*. ("Acta universitatis upsaliensis, Studia Doctrinae Christianae Upsaliensia," 4.) Stockholm: Diakonistyrelsen [1966].

Herrmann, Wilhelm, *Ethik*. Tübingen und Leipzig: J. C. B. Mohr, 1901.

Höffding, Harald, *A History of Modern Philosophy*. Vol. II. New York: Dover Publications, 1955.

Holl, Karl, *Gesammelte Aufsätze zur Kirchengeschichte. Bd. I, Luther*. Tübingen: Mohr, 1932.

Horton, Walter Marshall, *Christian Theology; an Ecumenical Approach*. Rev. and enl. edition. New York: Harper [1958].

Houm, Philip, *Hvem var han? På sporet etter mesteren fra Galilea*. Oslo: Aschehoug, 1968.

——, *Mannen fra Nasaret og Den norske kirke*. Oslo: Aschehoug, 1965.

Johnson, William A., *The Religious A Priori*. Unpublished Ph. D. dissertation, Columbia University, 1960.

Kant, Immanuel, *Critique of Pure Reason*. Rev. ed. New York: Willey [1900].

——, *Grundlegung zur Metaphysik der Sitten*. Riga: J. F. Hartknoch, 1785.

Kegley, Charles W., ed., *The Philosophy and Theology of Anders Nygren*. ("Library of Living Theology.") Carbondale, Ill.: Southern Illinois University Press (forthcoming).

Liljequist, Efraim, "Jacob Christopher Boström," *Svenskt biografiskt lexikon*, bd. 5, 521-40. Stockholm: Bonnier [1925].

Lindahl, Elder M., *On Relating Philosophical Inquiry to Religious Convictions, with Special Reference to the Early Writings of Bishop Anders Nygren*. Unpublished Ph. D. dissertation, Northwestern University, 1966.

Lindroth, Hjalmar, "Anders Nygrens kriticism i förhållande till Kants och Schleiermachers," *Nordisk teologi. Ideer och män*. Lund: Gleerup [1955].

——, "Logos—Ordet," *Ordet och tron. Till Einar Billing på hans sextioårsdag*. Stockholm: Diakonistyrelsen, 1931.

——, *Lutherrenässansen i nyare svensk teologi*. Stockholm: Diakonistyrelsen, 1941.

——, "Om teologien såsom en positiv vetenskap," *Festskrift tillägnad Axel Hägerström*. Uppsala & Stockholm: Almqvist & Wiksell, 1928.

——, "Religion och vetenskap en sista gång," *STK*, 7 (1931), 406-12.

LINDROTH, Hjalmar, *Schleiermachers religionsbegrepp*. 2 vols. ("UUÅ," Teologi, 1.) Uppsala: Lundequistka bokhandeln, 1926-1930.

——, *Verkligheten och vetenskapen*. Uppsala: Lindblad, 1929.

LJUNGGREN, Gustaf, *Synd och skuld i Luthers teologi*. Stockholm: Diakonistyrelsen, 1928.

LUTHER, Martin, *The Bondage of the Will*. Westwood, N. J.: Revell, 1957.

LYTTKENS, Hampus, *The Analogy between God and the World. An Investigation of its Background and Interpretation of its Use by Thomas of Aquino*. Uppsala: Almqvist & Wiskell, 1952. Also "UUÅ," 5, 1953.

——, *Nythomismen. En religiös filosofi*. Stockholm: Diakonistyrelsen, 1962.

——, "Religionsfilosofi," *Förslag angående utbyggnad och omstrukturering av de teologiska fakulteterna*. Mimeographed paper, Lunds universitet, Teologiska fakulteten (March, 1968), 27-28.

MARTENSEN, Hans Lassen, *Den christelige Dogmatik*. Kjöbenhavn: Reitzel, 1849.

NELSON, John Robert, *The Realm of Redemption*. London: Epworth Press [1951].

NØJGAARD, Niels, *Om Begrebet Synd hos Luther*. København: Gad, 1929.

Nordisk teologi. Ideer och män. Lund: Gleerup [1955].

NYGREN, Anders, *Agape and Eros*. Philadelphia: Muhlenberg Press [1953].

——, "Är evighetskategorien en religiös kategori?", *Kristendomen och vår tid*, 17 (1922), 220-49.

——, *Det bestående i kristendomen*. ("Religionsvetenskapliga skrifter," 8.) Stockholm: Sveriges kristliga studentrörelse, 1922.

——, *Commentary on Romans*. Philadelphia: Muhlenberg Press [1949].

——, "Diskussionsinlägg. Är den religiösa sanningsfrågan ett vetenskapligt problem eller icke?", *STK*, 4 (1928), 308-12.

——, "Diskussionsinlägg. Religionens sanningsfråga och religionsvetenskapen," *STK*, 4 (1928), 198-206.

——, *Dogmatikens vetenskapliga grundläggning*. ("LUÅ," n.f., avd. I, bd. 17, 8.) Lund: Gleerup, 1922.

——, "Egoism och religion," *STK*, 3 (1927), 129-50.

——, *The Essence of Christianity*. London: Epworth Press, [1960].

——, *Filosofi och motivforskning*. Stockholm: Diakonistyrelsen [1940].

——, *Filosofisk och kristen etik*. ("LUÅ," n. f., avd., I, bd. 18, 8.) Lund: Gleerup [1923].

——, "From Atomism to Context of Meaning in Philosophy," *Philosophical Essays Dedicated to Gunnar Aspelin*. Lund: Gleerup, 1963, 122-36.

——, "Hur är filosofi som vetenskap möjlig?", *Festskrift tillägnad Axel Hägerström*. Uppsala & Stockholm: Almqvist & Wiksell, 1928.

——, *Den kristna kärlekstanken genom tiderna*. Vol. I-II. Stockholm: Diakonistyrelsen, 1930-36.

——, "Om det levande förflutna. Till Schleiermacherminnet 1968," *STK*, 4 (1968), 197-203.

——, "Ragnar Brings teologiska insats," *Nordisk teologi. Ideer och män*. Lund: Gleerup [1955].

——, "Den religionsfilosofiska apriorifrågan," *Kristendomen och vår tid*, 17 (1922), n. p.

——, *Det religionsfilosofiska grundproblemet*. Reprinted from *Bibelforskaren*, 1919-1921. Lund: Gleerup, 1921.

——, *Religiöst apriori*. Lund: Gleerup [1921].

——, "The Religious Realm of Meaning," *The Christian Century*, July 16 (1958), 823-26.

——, "Till frågan om den transcendentala metodens användbarhet inom religionsfilosofien," *Bibelforskaren*, 40 (1923), 273-93.

NYGREN, Anders, "Till frågan om teologiens objektivitet," *Teologiska studier tillägnade Erik Stave, på 65-årsdagen.* Uppsala: Almqvist & Wiksell, 1922.
——, "Till teologiens metodfråga," *STK*, 32 (1956), 20.
NYMAN, Helge, "Teologisk litteratur. Ragnar Bring: Kristendomstolkningar i gammal och ny tid," *STK*, 27 (1951), 200-02.
OTT, Heinrich, *Denken und Sein. Der Weg Martin Heideggers und der Weg der Theologie.* Zürich: Zollikon, 1959.
——, "Was ist systematische Theologie?" *Zeitschrift für Theologie und Kirche,* Beiheft 2 (1961), 19-46.
OTTO, Rudolf, *Das Heilige.* 13th ed. Gotha: Leopold Klotz Verlag, 1925.
——, *The Idea of the Holy.* New York: Oxford University Press, 1958.
——, *Die Kantisch-Fries'sche Religionsphilosophie.* Tübingen: J. C. B. Mohr, 1909.
PATRICK, Denzil G. M., "Some Trends in Contemporary Theology," *The Student World,* 31 (1938), 363-77.
PFANNENSTILL, Magnus, *Luthers tro såsom förtröstan och kunskap.* ("LUÅ," n. f., avd. I, bd. 14, 4.) Lund: Gleerup. 1918.
PHALÉN, Adolf, "Kritik av subjektivismen i olika former," *Festskrift tillägnad E. O. Burman.* Uppsala: Akademisk Bokhandel, 1910.
POLANYI, Michael, *Personal Knowledge.* Chicago: University of Chicago Press [1958].
PRENTER, Regin, *Skabelse og genløsning.* 2 ed. København: Gad, 1955.
——, "Teologisk literatur. Benkt-Erik Benktson: Den naturliga teologiens problem hos Karl Barth," *STK*, 25 (1949), 258-64.
ROBINSON, James M. and John B. COBB, Jr., eds., *The Later Heidegger and Theology.* ("New Frontiers inTheology," 1.) New York: Harper & Row, 1963.
RODHE, Edvard Magnus, "En blick på de trenne sista decenniernas svenska teologi. I. Nittiotalet," *STK*, 3 (1927), 207-29.
——, "En blick på de trenne sista decenniernas svenska teologi. II. Efter sekelskiftet," *STK*, 3 (1927), 305-35.
——, "Ebbe Gustaf Bring," *Svenskt biografiskt lexikon,* bd. 6, 250-62. Stockholm: Bonnier [1926].
RODHE, Sven Edvard, "Teologisk litteratur. Ragnar Bring: Teologi och religion," *STK*, 15 (1939), 89-94.
RUNESTAM, Arvid, "Diskussionsinlägg. Troskunskap och vetenskap. 'Den allmänneliga kristna tron' ännu en gang," *STK*, 2 (1926), 90-98.
——, "Gudstro och självkännedom," *Ordet och tron. Till Einar Billing på hans sextioårsdag.* Stockholm: Diakonistyrelsen, 1931.
——, "Naturligt och kristligt," *Till ärkebiskop Söderbloms sextioårsdag.* Stockholm: Diakonistyrelsen, 1926.
——, *Psykoanalys och kristendom.* 2:a utökade uppl. ("Religionsvetenskapliga skrifter," 14.) Stockholm: Sveriges kristliga studentrörelse, 1931.
——, *Svensk kyrka och teologi i dag.* Stockholm: Diakonistyrelsen, 1953.
——, "Teologisk litteratur. Dogmhistoriens object," *STK*, 4 (1928), 376-86.
——, "Troskunskap och vetenskap. En inledningsfråga i Aulen's 'Den allmänneliga kristna tron'," *STK*, 1 (1925), 355-60.
——, *Wilhelm Herrmanns teologi.* Uppsala: Författaren, 1921.
RYDING, Erik, *Den svenska filosofins historia.* Stockholm: Natur och kultur [1959].
SCHLEIERMACHER, Friedrich, *Die christliche Glaube.* 2 vols. Berlin: G. Reimer, 1821-22.
[——], *Friedrich Schleiermachers Dialektik.* Leipzig: J. C. Hinrichs, 1942.
[——], *Schleiermachers kurze Darstellung des theologischen Studiums.* Berlin: G. Reimer, 1811.

Schleiermacher, Friedrich, *Über die Religion. Reden an die Gebildeten unter ihren Verachtern.* Berlin: J. F. Unger, 1799.
Schweitzer, Albert, *The Quest of the Historical Jesus.* New York: Macmillan, 1956.
Sundkler, Bengt, *Nathan Söderblom. His Life and Work.* Lund: Gleerup, 1968.
Söderblom, Nathan, *Naturlig religion och religionshistoria.* Stockholm: Bonnier, 1914.
———, *Studiet av religionen.* Stockholm: Ljus, 1907.
———, "Uppenbarelsereligionen," *Skrifter i teologiske och kyrkliga ämnen tillägnade C. A. Toren.* Uppsala: Schultz, 1903.
———, *Das Werden des Gottesglaubens.* Leipzig: J. C. Hinrichs, 1916.
Svensk teologisk kvartalskrift. Lund: Gleerup, 1925-.
Tegen, Einar, *Är en transcendental deduktion av religionen möjlig?* Reprint from *Bibelforskaren*, 1922, 300-19; 1923, 1-30. Uppsala: Författaren, 1924.
This is the Church. Philadelphia; Muhlenberg Press [1952].
Tillich, Paul, *Systematic Theology.* Vol. I-II. Chicago: University of Chicago Press, 1951-57.
Wallgren, Erik, *Individen och samfundet.* ("Studia theologica Lundensia," 16.) Lund: Gleerup, 1959.
Wendt, Hans H., *Christentum und Dualismus.* Jena: G. Neuenhahn, 1909.
Wetter, Gillis Peterson, *Tro och vetande.* Stockholm: Bonnier, 1915.
White, Morton, *The Age of Analysis.* New York: New American Library [1957, c. 1955].
Williams, Daniel Day, *What Present-Day Theologians are Thinking.* Rev. ed. New York: Harper [1959].
Wingren, Gustaf, *Creation and Law.* Philadelphia: Muhlenberg Press [1961].
———, *Einar Billing. En studie i svensk teologi före 1920.* Lund: Gleerup, 1968.
———, "Einar Billings teologiska metod," *Nordisk teologi. Ideer och män.* Lund: Gleerup [1955].
———, *Gott und Mensch bei Karl Barth.* ("Luthertum," Hft. 2.) Berlin: Lutherisches Verlagshaus, 1951.
———, *The Living Word.* Philadelphia: Muhlenberg Press [1960].
———, *Man and the Incarnation.* Edinburgh & London: Oliver and Boyd, 1959.
———, "Några karakteristiska drag i modern teologi," *STK*, 27 (1951), 241-47.
———, *Skapelsen och lagen.* Lund: Gleerup, 1958.
———, *Svensk teologi efter 1900.* ("Andra tider—samma tro," 20.) Stockholm: Sveriges kristliga studentrörelse, 1958.
———, "Swedish Theology since 1900," *Scottish Journal of Theology*, vol. 9 (1956), 113-134.
———, "Teologiens metodfråga, "*STK*, 32 (1956), 36-41.
———, *Theology in Conflict.* Philadelphia: Muhlenberg Press [1958].
Wittgenstein, Ludwig, *Tractatus logico-philosophicus.* New York: Harcourt, Brace; London: Kegan Paul, 1922.
World Lutheranism of Today. A Tribute to Anders Nygren. Stockholm: Diakonistyrelsen, 1950.
Wrede, Gösta, *Kyrkosynen i Einar Billings teologi.* ("Acta universitatis upsaliensis, Studia Doctrinae Christianiae Upsaliensia," 5.) Stockholm: Diakonistyrelsen [1966].

INDEX OF NAMES

(Listings in Bibliography not included)